Ancient Lahul
And
Himalaya

Ancient Lahul And Himalaya

Tobdan

Kaveri Books
New Delhi - 110 002

ISBN : 978-93-86463-14-2
First Published in 2021

Published by
Kaveri Books
4832/24, Ansari Road, Daryaganj,
New Delhi - 110 002 (India)
Ph. : 011-2328 8140, 4707 2321
E-mail : info@kaveribooks.com
kaveribooks@gmail.com
Website : www.kaveribooks.com

Typesetting at Creative Graphics, Delhi

PRINTED IN INDIA

Preface

The little known small territory of Lahul is located remotely at a great height in the Himalaya. In c.1900 CE there lived less than 6,000 persons to which we may add 1000, presuming the approximate number of persons inhabiting Chamba–Lahul, the part of whole Lahul. This small body of the population is divided into about half a dozen petty communities speaking the same number of distinct languages and practising the same number of diverse cultures. In its history it is not known if it had been at any time a single unified state, independent under a single native ruler or otherwise. It remained generally under the sway of the powerful neighbouring states. Even then Lahul was a divided state, a portion of it was ruled by one state and the other by a different state. Only its geography kept it united as one entity. The parts severed by history became reunited in the course of time to assume its complete shape after lapse of centuries. Lahul is a basin encircled by high mountain ranges covered with permanent thick layer of snow which can be crossed out of or into the area only in the summer through some traditionally identified high passes. The exit door of Chandrabhaga to Pangi was also not a route of normal communication.

Lahul has not been studied historically seriously. Perhaps because even if someone attempts to do so, in a situation as we have seen above, one may not be rewarded ordinarily with a satisfactory result even by putting great amount of labour and resources. Lahul has a little political history. But it has some significant amount of cultural history scattered in small pieces in numerous colours.

One healthy factor is that Lahul is endowed with a great natural characteristic that in the climate of Lahul grains and other things do not get rotten soon. Moreover the society here remained comparatively calm and undisturbed and unmolested by the historical marauders. Therefore many objects remained here preserved for long period in the shape of solid artifacts, cultural practices, traditions, etc. The volume of the available matter may be very small but it is rare, old and valuable. Another unique feature of Lahul is that it is a buffer land situated between two great international cultures, Central Asia on the one side and the Indo-Aryan of the Indian sub continent on the other.

Here we attempt to explore somewhat deeper past of Lahul. Despite all its geographical hindrances Lahul did not remain an unknown land even in the long past. A great international trade route linking the vast fertile plains of north India with the bubbling markets of Central Asia passed right through Lahul. Indian Buddhism in the ancient past also marched through the same much trampled path to the highlands of Central Asia.

Lahul is situated at the headwaters of river Chandrabhaga in the high Western Himalaya. The river received this name at its head, the place where Lahul is situated. The river possesses rich and long history. The ancient Pali literature provide that there lived Kinnaras on the banks of Chandrabhaga. This introduces us to a moment in the pre-historic period in the history of Lahul.

I am thankful to many friends for being helpful to me in many ways during the course of my study. I mention some of them here as: Ajeya Kumar Sumnam, Thakur Duni Chand, Premlal Yoterpa, Ashwani Kumar Negi, Bir Singh Rawal, Raju Rawal, Norbu Pankharpa, Dola Ram Tainta, Master Budh Ram, Gopi Ram Sakar, Sher Singh Milangpa, Gyaltshan Ghyap, Chhimed Dawa Goram, Jai Chand Kaistha, Khub Ram Khushdil, Surat and Pyarelal of Roghi, Gopal Kirshan and Sewa Buthid of Kalpa, Norbu Kukuji, Shakun singer, Nawang Jinba, Sonam Lamo, Sonam Hozer Hayar, Thinley Shashni, Tanzin Pagsang, Tanzin Damchhos Karpa, C. Dorje and many others. I am earnestly grateful to the Internet Archive and MCADD-PAHAR for the rare kind of undemanding Library services I availed from the sources. I am thankful to Shri Rakesh Goel, of M/s Kaveri Books, for accepting the book for publication.

Tobdan

Contents

List of Plates

1

Ancient Lahul and Chandrabhaga in the Himalaya

Lahul is situated on the headwaters of the river Chandrabaga. Chandrabhaga forms one among the seven rivers of the Vedic Saptasindhu and one of the five of Punjab rivers. The river originates in two headwaters named Chandra and Bhaga from either side of Baralacha pass situated at the head of Lahul. The two branches join at Tandi (Tangti) in the middle of Lahul to form the united Chandrabhaga. It exits Lahul at some distance after Tindi to Pangi in district Chamba. From there it goes to Paddar in Jammu and Kashmir from where it is known as Chenab. Lahul comprises the region of two feeders Chandra and Bhaga and a portion of the combined Chandrabhaga from Tandi to a little ahead of Tindi. Thus Lahul wholly lies in the upper drainage part of the river Chandrabhaga. The river records a long and rich history which is greatly helpful in understanding some aspect of the past of the remotely located and little known region of Lahul in Himachal Pradesh, in the Himalaya. The Seven rivers of Saptasindhu, in one system, are named as: Indus, Jhelum, Ravi, Chandrabhaga, Beas, Satluj and Sarasvati. The list includes the five rivers of the Punjab. Chandrabhaga is referred in both the lists. In Lahul even though every stream, every piece of field and the pieces of wastelands, all are named but the main river is not known named in any of the existing local languages of the area. It is known generally by 'river' in their respective language like gtsang-po (= river) in sTod. The river for most of its length in the lower part is known as Chenab, but the ancient name Chandrabhaga is still retained at its head, the part flowing in Lahul. In Pangi both the names are used but in Kishtwar after crossing Pangi it becomes Chenab for whole of its length till it joins the Indus.

Asikni (Asiknī): The earliest name given to the river, as is generally known, was Asikni. Asikni is Vedic name, recorded in Rigveda, the earliest of all. Later it received the other name Chandrabhaga. During the time of Alexander (BCE 326) both these names, Asikni and Chandrabhaga, were current in north-west India. Greek authors like Pliny, Ptolemy, Arrian, etc, have recorded the former name modified as Akesines and some others the latter one in their writings. Asikni is another form of the word asita which the lexicons translate as 'dark-coloured'. Mc Crindle translates Asikni also as 'dark-coloured'. Monier-Williams while explaining the term asita in his well known work also takes it for Chandrabhaga. Both these words mean 'dark-coloured' and therefore it may be presumed that the river received these names due to its particular characteristic of being dark-coloured.

It indicates that the river was observed to have been generally greatly disturbed and therefore muddy. The early inhabitants of the region where the two rivers, Chandrabhaga and Sindhu, merge with each other, watched the behavior of the two closely and distinguished them by one of their major characteristics. Accordingly they named the one as Asita (dark-coloured) and the other Sita (white). These were the initial and informal folk names given to the two great rivers according to the perception of the inhabitants of the region living around the place where the two great rivers join. Thus Asita was the first and the earliest name of the river. Monier-Williams writes that asita is the original word and is not compound of *a* and *sita*. This however makes little difference here. The two names must have been proposed simultanerusly because the two rivers were both flowing in front of the observers and the names are conjunctive and opposite in meaning to each other displaying the apparent distinctive characteristics of the two.

Asita, however, merges here with the Sita and loses its identity. Asita the name also was forgotten soon. The other name Sita continued in existence throughout the history, sometimes transforming to Śīta or Sītā, and kept on confusing the scholars. Sometimes the name was also applied to some other river. The scholastic names Asikni and Sindhu were received by the two rivers later perhaps alongwith the names of the other rivers of Saptasindhu.

These names Asita and Asikni, intended to give expression to one of its principal features, were given to the river at its last end at the point where it joins with the Indus and loses its identiy.

Chandrabhaga: The river received its early names Asita and Asikni at its extreme end. But it received its other name Chandrabhaga at its head. From the fact that the two headwaters of the river were named distinctly as Chandra and Bhaga and the combined name of the two became the name of the main river, it becomes apparent that the river Chandrabhaga received this name at its head. From here we can understand the importance the history assigns to the river at its head. It appears that the early geographers had surveyed the region and acquired first hand knowledge of the remote and inaccessible region of the headwaters of the river.

Visvesvaranath, describing the Vedic rivers, states, quoting from Nirukta (9 and 26), that the other name of Asikni is Chandrabhaga, (Visvesvaranath, 1967: 114, Note-6). Thus according to Visvesvaranath the name Chandrabhaga originated in Vedic period. The statement appears to be reliable because this second name too was current during the time of the Greek historians of the time of Alexander's Campaign, before the Mauryan period. Ptolemy calls it Sandabala and Pliny has Cantabra or Cantaba.

Greek Authors on the river Chandrabhaga

The distinctive feature of the river on the basis of which it received its original name is well testified in the descriptions of the ancient Greek scholars. They give account of the dangerous scenes they witnessed created on the river. McCrindle writes that Aristoboulos and Nearchos, the two writers, speak about the rising of the rivers. Nearchos while writing about the river Chandrabhaga says that when they encamped near the Akesines, they were obliged to shift their quarters to higher ground when the river rose, and that this occurred at the summer solstice. Aristoboulos even sets down the measure of the height to which the river rose above its former level and this was forty cubits, of which twenty filled the channel up to the brim and the other twenty inundated the plains. They concur also in stating that the cities built upon mounds become islands. The inundation eases after the setting of Areturus when the waters subside, (McCrindle, 1901: 23). The Greek authors of Alexander's time transformed the name to Akesines from Asikni.

A much disastrous scene occurred on the same river on another occasion. When Alexander crossed Chandrabhaga many of his soldiers perished in the inundation of the river. "Alexander himself advanced towards the river Akesines. This is the only Indian river of which Ptolemy has mentioned the size. He states that where Alexander crossed it with his army in boats and on inflated hides the current was so rapid that the waters dashed with foam and fury against the large and jagged rocks with which the channel was bestrewn. He informs us also that it was 15 stadia in breadth, and while the passage was easy for those who crossed upon inflated hides not a few of those who were carried in boats perished in the waters, as many of the boats were dashed to pieces by striking against the rocks," (McCrindle, 1893:112-113).

Of the two names the Greek authors had preference for the former name Asikni from that of the latter Chandrabhaga, writes McCrindle. He writes that in Greek this latter name would be represented by Sandrophagos. But perhaps on account of the disaster which befell the Makedonian fleet at the turbulent junction of the river with the Hydaspes it is said that the followers of the great conqueror discerned an evil omen in the name of Chandrabhaga on account of its near similarity to their own word Sandrophagos or Alexandrophagos, 'devourer of Alexander' and hence preferred calling by the more ancient of the two names, (McCrindle 1926: 198-Note).

The river Chandrabhaga is referred to in ancient great Sanskrit works like: the Puranas, Mahabharata, Rajatarangini, etc. References are also found in the ancient Pali works. The references in Pali are much detailed and more descriptive.

A Pali work Milindpanha writes that, 'Five hundred rivers flow down from the Himalayan slopes, yet of these five hundred rivers, only ten are counted as rivers, that is to say the Ganges, Jumna, Aciravati, Sarabhu, Mahi, Sindhu, Sarassati, Vetravati, Vitamsa and the Candabhaga, while the remaining rivers are not counted as rivers, (Horner, 1963-I:159). Another similar work Apadana gives, the names viz. Sindhu, Sarssati, Candrabhaga (Candabhāgikā), Ganga, Yamuna, Sarbhu (Saryu) and Mahi, (Kashyap:1959-I: 32).

Chenab: Chenab is its fourth and the latest name. This name was given perhaps in the medieval time. Alberuni still names the river as Chandrāha i.e. Chandrabhaga (Sachau, 1888: 250-251). The earlier name Asikni appears to have become disused. Abul Fazal during the time of Akbar writes it as Chenab and says that its ancient name is Chanderbhaga. He writes that, from the top of the mountains of Kishtwar (Khatwar) issue two springs, one called Chandar and the other Bhaga which unite near Kishtwar, from thence they flow down, (Jarrett, 1891-II: 310-311). By this time the river was known by this new name. The name Chenab was given probably on the assumption that it originated in China (Cīna), (Cīna +'ab = water coming from China). China here stands for Tibet. It may be remarked here that the vague references to Cīna or even to Mahācīna in the ancient Indian literature may be understood generally for Tibet.

Chandrabhaga, geography: Chandrabhaga, the third name of the river, was conferred to it in its uppermost region in the region of its origin. The area might have been then mostly desolate. Some part of the uppermost portion of the riverhead is still unhabited. The uppermost inhabited part known by the name of Lahul is populated even today very thinly. Corresponding to the two heads of the river there are two lakes connected with the two streams named similarly. The propounders of the name might have initially acquired detailed geographical knowledge of the river including the region of its head streams. This is self-evident from the name of the river itself. Names were given to the various landmarks around it viz. the lakes and mountain in the region based on a single theme of 'Chanda' or 'Chandra', the Moon. Possibly some special objective could have been in view.

From an important Pali source, the story of Chanda-Kinnara Jataka, we learn that the name of the mountain, situated in the middle at the confluence of the two rivers Chandra and Bhaga, was Chanda-Parvata, (Tobdan, 2008: 459-464). In Pali accounts the river Chandrabhaga appears to receive much consideration.

Geographically the river possesses some distinctive features. Chandrabhaga is one of the most powerful and the longest of the Punjab rivers. All the rest of the Punjab rivers merge into it. It retains its identity in its name till it merges with Indus the sixth river of Saptasindhu. Sarasvati, the seventh of the group, having been lost.

McCrindle writes that Chandrabhaga, the Akesines, now the Chenab, is the largest of all the Panjab rivers. It issues high up on the mountains and reaches the level country after a descent of 300 miles. It is joined by all the other Punjab rivers receiving on the right the Hydaspas (Jhelam) on the left the Hydratis (Ravi), and further down on the same side the mingled waters of Hyphasis (Beas) and the Satadru or Satluj. In Alexander's time it joined the Indus near Uchh but now the point of junction is lower down near Mithankot, whence the distance to the sea is 470 miles, (McCrindle, 1901: 23, Note-2).

Etymology: The name Chandrabhaga is composed of two words Chanda or Chandra and Bhāgā. There is no doubt about the form and meaning of the first part Chanda or Chandra which means 'the Moon'. But the form of the second word Bhaga is uncertain therefore also its meaning. The main issue before us is whether it is Bhāga or Bhāgā, because we find scholars using both forms of the term.

We always pronounce the word as Bhāgā for the river Bhāgā and also as part of the compound word Chandrabhāgā. But there exists disagreement among the scholars. Sanskrit scholar Amarsingh in his celebrated work Amarkos (Varivarga:34) writes Bhāgā but Varahmihir in his Brhatsamhita (Grahbhakti:27) writes Bhāga. The Pali work Apadana (Apadāna) uses the term at several places and in the two versions of Kashyap and Rhys Devids it is found used as Bhāgā. Similarly the renowned Pali scholars Malalasekera (1937-I: 850) and BC Law (1954: 72), both write Candabhāgā.

Varma in his Hindi Lexicon of five volumes retains both the words in the compound words Chandrabhāga and Chandrabhāgā. By Chandrabhāga he means the region in the Himalaya from where the river Chandrabhāgā originates which we may translate as the portion of the Moon or Moonland. By the latter term Chandrabhāgā he means the name received on account of its being originating from the region of Chandrabhāga in the Himalaya, (Verma. 2007-II: 186). The explanation is credible. McCrindle takes the word as Chandrabhāga and translates it as lunae portio, to mean as 'share of moon', (McCrindle, 1927:89).

As both the forms of the word are seen used by the scholars through different periods of history, it appears that both are indispensable. We in our use here write as Chandrabhāgā and Bhāgā. It is difficult to explain the two terms Bhāga and Bhāgā literally as independent words and their relevance to the nomenclature at the present level of our knowledge. McCrindle writes it as of Sanskrit (McCrindle, 1927: 89). Monier-Williams appears to omit this word from the list of the Sanskrit words in his celebrated work.

Surajbhaga: The nomenclature Bhaga has received recently a new interpretation and form to be designated as Surajbhaga. As a further extention the lake from which the river originates is named as Surajtal. The first such information is gathered from Moorcroft and then from Alexander Cunningham.

Moorcroft and Trebeck while going to Ladak in 1820 passed through Lahul. They name the river Bhaga, the second feeder of the river Chandrabhaga, as Surajbhaga. 'We descended to the Surajbhaga by an almost precipitous path and crossed it by another plank bridge where it was about thirty feet broad, deep and rapid, but full of blocks of stone', (Moorcroft: 1841-I: 205-6). Then they passed through the lake from which the river Bhaga originates. They write, 'Following the other branch we soon came to a place where it issued from the middle of a natural dike, which filled up the space at the foot of two mountains, ascending to the summit of which we beheld a basin of clear water of a deep green hue about a mile in circumference. This small lake, also called the Chukam, collects the water from the surrounding heights, and may be regarded as the source of the Surajbhaga portion of the Chinab. From the lake we ascended a steep pass that led over the rounded back of a part of the Bara Lacha ridge. According to the barometric metrical measurement we had attained here the elevation of sixteen thousand five hundred feet, (Moorcroft, 1841-I: 215).

The arrangement of naming the two rivers as Sun and Moon, although plausible, appears to be a recent invention. There is not even a slight indication to this fact among so many ancient instances we have been able to refer. This does not appear to fit in the thematic plan of the ancient propounders of the whole complex of the names. Bhaga cannot be made to mean Suraj (Sun) even by adding the term Suraj to it.

The Two Lakes, Suraj Tal and Chandra Tal: Cunningham writes about the two lakes that, Suraj Dal is a small oblong sheet of clear green water, dammed at the western end by masses of splintered rock that have fallen from above. It is about a quarter of a mile long and only half as broad. A small rill of melted snow flows into it from the east; but the rill is altogether so insignificant that the Suraj Dal may fairly be considered as it is reputed to be, the source of the Bhaga river. But the Chandra Dal, although double the size of the Suraj Dal, is situated at least twenty five miles below the real source of the Chandra river, in the Bara Lacha Pass. It is, however, always spoken of as the source of the Chandra river. The Dal is a Kashmiri term for any sheet of water, whether large or small, but it is also a Tibetan word, signifying still, quiet, (Cunningham, 1854a: 143-144). In fact the river Chandra passes about half a kilometrer below from the lake without touching it and is additionally fed from the Lake.

The rivers Chandra and Bhaga: Cunningham provides detailed geographic data about the rivers—the two river heads and the main river—covering the complete course from its origin to the point of its junction with the Indus. He writes, "Chandra and the Bhaga rise on opposite sides of the Bara Lacha pass, in N. latitude 32°15′ and E. longitude 77°22′ at an elevation of 16,500 feet above the sea. The Chandra flows at first to the south for fifty five miles and then sweeps suddenly up to the north west for sixty miles further, to the junction of the Bhaga river at Tandi. The fall to this point is 7500 feet, or sixty five feet per mile, for the Chandra river, and 125 feet per mile for the Bhaga river, which has a course of only sixty miles to the southwest. At Koksar, twenty five miles above Tandi and 10,000 feet above the sea, the Chandra river averages 200 feet in width, with a mean depth of two and a half feet, and a current of not less than four miles per hour in October when it is fordable with very great difficulty. The discharge at that time is therefore not less than 2000 cubic feet. From Tandi the Chander Bhaga pursues a north westerly course to Kishtwar, a further distance of 115 miles. The whole length to this point is 330 miles, and the fall is 11,500 feet, or 34.8 feet per mile.

'Between Tandi and Kishtwar the Chandra Bhaga receives many snow fed torrents of considerable size, of which the largest are the Chukam (Tso-khang, and also Thirot) and Chatrgarh rivers. The discharge at Kishtwar cannot therefore be less than 4,000 cubic feet or just double that at Tandi which is halfway between the source and the town of Kishtwar. Below the town it receives from the north the large river of Wardwan, about sixty miles in length, by which the discharge is probably increased to 4,500 cubic feet.

'At Koksar 10,000 feet above the sea which is the highest inhabited village on the Chandra river, a suspension bridge of twisted birchen rope is annually constructed. A second suspension bridge of the same kind formerly spanned the mouth of the Bhaga river at Tandi, but this was carried away some time after Dr. Gerard's visit in 1830. In 1839 I saw the ropes lying high and dry on the northern bank, but when I visited Tandi again in 1846, there was no trace of them. A small wooden bridge of thirty eight feet span, and forty feet above the stream is thrown across the Bhaga river above four miles from Tandi. Fifteen miles below Tandi, and five miles above Triloknath, the Chandra Bhaga is crossed by a couple of spars covered with loose planks. The bridge is eighty five feet long and forty three feet above the water. Two miles above this bridge the river was not less than 300 feet broad. Above Chatrgarh and opposite Kishtwar, the Chandra Bhaga is crossed by suspension bridges.

'From Kishtwar the river sweeps suddenly round to the south-west as far as Doda. It then turns due west towards the fort of Riyasi, where it resumes its south westerly course to Aknur at the foot of the hills, a total distance of 150 miles. From Baralacha pass to Aknur the length of the Chenab is 380 miles, and the whole fall is 15,500 feet, 40.8 feet per mile. From Aknur to Mithankot the length is 570 miles in a south-south-west direction, and the whole length from its source to its junction with the Indus is 950 miles", (Cunningham,1854a: 119-120). At Udaipur Miyar Nala, a big tributary, joins it.

In Lahul the rivers Chandra, Bhaga and Chandrabhaga are highly tamed and flow quite gently. They are not known to have been in flood as the Gazetteer also reports, 'floods are not common in Lahul'. This may also be observed from the undisturbed conditions of the course of the river. In this context we quote here an example showing Bhaga flowing nearly in the same position since the early prehistoric times. Below Kolong on the right bank of the Bhaga at a place called Mangalag (Manga-lhag, meaning?), close to the river bank, at a height of about 100 feet, there are some big boulders on which are seen rock carvings of the pre-historic period. There are some similar carvings at Muntsi on its left bank near Tinno. The rivers are generally blue except in the summer when they become muddy. In the summer, as the summer gets warmer, the side dokpos, streams, become more and more powerful and turbulent. The small bridges put up near the villages by the inhabitants with great labour every year are carried away and communications are broken in the bright daylight. The cattle and the shepherd and some villagers working on the fields become stranded. The dogpos sometimes even dam up and block the main river. In Jispa the whole village was drowned in the lake created on the Bhaga by the flood from Marshang dokpo just below the village in 1965. The houses were shifted from the plain to the higher slopes. People quote instances of similar earlier happenings. The inhabitants are well aware of all these unusual phenomena occurring regularly in the nature. Thakur Duni Chand of Sissu tells that the Chandra sometimes gets blocked by the snow flood in the winter and lake is created. Once the temporary lake, created at Zankhar Phalong or Gupha Hotel, near Sissu towards Khoksar, in the winter rose so high that it submerged the site of the dhaba, the eating shop, which lay above the highway. The height of the mouth of the north portal of Rohtang tunnel under construction on the other side of the river is visibly lower than the level attained by the artificial lake, tells history.

The Great Triangle: Chandra and Bhaga encircle a great mass of land. A large part of it is uninhabited. The old Gazetteer gives geography of the region stating that, 'The great triangle formed by the Candra and Bhaga is filled up by an off shoot from the range to the north; its peaks rise to 21, 20 and 19,000 feet, and its numerous lateral valleys are all filled with glaciers. It is one great ice-bed, broken here and there by lofty heights of impassable rock and snow. To the south of the highest peak, 21,415 feet, stretches a vast glacier, 12 miles in length, which is met by another of even greater dimensions. The most noted peak, though not the highest, is the Gephang Lha, or God Gephan, in whose honour the Lahulis hold feasts and make sacrifices. This is the snowy cone which can be seen from the Kulu valley through a gap in the mid-Himalaya. The most noted glacier in Lahul is that known as the big Shigri at the bend of the Chandra on its south side. It is nearly two miles wide and runs right down to the river; the marks are still to be seen throughout Lahul of the destruction caused many years ago by a portion of the glacier having fallen across the river and dammed up the water until the melting of the ice released the pent-up flood', (Gazetteer, 1898: 2-3).

The Present Habitation: The old Gazetteer writes that the first signs of permanent habitations on the Chandra river are met with opposite to the Hamta Pass at Old Khoksar, where there is a village occupied by five families, some 14 miles above Khoksar at the foot of the Rohtang Pass, (Gazetteer, 1898- III: 3). This village of Old Khoksar in local custom was called Ya-ri Khoksar (gYa'-ri = wild vacant land) which was situated on a slope. Today the village does not exist. But a settlement named Chhatru of a few seasonal shops has come up on the right bank of the river beside the bridge. At Chhota Dara (Phooti Rooni) there is a govt. rest house. At Bathal (Karche) there is a temporary seasonal settlement situated nearer to the base of the Kunzom pass. All the three settlements are for the benefit of the travelers and all are situated on the right side of the Chandra. Khoksar and thereafter Grampbhug, presently known as Khoksar, are the existing settled places first met in the valley.

The first inhabited village on the Bhaga is Dar-se (folk), Dar-tse (literary), Darcha (common name) where there is the confluence of three rivers of Bhaga in the middle, on its left joins the Yotse and on the right the Zanskar. The dokpo coming from the side of north-west is called locally as Rarig, Bartsi, Kado, Kakthi, or Zanskar dokpo or chhu. The stream coming from north-east direction is called Yotse dokpo which is combination of two dokpo of Mulki chhu and Milang chhu. The river Bhaga presently is not known by any name. Moorcroft, however, records its local name as Chukam and identifies the lake from where the river originates by the same name. This term Chukam here cannot be explained. Moorcroft writes, "On the 4th we passed the junction of the two rivers which form the Darcha river; one of these the Chukam, we followed, the other the Kakthi, is said to come from the snows, about two kos to the north-west.", (Moorcroft, 1841-I: 214). Here Kakthi may be identified with Zanskar chhu. The author further writes, "This small lake, also called the Chukam, collects the water from the surrounding heights, and may be regarded as the source of the Suraj-bhaga portion of the Chinab."

This unique site, confluence of three rivers, is identified for hydro-electric project or a dam which is likely to engulf the whole of sTod valley, one complete society of a distinct ancient culture.

Importance of the Himalaya: Himalaya, the Lord of the Mountains, is greatly praised in the ancient Indian literature. It was known by several names: Himavata, Himavanta, Himavāna, Himvā, etc. Himalaya, the existing name, occurs perhaps for the first time in the work of the celebrated Sanskrit poet-author Kalidas of the first half of sixth century CE in his work Kumārsambhavam. The name got popularity during the British period. Alberuni calls it Himvanta. Whatever was it named, the Himalya always inspired and benefitted the inhabitants of Bharatvarsa through the ages. Therefore the Himalaya has been praised in many works by the learned scholars of all faiths.

In the Buddhist tradition the monks used to go from the lower hills and the plains to the Himalaya for meditation and leading meditative solitary life. In the story of Milindapanha ca. 2nd BCE it is told that when king Milinda of Sagala enquired about the learned men of his kingdom with whom he could converse on the matters on which he had some doubts, he came to know that 'the monks had mostly gone to the Himalayas', (Horner, 1863-I:8). It is also told that, "at that time a hundred myriad arahants were living on the

'Guarded Plateau'[1] on an Himalayan mountain-slope," (Horner, 1863-I: 8, Note-6). Assagotta also held a conference of the monks there to discuss this issue of searching an able monk to converse with the king Milinda. There is also a tradition in which it is said that Arhatas live on the Kailas.

The region of the headwaters of the river may have been explored or re-explored by some missionary adventurers of Buddhism, may be of the time of the Emperor Asoka or some other period. Canda-Kinnar Jatak, an important story relating a former life of the Buddha was plotted in the environment of this region. Another important work identifies the inhabitants of the headwaters of Chandrabhaga as Kinnars and there also are teachers belonging to the community practicing the Doctrine.

Apadana: Apadana (Apadāna) in this respect is an important work in the ancient Pali lietature. It possesses a number of references to the Himalaya and particularly river Chandrabhaga. Of special interest is that it makes references to Kinnaras, the inhabitants of the region of the headwaters of this river. Kinnaras otherwise are rarely seen as the subject of history. Malalasekera and BC Law say that the Apadana is regarded as one of the latest books in the collection of Canonical works. But it is also said that the different legends in the work are of different dates. The work, however, covers the Himalaya quite widely. It also mentions Vitasta, Jhelum, in the west and Bhagirathi in the middle of the Himalaya.

Apadana is an anthology of about 600 legends in verse of Theras and Theris, male and female monks. This is divided into two sections of Therapadana and Theriapadana: Stories of monks, male and Stories of monks, female. Out of the total number of stories 40 belong to Theris. The narrations include the stories of some exalted nobilities of the Doctrine. The lives are mentioned as having lived in the life time of the Buddha. There are also separate Buddhapadanam and Pachchekbuddhapadanam in the work.

Himavanta, Himalaya, is referred to in the work, in the Thera section, more than 36 times, and Chandrabhaga 17 times in the Thera and 3 times in the Theri. Kinnari is mentioned in the Theri section 3 times. Kinnara is mentioned, in the Thera section, once living in the Himavanta and 4 times on the banks of Chandrabhaga.

The Apadana reveals that many monks, both male and female, lived on various mountains in the Himalaya meditating. Some of these mountains are named as Lambaka, Nisabha, Kukkara, Gotama, Vasabha, Kukkata, Bhutagana, Romasa, etc. The monks had built their huts of grass and lived there meditational solitary life. Some of them lived on the banks of the Chandrabhaga.

These monks are of two classes. One is that of the migrant monks. They have come from the lower regions and have temporary residences to live for practicing meditation. Some others are Kinnar and Kinnari. They were born here and are inhabitants of the place. This is evident from the description given in the story of each monk which says, 'I was a Kinnara' or 'Kinnari then'. The Kinnars lived in a wider area in the Himalaya but the concentration of their habitation is shown on the banks of Chandrabhaga, certainly at the headwaters of the river.

The following is the description of the residence of a monk on the Himalaya who has made a residence for meditation. The description is common for all such kind of monks residing on a mountain in the Himalaya.

"Close to the Himalayan range,
The mountain called Lambaka,
My ashrama is very well made,
A well constructed hall of leaves", (Walters, 2018a: Sariputta-19).

Here we take liberty to make a little modification in the translation in the first sentence replacing with the one as 'in the middle of the Himalaya'. This is because the texts mention the residence of the meditators on a specifically named mountain which is situated somewhere in the Himalaya, and also following the text.

On the Himvanta there also lived a monk named Devala who adored the Buddha, had many pupils, and carried heavy weight of 'jattā', knotted hair, on his head and carried a Kamandala, a vessel, for begging alms. The monk in the archaic dress or in the dress of heretics, is unique. The instance is not an exception.

The following description indicates that the monk was born in the tribe or class of Kinnara in the Himalaya. His habitat was on the

Himalaya but it was at a distance from Chandrabhaga where there lived most of the Kinnara and Kinnari monks of the description.

On a Himalayan mountain,
I was a kinnara back then.
I saw the Buddha, Stainless One
Bright but cool like a rayless sun,
(Walters, 2018a: Padapujaka, 389-390).

Chandrabhaga: Just as there lived monks on the various mountains in the Himalaya there also lived monks and nuns on the banks of the Chandrabhaga. In whole of the work there are shown four Theras and three Theris of Kinnara class who live on the banks of Chandrabhaga. The representation given to the number of Kinnara and Kinnari monks among the highly ranked Theras and Theris is a matter of great significance to the Kinnaras, the residents of the headwaters of Chandrabhaga. The following is the kind of description of residence of a Kinnari:

On Candabhaga River's bank
I was a kinnari back then,
I saw the stainless Buddha there
Self-become, the Unconquered One,
(Walters, 2018b: Tinimalamalika-11, Salamalika-34).

Following is the type of description of the residence of Kinnara residing on the bank of Chandrabhaga.

On Candabhaga River's bank
I was a kinnara back then,
I lived on flowers as my food
And dressed in clothes made of flowers,
(Walters, 2018a: Candanapujaka- 254).

The Kinnaras and Kinnaris described in the Apadana are inhabitants of the Himalaya and residents of the uppermost region of the Chandrabhaga river. The characters describe themselves as a Kinnara or a Kinnari and living on the banks of Chandrabhaga. They lived in their own habitat. The place given to the Kinnara folk in the famed work Chanda-Kinnara Jataka and the amount of representation given in the Apadana among the noble class of the learned and honourable monks is a matter of great importance for the class of people who lived in the high altitude regions unknown to the world.

There is some variation in the treatment of this class of the Kinnar race in the ancient literature in Pali and Sanskrit. The presently quoted two Pali sources as above treat the class as any other group of human race. They are a historical people. But some other Pali and Sanskrit works place them in the class of non-humans. Perhaps the two sources just referred to belong to an earlier period.

The authors of Pali literature were well aware of the geography of the region of the headwaters of Chndrabhaga. This we learn also from a different work, the Chanda Kinnara Jataka. The plot of the story was set on mount Chanda which has been identified with the mountain situated between the rivers Chandra and Bhaga at the place of their confluence in Lahul. The two works appear to refer to the same geographical region, which has been discussed in the work separately.

The story of Chandra and Bhaga: There exists a story relating to the present subject in folklore in Lahul. Chandra, a beautiful damsel, and Bhaga a handsome but proud youth, lived in devaloka and were in love with each other. They could not marry in the heaven. So they decided to descend on the earth. The resident gods of devaloka gave a golden tray to Chandra and a golden rod to Bhaga to meet their expenses on the earth. They descended on the Baralacha pass and met at Tandi, (Tashi Dawa, 1994: 37-38).

The story has been transformed slightly to make it a little more logical. Chandra is daughter of Chandra, the Moon, and Bhaga son of Suraj, the Sun. They lived in the world of gods. They grew as friends from the childhood. But when they grew young and decided to marry they came to realize that they could not marry because of their inherent strong and opposite characteristics. One of the wise gods advised the two to transform themselves into the form of human beings and go on the earth to live there. The two descended on the Baralacha pass, and became united at Tandi. They turned Lahul into a settled region and lived for ever on the earth, (Tobdan, 2016: 17-18).

We gather, looking at all the sources, viz. the story of Chanda-Kinnara Jataka, the folkstory, the aggregation of the existing nomenclatures of the complex section of the head of the river Chandrabhaga, etc., that the central theme of all the names is Chanda or Chandra and its image is the central figure in the cluster of geographical names. The Jataka story names the Great Being as Chanda in the tribe of Kinnar and his spouse Yashodhra, a Kinnari, as Chandā. The same name Chanda is used both in masculine and feminine forms. Thus in the figure Chanda, or Chandra we visualise the images of both the Great Beings. No second symbol is intended here by the founders.

In summary we may say that river Bhaga, the counterpart of Chandra, is Bhaga, a share, a protion of the whole Chandra, and Chandrabhaga comprises Chandra and its portion, Bhaga. Suraj or the Sun is not intended here to be included in the picture. This we derive from various sources, the compositions of the ancient scholars as witnessed above.

Hence we may explain the various terms existing in the region as we understand. The name of the river Chandra may be read as such with its original meaning. This could also be taken for Chandā. Bhaga is read always as Bhāgā, as it is convenient. Chandratal the traditional name of the lake and Surajtal, the recently assigned name, may be retained as such. The section of land encircled by the rivers Chandra and Bhaga and the nearby, going with McCrindle and Varma, may be read as Chandrabhāga, portion of the Moon. The mountain presently known as Gandhala may be identified as Chanda or Chandra Parvata, the Moon mountain, going with the Chanda-Kinnara Jataka. The inhabitants were called Kinnara. Presently the whole area falls in Lahul.

Indian Buddhism in Lahul: Indian Buddhism in Lahul arrived before that of Tibetan Buddhism. This is evident from the standing monuments related to the subject in the area and other evidences. Lahul lies on the ancient trade route between northern India and Central Asia through which also travelled the Indian Buddhism. Lahul has been considered a difficult, remote and inaccessible area and in the modern times, a station of punishment posting. This may be one of the reasons that some of the ancient customs, practices, artifacts, monuments and other kinds of remnants of historical importance remained here to some extent unspoiled and preserved, till the people were unaware of the phenomena like development. Therefore we find some evidences of existence of the form of the Doctrine in the area in the past.

The following are some examples which indicate the existence of Indian Buddhism in Lahul. In 1857 Major Hay who was posted as a 'Political Employ' in Kullu subdivision which included the area of Lahul and Spiti, 'heard that some curious ancient vessels had been found near the junction of the Chandra and Bhaga rivers,' at 'Goondlah.'[2] 'In a great landslip a vaulted chamber or hollow had been laid bare, in which were found this brass vase, and some dishes of kansa, or mixed metal.' Major Hay could get the vessel only. Some other valuable articles had been lost. This contains fine engravings. Charles Horne dates it 200-300 A.D., (Charles Horne, 1871: 367-375). This bronze vessel after re-examination has been predated to 1st century BCE, (Errington and Cribb, 1992: 163-164).

There exist rock carvings of the Buddhist deities at Gundhla, Kardang, Kyelang and Srangbar (Khangsar). These are works of Indian Buddhism, prior to the advent of Tibetan Buddhism. Christian Luczanits in his correspondence with Nawang Jinpa places the rock carvings of Gundhla to the period from 10th to 12th century, (courtesy Nawang Jinpa).

The temple at Rebag, Triloknath, which was earlier known as Vihar, is dedicated to Arya Avalokitesvara. The scholars affirm that, 'The temple of Triloknath is .... Obviously of Buddhist origin, clearly indicated by the Buddhas in the brackets of the columns and the main image, the Nagara temple with the conspicuous tower also attracts Hindu pilgrims,' (Widorn & Kozicz, 2012:29). The present principal statue of Avalokitesvara is made of marble (rdo ka-ma-ru or ka-ma-ru-pa = marble stone). There is a similar statue of about the same size made of stone in black colour. This is told to be the older principal statue. There is another conspicuous stone sculpture, a carving on the flat stone slab (Plate 1). Christian Luczanits's comment is: "This likely is a depiction of the Bodhisattva Avalokiteśvara, with the gesture of giving (varadamudrā) and a lotus shown with a closed blossom. It is rather generic and there are other Bodhisattvas with very similar iconography, but Avalokiteśvara is the most popular,' (personal communication). We have a view to add. From appearance the object is indicative of remnant of a much earlier period. This image is in appearance like those of the Kushan kings existing elsewhere. Here he is exalted and represented in the appearance of Avalokitesvara. This is an important object.

The date of foundation of the temple is evidenced by the inscription in Sharda script inscribed on a wall stone near the base on the right side of the entrance of the temple, left side of the devotee (Plate 2). The inscription was read and translated by Acharya Diwakar Nath. Following is the translation of the inscription:

"Success ! Reverence to the glorious Avalokitesvara!

'Because he is intent upon others' glorious benefit a man of incomparable stainless vigour, who has given up the slightest passion for belongings and is rich with hundreds of powerful virtues, Dvamgra Rana in person has built an excellent towering temple for you, without hesitation as high as the importance of Lahuna. The second day of the dark half," (courtesy Nawang Jinpa).

The translator remarks that the inscription retains features of late Gupta script. So he calls it proto-Sharda and gives date around the end of the ninth century. The temple was built by Dvamgra Rana dedicated to the Lord Avalokitesvara, as high as the importance of Lahuna (Lāhuṇa). Lahuna, here may be taken for Lahul and its fame. Lāhuṇa may be the original form of the name of the area presently known as Lāhul, also recorded by Hiuen Tsiang.

At Chhokhor near Sissu in Tinan valley there is a small monastery in Tibetan style almost all of whose worship objects, i.e. the idols, however, are wholly remnant of a temple of Indian Buddhism. The main statue of Tara of metal in sitting posture with a Bodhisattva on the crown is a work of Indian Buddhism. It is so heavy that it is difficult to lift up by an ordinary person. There are some small images of the Bodhisattvas, one of stone and another of marble. The one of stone contains engraving in Sharda in which the letters are engraved deep in reverse perhaps to obtain a mark. It was discovered by GCL Howell, Asstt. Commissioner, Kullu and A.H. Francke and was examined by Vogel, (Francke, 1926-II: 214).

Rahul Sankrityayan also visited and examined the inscription. All say that it is a sacred formula and Rahul Sankrityayan reads a part of it as 'Hum phat svah!' (Rahul Sankrityayan, 1956b. 34).

At Margul in the temple of Mrikula devi there are carvings on wood on the ceiling depicting scenes from the life of the Buddha. Chhukutsi gonpa is also in possession of some objects which may lead its history touching the period of the Indian Buddhism.

The Bodhisattva bust of marble of unique features discovered at Gandhala belongs to Indian Buddhism. Snellgrove writes, "There are remains of ancient wood-work without, and inside standing amongst images of recent workmanship on the altar is the head of a bodhisattva which had been dug up in the valley below (pl.24)", (Snellgrove, 1957: note 39, p. 293). Snellgrove links it with the period of presence of Indian Buddhism in Kulu. The object has now been lost to big thieves.

At Karing there is a big structure of abour 10'x10'x6'(ht.) of maane over which are placed two sections of two beautifully carved pieces of stone pillar bases like those belonging to some palace (Plate 3). The place, situated on a flat plateau overlooking the valley and safely located, looks, from the left over unusable wall stones, like a ruin of some important structure.

All these indicate to the advent of Buddhism in Lahul in some early period and having evolved for long period. When the practice of Buddhism started weakening on the soil of its birth its practice had been flourishing in the countries in the north. The practice of Indian Buddhism in Lahul was gradually taken over by Tibetan Buddhism. The practice of Buddhism continued in Lahul incessantly since its advent. To the remote ancients, Lahul was not so remote and inaccessible.

Below we quote a stanza from an ancient prayer or song titled Lha-rgyas (= great god), a ceremonial prayer from the area of sTod. The prayer song is sung in the gatherings on auspicious occasions, specially on the occasion of Losar, New Year festival. It is purely folk in content. The following is an example of its contact with the Indian Buddhism.

The text

brag-dmar 'dabs-su bzhugs pa'i,
btsun-pa spun gsum de.
snams-me snams-la ci snams.
snams-me snams-la ras gzan rkyang gcig snams.
'don-ne 'don-la ci 'don,
'don-ne 'don-la 'bras dkar hro-lo 'don.
skyem-me skyem la ci skyems.
la skyem-me skyem-la sing-chang sing-ma skyems.
ta-li lang-la, la ta-li bkra-shis brjod.

Translation

Sitting beside the red rock,
The three monk brothers,
They wear, but what do they wear?
They wear, they wear a single length of cotton cloth.
They eat, but what meal do they eat?
For meal they take white rice, each grain separated.
For drinking what do they drink?
For drinking they drink thin beer.
Say auspiciousness!

From the above description it appears that the three monks belong to the regions lower to Lahul who are habitual to wear cotton clothes of monks as their dress and eat rice, which are foreign to Lahul. This points to the presence of the Indian Buddhism in the area.

Kinnara in history: Kinnaras are inhabitants of the high Himalaya. They are known as beings different from the humans. Sometimes they are described as a strange and mythical beings, half human and half animal. Sometimes they are seen among the gods in the drawings and paintings in the temples. They had their land named Kimpurusavarsa. In the time of composition of the two works Canda-Kinnara Jatak and Apadana the Kinnaras are known, like any other class or tribe, a people, living in the Himalaya on the banks of the headwaters of the Chandrabhaga and nearby.

The Canda-Kinnara Jataka assigns them a honourable place in that the Tathagata Buddha and Yashodhra take birth in the life of Kinnara and live in the country of the Kinnara. The other work Apadana selects Kinnara Theras and Theris, descriptions of whose lives have been given honourable place among the class of the most honoured and learned class of monks of the Doctrine and the amount of representation given to them is also of high degree. Ordinarily we may presume them belonging to an illiterate tribe of high mountain region.

We are prompted here to remember also the wonderous deeds of Majjhima and his four companions, the missionaries of Asoka the Great, the Great Emperor, under whose aegis, the farsighted Moggaliputta, sent a team to the high Himalaya.

Thus a small culture of the Buddhist Kinnaras flourished since the ancient times in the region of headwaters of the river Chandrabhaga at a great height in the Himalaya. Lahul, the Lo-u-lo of Hiuen Tsiang and Lahuna of the inscription of the Vihar, became a famed place. Geographical importance of the region was identified by the wise ancient observers. The river was assigned the name Chandrabhaga at its head. But before this, independent names of its two heads were devised and then the name of the main river was commissioned by combining the names of its two headwaters. The river could not have been named in this manner by the Kinnars inhabiting the river banks, who were perhaps illiterate and not possessing as much knolwedge. It was named by the educated adventurers who came from the lower regions.

The second is the site of the famous monastery of Lahul situated in the middle of the height of the mountain on the confluence of Chandra and Bhaga. In the old local Bhoti writings it is written as Gandhala and is still pronounced similarly in sTod. This is possibly a remnant of a name of Indian Buddhism, some Pali or Sanskrit term. The term became confused with Gondhla to be corrupted to Gandhola.

The peak is named as Drilbu Ri (Ghanta Parvat). This may be a later name. There resides Chakrasamvara here. The plateau slightly above the riverbase having a level ground is named Tubchiling (folk tradition) or Tukiling (literary). The new Gandhala monastery has been founded here at Tubchiling. The articles brought from the Gandhala monastery from above are placed here. The old monastery of Gandhala still exists at its old place. The ancient site of the monastery is not known.

Notes

1. **'Guarded Plateau':** The term 'Guarded Plateau' here is translation of the original word "Rakkhitatala," writes the translator, (Horner, 1863-I: 8, Note-6). This term Rakkhitatala may be identified with the name of the sister lake of Manasatala or Manasarovara on the Kailas-Manasarovara which has now become corrupted as 'Rākśasatāla'. Rakkhita appears to be the proper word for this name is found associated with the names of several noblemen in the works referred above.
2. **Gandhala:** With the modern speakers and writers the term has become complex and confusing. There are two places with almost similar names. The first is Gundhla also known as Tinan and Gondhla. This is the seat of the Thakurs of the Tinan valley, i.e. Chandra valley. Gondhla or Goondhla is a distorted medieval name. Tinan is old and traditional name of the area and also name of the place presently known as Gundhla. Its proper form is Gundhla. All the documents from the house and other older writings from the area write Gundhla.

2

The Four Great Rivers of the Himalaya in Jambudvīpa

Himalaya, the immense complex of mountain chains, with the highest mountain peak in the world, is a precious crown of Bhāratavarṣa in Jambudvīpa. On the high plateau in the middle of the mountain are situated some of its grand monuments: mount Kailas, lakes Manasarovara and Rāksśasatāla. Sources of some great rivers are situated at some distance around them. This unique physiography of the Himalaya probably could have been one of the sources of inspiration for the ancient geographers of India for creation of the geographical map of the world. Four famous rivers emanating from the great height of the Himalaya are greatly praised in the ancient literature of India. They hold in fact the same magnificent position in their real geographical situation. They are reckoned among the world's largest and the longest rivers. According to the Puranas they are named as Gaṅgā, Cakṣu, Sītā and Bhadra Somā. According to Vasubandhu's (ca. 350-430 CE), born at Puruspura in Gandhara, Sanskrit work Abhidharmkośbhāṣya they are named as: Gaṅgā, Sindhu, Vakṣu and Śītā. The two sources exhibit some dissimilarity in naming the four rivers. The difference in the system of naming is one reason, scholars and specialists confront many problems in correlating these names with the real geographical entities and their modern names.

The World according to Hindu Cosmolgy: According to the Puranas, explains S.M. Ali, the world comprises of seven dvīpas and seven seas, arranged alternately in circle. The dvīpa in the centre is famous as Jambudvīpa which is surrounded by an ocean of salt water. Thereafter comes the second dvīpa encompassed by the ocean of sugarcane—juice. The series of seven dvīpas, and seven oceans of different kinds, are thus arranged similarly one after the other. Their areas also increase in simple geometrical progression as we move outwards from the centre. The last ocean is of fresh water, (S.M. Ali, 1966: 26).

Jambudvīpa, perhaps the largest, according to S.M. Ali, corresponds to the continent of Asia. It is divided into nine Varṣas or divisions of land and has the same number of mountain ranges, each forming a boundary of a Varṣa.

In the series of nine regions and nine mountains Bhāratavarṣa, the last of the regions, is situated in the south of Himavat, the Himalaya. The high and the sacred mount Meru is situated in the middle of Jambudvīpa. Before Himalaya is situated the land of Kimpuruṣa and before it is the mountain of Hemkūṭa wherein is located the Kailas. There is a big city full of rows of big houses decorated with gold and diamonds. This rich city belongs to the great god Kubera, the king of Kinnaras and the Lord of wealth. Bhāratavarṣa corresponds to the Indian sub-continent.

River system: According to the Puranas, four great rivers originate from mount Meru. They flow in the four directions towards east, south, west and north. Indeed these rivers are four branches of the original river Swarga-gaṅgā or Mandākinī. It rises from under the feet of Viṣṇu, at the polar star. Passing through the circle of the moon, it falls upon the summit of Meru, where it divides into four streams which flow towards the four cardinal directions. But before the heavenly stream divides into these four branches, it encircles Meru through seven channels for a space of 80,000 yojanas. After its division, each stream falls from the immense height of Meru into separate lakes from where they flow towards their respective directions. Thus there are four corresponding lakes Aruṇodā, in the east of Meru, Manasā in the south, Sitodā in the west and Mahābhadrā in the north. The Puranic accounts also propose that these four rivers after originating from the four lakes pass through the heads of various animals, writes S.M. Ali.

S.M. Ali identifies Meru of the Puranas with the Great Pamir Knot of Asia. He writes, "The Pamir is the focal point of Central Asian drainage. Major rivers flow from it towards west (Oxus), south (Indus), east (Tarim) and north (Syr Daria)", (S.M. Ali, 1983: 52).

The World according to the Buddhist Cosmology: Vasubandhu explains the world system in his celebrated work Abhidharmkośbhāṣya while explaining the process of transmigration of a life from one world to another as a cause of one's karmic actions. The physical world in which the living beings reside is named as Bhājanloka. Over the golden plane which lies over the sea of water there are seven concentric rows of mountains with interval of seas in between. Sumeru the eighth mountain is in the center. This whole system is surrounded by a vast ocean of salt water which is encircled by the ninth mountain of iron called Cakravāḍa, the outer wall.

The Four Continents: In the outer salt sea, corresponding to the four sides of Sumeru, are four continents. Jambudvīpa (Rose Apple Tree Continent), among them, is situated in the south of Sumeru in the form of a cart. Jambudvīpa is flanked by two sub-continents, Cāmara and Avaracāmara. All these continents are inhabited by humans.

Jambudvīpa: Jambudvīpa is almost triangular in shape with its base towards the north and the apex downwards, towards the south. But this apex is not exactly an angle and greatly coincides with the map of India. The author calls it a shape of cart. Moving north from the south there are three mountain ranges. Further up is the great mount of Himavat, the mountain of Snows, our Himalaya. Beyond this is the great Lake Anavatapta, Mansarovara. Still beyond this is situated the mountain Gandhamādana, (Sangpo, 2012-II: 1049-1057). Jambūdvīpa here is identical with the Indian sub-continent.

The Rivers: From the lake Anavatapta, Lake of 'No Heat', flow four great rivers named: 1. Gaṅgā, 2. Sindhu, 3. Vakṣu, and 4. Śītā, which the translator of this work equates the first three with Gaṅgā, Indus and Oxus. The fourth Śītā has been left with some references who locate the river in the area of Central Asia, (Sangpo, 2012-II: 1057).

Pali sources provide us some interesting information on the subject. Malalasekera, quoting from the Pali literature, explains that Anotatta i.e. Anvatapta or Mansarovara is one of the seven great lakes of Himavā i.e. Himalaya. The water of this lake is always cool, hence the name. Many bathing places are found therein free from fish and tortoises, with crystal clear waters, where Buddhas, Pratyek Buddhas and Arahatas bathe and whither devas and yakkhas, come for sport. Four channels open out of the lake in the direction of the four quarters which are named: Simhamukha, Hathimukha, Assamukha and Usabhamukha i.e. head of lion, elephant, horse and cattle. Four rivers flow from these channels and animals of the respective names abound on the banks of these four rivers. The eastward river encircles the lake three times, waters the non-human regions of Himavā and enters the ocean. The rivers that flow north and westward flow in these directions through regions inhabited by non-humans and enter the ocean, (Malalasekera, 1937: 96-97). The inhabitants of the lands through which the three rivers flow, other than the one flowing towards south, are stated to be non-humans. Malalasekera does not give name of the rivers. It is noteworthy that the inhabitants of the whole region of the High Himalaya are here placed among the non-humans.

The river flowing towards south is not named here. However, it may be inferred from the previous descriptions and understood, as Gaṅgā. The river appears to be very vast which flows through extensive land and spreads into several big branches. It has been greatly glorified. Malalasekera writes that, "This river, like the one of eastward, flows three times round the lake Mansarovara and then straight south over a rocky channel for sixty leagues and then down a precipice forming a cascade six miles in width. For sixty leagues the water dashes through the air on to a rock named Tiyaggala, wherein by the force of the impact of the waters the Tiyaggala Pokharaṇī, a lake, has been formed, fifty leagues deep. From this lake the waters run through a rocky chasm for sixty leagues, then underground for sixty leagues to an oblique mountain, Vijjha, where the stream divides into five branches, like the fingers of the hand. Names of the different parts of this river starting from its origin are given as under. The part which encircles the original lake Anotatta is called Āvaṭṭagaṅgā; the sixty leagues of stream which runs over the rocky channel, Kaṅhagaṅgā; the thirty leagues of waterfall in the air, Ākāśgaṅgā; the sixty leagues flowing out of the Tiyaggala-Pokharaṇī and through the rocky gorge is called Bahalagaṅgā, and the river underground, Ummaggagaṅgā. The five streams into which the river is divided after leaving the oblique mountain Vijjha are called Gaṅgā, Yamunā, Aciravatī, Sarabhū and Mahī", (Malalasekera, 1937: 97).

The Four Great Rivers in the Puranas: In the Puranas as well the four rivers have been described as emanating from the heads of various animals. S.M. Ali writes that the Puranic accounts suppose that these rivers emanate from the heads of four different animals. "The Gaṅgā running towards the south passes through a cow's head, hence India is called the Land of Cows. In the west is a horse's head from which flows the Chakṣu, and the inhabitants of the countries bordering on it are of course Aśvas or Turaṅgamas, horses or rather horsemen. Towards the east is the head of an elephant, from which flows the river Sita. To the north is the lion's head, from which flows the Bhadra Somā, hence this country is called the country of the Lions, and there is actually a powerful Tartarian tribe there, called the 'Tribe of the Lion'. All the four rivers after running through the various regions of Jambūdwīpa, fall into their respective oceans", (Ali, 1983: 61-62).

The Four Rivers in Tibetan tradition: The tradition of referring to the narrative of origin of the four great rivers in Indian literature had lapsed since long back. The Tibetan writings revived the Indian tradition and it survives in their tradition in their own garb and also by adding or changing somewhat in their own manner.

Gangri (gangs-ri)— mount Kailas, and mTsho Ma-pham — lake Mansarovara, are very important pilgrimage places for the Tibetan devotees. Parnavananda informs that, circumambulation of the 51 kms. circle of the Gangri, Kailas, was completed in three or more days. Circumambulation of the mTsho Ma-pham, Manasarovara, of 86 kms. was performed when the numerous streams flowing to the lake were covered by the thick sheet of ice, in late Autumn or early Spring, but mostly it was done in the winter. Many great Teachers are known to have visited the place. Padmasambhava's name is also associated with the sacred place. It was specially important for the sgrub-thobs, Tantrik sādhakas, practitioners, who know it as "ti-se'i sgrub-gnas", "Kailas — the place for meditation". Pranava Nanda, ca. 1947, found five monasteries around the Kailas and eight on the shores of Mansarovara.

Regarding the four great rivers the Tibetan authors trace their origin from mount Kailas or the lake Mansarovara. Sum-pa mKhan-po (1704-1788), a renowned historian, writes that in Zhang-zhung i.e. Guge, there is the mount Kailas, and in front of it is the lake Mansarovara. Four rivers rise from the four sides of Kailas. Ganga rising in the east flows through Guge to India. Sindhu emanates from the south and flowing along snowy mountains of Purang passes through Monyul (the country of Mons, the inhabitants of the Indian Himalaya) to India and falls in the ocean. Pakshu, originating from the west, flows towards north and goes through Ladakh and Mo-dkar(?) to Shambhala. Sita originating from the north of Tise moves from behind Tashi Lhunpo to eastwards, turning right joins the river coming from dBus (Central Tibet). Then going through bSam-yas and Tsari, enters India. Sakya Panchen says that each of the four rivers takes seven turns round the mountain before resuming journey to their respective directions. It is difficult to argue on this point, (Dorje, 1978: 69-70).

Sumpa mKhanpo here takes the names of the rivers in their Indian form and does not follow the usual Tibetan tradition of naming them with the names of animals, through one of the parts of whose body they are presumed to originate. They have been shown emanating all from the four directions of mount Kailas. Here Si-ta has been taken for Brahmaputra, Pakshu for Sindhu, and Sindhu for Satluj.

Another important Tibetan source on the subject is the 'Digung Karchag of Gangri', 'The Guidebook of Kailas of the Digung Sect', (Filibeck,1988). The author combines knowledge from both Indian and Tibetan sources. A common name has been given to the four great rivers as kha-'babs, mouth-falling, a river falling from the mouth or head of an animal. The work provides:

1. **Ganga: River Ganga, the eastern kha-'bab.** Formerly having descended from the lake (Mansarovara) itself came out in the valley of a hardened soil in the eastern side and became famous as 'chu-mig mthong-ba rang grol' — the 'self-born spring.'

   Thus it making its way from the middle of the lake, splitting the water apart. flowed towards the west. It passed at Dulchu on the north of Guge through a hill like the mouth of an elephant and came to be known as lang-chen kha 'bab, falling from the mouth of Elephant, and became famous everywhere as river Ganga of India.

2. **Sindhu, the river kha-'bab of south.** The river originating from the north of the lake, flows southwards. Passing through Purang across a hill like the mouth of a peacock or a bull, passes through Nepal, enters India, moves to the west and reaches the country of Sindhu. It is famous as Sindhu and also as rma-bya kha-'bab, river falling from the mouth of Peacock.
3. **Pakshu, the river kha-'bab of west.** The river originating from the west of the lake, flows to east. Passing through a rock like the mouth of a horse, goes to Tsang, dBus and Khongpo of Tibet and, enters India from the eastern side in Kamarup and is named rta-mchog kha-'bab, falling from the mouth of an Excellent Horse, and is known also as Lohita, Tsangpo or Pakshu.
4. **Si-ta, the river kha-'bab of north.** The river originating from the southern side of the lake runs north and passes through a hill like the mouth of a lion behind the Kailas and then passing through Ladakh and Baltistan goes to Hor, Mongolia, and falls in the ocean in the north, and is famous as Si-ta (Filibeck,1988: 23).

Pranava Nanda found in the Tibetan sources a somewhat different interpretation of the source of the four rivers indicating to their having one common source, "The Tibetan Kailas Purana says that the Ganga had at first descended from Kailas to the Spring Chhumik-thongtol; that four rivers emerged out of this spring in copper pipes through the Lake Manas," (Pranava Nanda, 1949: 14).

Tanzin Thinley, in another source, describes, stating to quote from mdsod-'grel (Abhidharmkośbhāṣya), that there originate from the four sides of Kailas the four rivers in sequence from the rocks looking like the faces of 1. Elephant, 2. Bull, 3. Horse, and 4. Lion; or as, 1. Elephant, 2. Horse, 3. Peacock, and 4. Lion. They are named respectively: 1. Ganga, 2. Sindhu, 3. Pakshu, and 4. Sī-ta (Tanzin Thinley, 1980: 167-168). Taking view of the statements from various Tibetan sources it is difficult to reach at any definite conclusion.

Names of the four rivers currently followed in Tibetan literary tradition are given as under:

East: rTa-mchog kha-'babs, falling from the mouth of an Excellent Horse - Brahmaputra.

North: Seng-ge kha-'babs, falling from the mouth of Lion — Sindhu.

West: gLang-chen kha-'babs, falling from the mouth of Elephant — Satluj.

South: rMa-bya kha-'babs, falling from the mouth of Peacock — Ganga i.e. Karnali.

Scientific Study: Scientific study of the geography of the region of Kailas-Mansarovara by the European explorers began during the British period. William Moorcroft and Hearsay were the earliest who visited the area in 1812, (Moorcroft, 1818: 380). Some other important explorers were: H. Strachey in 1846, R. Strachey in 1848, C.A. Sherring in 1905, Sven Hedin in 1906-07, etc. Swami Pranava Nanda visited the region several times, through different routes, and spent long times in the area during the period around the Independence of the country and gathered much useful data about the region.

Geography of the Kailas Manasarovara region: Himalaya, Nāgadhirāja, the Lord of the Mountains, is known in ancient Indian literature by several names as we have seen. Himalaya, the existing name, occurs perhaps for the first time in the work of the celebrated poet-author Kalidas of the first half of sixth century CE in his work Kumārsambhavam. S.M. Ali identifies the Puranic Himvān or Himavat with the geographical Himalaya which represents the existing Great Himalayan ranges. In Tibetan it is called hi-ma-la or ri-bo gangs-can.

Kailas: The great mount Kailas is known in Tibetan as Gangri (Gangs-ri = snowy mountain), Ti-se, Ti-rtse or Gang Rinpoche. The sacred mountain is the Abode of Shiva and there live the Arhatas. According to Lha-rgyas, an ancient song from sTod, there lives the deity of the middle region, the region between the earth and the firmament, bTsan.

Manasarovara: Mansarovara or Mānasa is known in Tibetan as mTsho Ma-pang, Ma-vang or Ma-pham and also as Ma-dros as translation of Sanskrit 'Anavatapta'. The adjective g-yu-mtsho, turquoise lake, is added like a jewel. In the folk tradition of sTod, Lahul, there resides in the lake the powerful Naga, the king of the nether world.

Rākśastāla or Rāvaṇahṛd: It is known in Tibetan as La-ngag. According to one source, quoting from a Puranic source, Rākśastāla is also known as Lohitya-sarovara and that river Brahmaputra originates from it. Rakkhitatāla, the Pali name, appears to be its original name.

Place of origin of the Four Great Rivers: Most of the Puranas hold that the four great rivers originate from mount Meru. We locate Meru, for our purpose, on the Himalaya. Like Pamir Knot four rivers also emanate from the Himalaya from around the Kailas and Manasarovara each flowing to four different directions. Tibetan sources while dealing with these four great Indian rivers know only of the Himalaya as their source and make no mention of Pamir. Swami Pravavanand follows the Tibetan tradition. Moreover we treat the four rivers as a single group as has been dealt with in the Puranas. Therefore they all originate from one place. In this regard it is noteworthy that Agrawala, in his study on the Matsya Purana holds that, among others, the four great rivers Ganga. Sindhu, Satadru and Lauhitya (=Brahmaputra) all rise from the Himalayas, (Agrawala, 1963: 194-95).

In this regard the modern explorers have now established that it is true that the four rivers originate from the summit of the Himalaya but none of them originates either from Kailas or Manasarovara. They originate in the neighbourhood of the region at some distances from these great landmarks.

On the great plateau on the summit of the Himalaya, the grand Kailas is situated somewhat on northern direction and lake Manasrovara on its south at a distance of about 32 kms. The sister lake Rākśastāla, slightly smaller in size, is situated at some lower level on the western side of Mansarovara. The two lakes are connected by a stream named Barkha or Ganga-chhu in Tibetan of about six kms. long flowing from the former to the latter but occasionally becoming subterranean. On the south of Manasarovara is situated mount Gurlā Mandhātā and on its east are some smaller hills. Thus the heavenly lake Mansarovara naturally being surrounded from all the sides by high mountains is described in the Pali sources figuratively. Malalasekera writes, 'Anotatta is one of the seven lakes of Himavā. It is surrounded by five mountain peaks... overshadows the whole lake, which is also hidden by other peaks. ...The light of the Sun and of the moon never falls directly on the water but only in reflection. This means that the water is always cool, hence the name'. It is an example of the deep and intimate knowledge of the ancient scholars even of such a remote and difficult area as the region of Kailas-Manasarovara.

Pranava Nanda, drawing from the Tibetan sources, as he says, gives the direction and approximate distances of the sources of the four great rivers from the holy lake. He writes, Indus rises in the north-east of Kailas about 100 kms. from Manasarovara; Brahmaputra 107 kms. south-east of Manasarovara; Satluj at Dulchu 48 kms. in the west of Mansarovara or Rākśastāla and Karnali at 48 kms. south-west of Mansarovara. Thus they are situated within the radius of 72 kms. as the crow flies, from the Kailas-Mansarovara region, (Pranava Nanda, 1949: 16).

Naming the rivers: On this aspect of naming the rivers S.M. Ali writes that the nomenclature of the rivers have been a source of constant trouble. It is not peculiar to the Puranas alone. Even today in certain regions the main channel of a river assumes a different name after every bend. In Ladakh the Indus is known by many names, so is the Sutlej. The names Karnālī, Gogra, Śāradā and Kuriali all pertain to one river, and these are in addition to their purely Tibetan names.

S.M. Ali further writes, 'The name Gaṅgā has been given ever since ancient times to many large rivers particularly to those which have been considered sacred. In Bhāratavarṣa alone we have the Pen-Gaṅgā, Waingaṅgā, Rāmagaṅgā, Kṛṣṇagaṅgā, Viṣṇugaṅgā and a number of other Gangas which we can easily locate on any modern map. The Gaṅgā of the Puranas may be easily taken to denote any river of the Seven Dvipas which is as big, and as beneficial as the Gaṅgā proper', (S.M. Ali 62-63). We have seen above the Pali version of the description of Gaṅgā. S.M. Ali locates Gaṅgā of the Puranas outside the Indian sub-continent, as witnessed above.

The Ancient and Modern names: The Puranic geographers deal with the four rivers collectively as a set. They explain that the four rivers originate from one common place named mount Meru which is situated in the middle of Jambudvīpa and each one flows to the respective four cardinal directions. Therefore we cannot divide these four great rivers, some originating from one place and others from a different place. The scholars identify the Puranic Jambudvīpa putting it in a wider perspective, with the continent of Asia and thus S.M. Ali identifies Meru with Pamir Knot. Thus the four Puranic rivers emanate from there. Sangpo identifies Ganga and Sindhu perhaps with those emanating from the Himalaya, but he places Pakṣu and Śītā in the Central Asia.

The two names Ganga and Sindhu remained unchanged throughout the history till the modern times and are well known Himalayan rivers. Modern geographers identify Gaṅgā with Karnāli, also called Gogra, as Gaṅgā does not originate exactly from the place cited. The Puranic and some other sources also apply some different names for some of the famous four rivers. These are Bhadra Somā, Pakṣu or Cakṣu or Vakṣu, and the third is Sītā or Śītā. The name Bhadra Somā, first of the three names, perhaps belongs only to the Puranas. Therefore it remained obscure. The other two are famous and have been dealt with by numerous scholars. They mostly place them in Central Asia. The names of Satluj and Brahmaputra do not appear in their recognizable form in the lists of rivers in the ancient sources. There appears a slight difference in the system of naming the rivers in the Vedic and the Puranic, and there also could be some different stages of naming in each of the two.

The name Peacock for the source of Ganga is found only in the Tibetan sources. Some Tibetan sources deal with these ancient Indian names of the rivers. But lack of consistency is observed among the sources. The two names Ganga and Sindhu in Tibetan tradition at places have been found misplaced. The Tibetan authors also disagree among themselves regarding the identification of the two ancient Puranic names of rivers Pakṣu and Sītā. Sumpa

Khanpo recognizes Pakṣu with Sindhu and Sītā with Brahmaputra. Swami Pranava Nanda, however, on the strength of two Tibetan guidebooks which he names as 'Kangri Karchhak', (Guidebook of Kailash) identifies Indian names of the rivers with the modern names as Pakṣu with Brahmaputra, and Sītā with Sindhu, (Pranava Nanda, 1949: 14-16). This is the pattern also followed in the Digung Gangri Karchag.

We look at the Puranic list of names again placing them in serial order in the sequence as they appear originally, as shown by S.M. Ali, in tabular form. Then we compare them keeping the present names of the four rivers and their directions against each of them, as under:

Direction	**Modern Name**	**Puranic Name**	**Animal Name**	**Lake Name**
South	Ganga	Ganga	Cow	Manasa
West	Satluj	Cakṣu	Horse	Sitoda
North	Sindhu	Sītā	Lion	Mahabhadra
East	Brahmaputra	Bhadra Somā	Elephant	Arunoda

In the last two columns the names of animals and lakes have been placed as they appear. Here we porpose a slight change. We are now firm, as we have seen in the previous chapter, the first and original name of Sindhu with its proper form and meaning is Sita. The name survived throughout the history till today. But the scholars at different times changed it to Sītā or Śīta, etc., and sometimes they took it for a different river. For example Alberuni quoting from Matsyapurana writes that three rivers 'Sita, Chakshu and Sindhu' rise from the Himavant, flow westwards and fall in the western ocean. Here Sita and Sindhu are taken for two different rivers. Therefore we have to abandon the other forms of the name Sita. As such the lake related to the river Sita or Sindhu should be Sitoda. Therefore we replace Mahabhadra with Sitoda alongwith the associated name of the animal. Thus the table may be presented finally as:

Direction	Modern Name	Puranic Name	Animal Name	Lake Name
South	Ganga	Ganga	Cow	Manasa
West	Satluj	Cakṣu	Lion	Mahabhadra
North	Sindhu	Sītā	Horse	Sitoda
East	Brahmaputra	Bhadra Somā	Elephant	Arunoda

Regarding Ganga no clarification is necessary. Sindhu in Ladakh is still known as Sita or the like and it is in usage with a class of persons there. Hence Sita and all its other forms may be taken for Sindhu. All the forms of Caksu, Vaksu, Paksu, etc. may be taken for Satluj. In this manner the habitation of the respective animals also matches with that of the river. The Puranic names thus may be matched with their modern names here as: Ganga (= Ganga), Satluj (= Cakṣu), Sindhu (= Sita, Sītā or Śītā) and Brahmaputra (= Bhadra Somā). The matter, of course, needs much wider and deeper inquisition.

3

Chanda Kinnara Játaka and the Chanda-Parvata

The upper portion of the Satluj valley, between Shipki La (Pass), on the border with the Chinese Tibet and Rampur in Shimla district of Himachal Pradesh, is today designated as district Kinnaur. It formerly comprised a part of the Bashahar state. The residents of the district are recognised as a tribe under the Constitution of India. The people know themselves as Kanauring in their own language and to their neigbours they are known as Kanaurá. The term Kanauring is applied for their country as well as their language. Rahul Sankrityayan quoting from a Pali book writes that in the second century BCE there lived Kinnaras on the bank of river Chandrabhaga.

The valleys of Chandra and Bhaga, the headwaters of Chandrabhaga, and a portion of it after the confluence of the two is today known as Lahul. Ethnically and linguistically they do not seem to be much different from the Kanaurás. They speak languages, which are although not the same, close to each other. The Lahula and Kanauri languages are composed of at least three elements of which an important element is the archaic 'su' (=god), as Rahul Sankrityayan calls it. The linguists classify the two dialects of Kanauri and Lahuli under the pronominalised Tibeto-Burman family. The character of pronominalisation, which distinguishes it from some other languages of the same family, is supposed to have been acquired while these tribes, or the tribe, came into contact with the ancient Indian tribe of the Munda, who today inhabit the Central Indian localities. The region of Chandrabhaga touches that of Satluj. Therefore, it is not impossible to suppose that the same tribe of Kinnara inhabited the Chandrabhaga and the Satluj valleys. Retaining the traits of Kinnara generally, the Lahulas have lost their original name in the course of their long history. Rahul explains that the area of the Kinnaras extended even beyond their present habitat, as we find some linguistic remnants in the areas of Uttrakashi and further east.

Thus we observe that the Kinnaras have been inhabiting the same geographical territory in the Western Himalayas since they were observed the earliest, more than two thousand years back.

Kinnaras have been a popular subject of description in the ancient literature of all the major religions of ancient India, Hinduism, Buddhism and Jainism. All of them locate them in the Himalayas. There they have been identified as the neighbours of the gandharvas, yakshas and kiratas.

Scholars have attempted to identify the existing Kinnaras with the classical Kinnaras and establish a relationship between the two. Rahul says that the modern term Kanaur is the corrupt form of Kinnara (Rahul 1956: 292). Das too is confident and says, 'Under the circumstances it may not be unjustifiable to identify the Kinnaras of early literature with the modern Kanauris who are the inhabitants of the modern Kanaur valley belonging to the Bashahar state on the bank of the upper Satluj, the land of the Kanauri speaking hilly tract which is rugged in an extraordinary degree. The descendants of the old Kinnaras live today in this Kanaur valley extending upto the Shimla hills. They are known today as Kinnauris. They speak a Tibeto Burmese language closely allied to those of Lahul and Malana. So the Kanauris seem to be the true descendants of devagayakas or svarga-gayakah, i.e. the celestial singers,' (Das, 1954: 44-45).

The Chanda-Kinnara Játaka story takes us further in strengthening our above proposition of the relationship between the ancient Kinnara race and the present Kanaura tribe. In the story we also come across an unidentified mountain named Chanda-parvata which was the habitation of the Great Being in his incarnation as a Kinnara. Lord Buddha, in one of his former lives as a Boddhisattva was born in the Kinnara tribe and was named Chanda and his beloved Yoshodara was named Chandā. The two lived in the Himalaya on the mountain named Chanda, the Moon.

The story goes like this, (Cowell, 1993: Jataka No. 485), 'This story was told by the Master, while dwelling in the banyan grove by Kapilapura about Rahula's mother when she was in the palace.

'The Master, seated in his fathers' house, recounted after the meal was done: 'I will praise the noble qualities of Rahula's mother in her own house, by telling the Chanda-Kinnara Birth.'

The Master said, "It is no marvel, great king! That now in my last existence the lady should love, and should be of faithful heart and led by me along. So also even when born as an animal, she was faithful and mine alone." Then at the king's request he told the story of the past.

Thus goes the story, "Once upon a time when Brahmadatta was king in Benares the Great Being was born in the region of the Himalaya as a fairy, Kinnara. His wife was named Chandā (which means the Moon). These two dwelt together on a silver mountain named Canda-pabbata, or the Mountain of the Moon. At that time the king of Benares had committed his government to his ministers, and all alone dressed in two yellow robes and armed with the five weapons (sword, spear, bow, battle-axe, shield), he proceeded to the Himalayas.

'Whilst eating his venison he remembered where was a little stream, and began to climb the hill. Now the fairies that live on the Mountain of the Moon in the rainy season remain on the mountain, and come down only in the hot weather. At that time this fairy Canda, with his mate, came down and wandered about, anointing himself with perfumes, eating the pollen of flowers, clothing himself in flower-gauze for inner and outer garments, swinging in the creepers to amuse himself, singing songs in a honey voice. He too came to this stream, and at one halting-place he went down into it with his wife, scattering flowers about and playing in the water. Then they put on again their garments of flowers, and on a sandy spot white as a silver plate they spread a couch of flowers, and lay there. Picking up a piece of bamboo, the male fairy began to play upon it, and sang with a honey-voice; while his mate waving her soft hands danced hard by and sang withal. The king caught the sound, and treading softly that his footsteps might not be heard, he approached, and stood watching the fairies in a secret place.

He immediately fell in love with the female fairy.' I will shoot the husband," thought he, "and kill him, and I will live here with the wife." Then he shot the fairy Canda, who lamented in pain.

'Lying upon his couch of flowers, he lost consciousness, and turned away. The king stood where he was. But the other fairy did not know that the Great Being was wounded, not even when he uttered his lament, being intoxicated with her own delight. Seeing him lie there turned away and lifeless, she began to wonder what could be the matter with her lord. As she examined him she saw the blood oozing from the mouth of the wound, and being unable to bear the great pain of sorrow for her beloved husband, she cried out with a loud voice. "The fairy must be dead," thought the king, and he came out and showed himself. When Canda beheld him she thought, 'This must be the brigand who has slain my dear husband!" and trembling she took to flight. Standing upon the hill-top she denounced the king.

'Hearing these words the king departed indifferent. Canda so soon as she knew him gone came up and embracing the Great Being took him up to the hill top, and laid him on the flat land there, placing his head on her lap, she made her moan.

'So did she make her moan; and putting the hand of the Great Being on her breast she felt that it still was warm. "Canda lives yet!" she thought. "I will taunt the gods until I bring him to life again." Then she cried aloud, taunting them, "Are there none who govern the world, are they on a journey? Or per adventure they are dead, and therefore save not my dear husband!" By the power of her pain Sakka's throne became hot. Pondering he perceived the cause; in the form of a Brahmin he approached, and from a water pot took water and sprinkled the Great Being with it. On the instant the poison ceased to act, his colour returned, he knew not so much as the place where the wound had been, the Great Being stood up quite well. Canda seeing her well-beloved husband to be whole in joy fell at the feet of Sakka, and sang his praise".

"Praise, holy brahmin! Who didst give unto a hapless wife.

Her well-loved husband, sprinkling him with the elixir of life."

Sakka then gave this advice "From this time forth go not down from the Mountain of the Moon among the paths of men, but abide here." Twice repeated this, and then returned to his own place. And Chanda said to her husband, "Why stay here in danger, my lord? Come, let us go to the Mountain of the Moon," reciting the last stanza.

"To the mountain let us go
Where the lovely rivers flow,
Rivers all overgrown with flowers
There for ever, while the breeze
Whispers in a thousand trees,
Charm with talk the happy hours."

'When the Master had ended this discourse, he said, "Not now only, but long ago as now, she was devoted and faithful of heart to me." Then he identified the Birth, 'At that time Anuraddha was the king, Rahula's mother was Canda, and I myself was the fairy."

The above Játaka tale appears to enjoy high reputation among the followers of the Doctrine. Discovery of a drawing of the story in a relief in Gandhara is a testimony to this fact. Das says, 'Canda-Kinnara' Játaka describes their sportive habits. This story of the Játaka has been well preserved in a Gandhara relief preserved in the Indian Museum (No. 5130). The relief depicts the "abduction of a woman" by a king after her male companion was shot by him in a forest country where the couple had gone to indulge in music and dance,' (Das, 1954: 42).

The value of the story is further enhanced from another fact, that the present Játaka story is considered to belong to the earliest Epoch, among the three Epochs of existence of the Buddha in the Buddhist world, 'the Distant Epoch, (durenidanam), extending from the time when he fell at the feet of Dipankara to his birth in the city of the tusita gods." The Middle Epoch (avidure) extends from that time until he obtained Buddhahood, and the Near Epoch (santike) until his death, (Cowell, 1993: note-i, 179).

The outline of the above story reveals that once the Buddha, in his former lives took birth in the region of the Himalaya as a fairy, a Kinnara named Chanda. His beloved was named Chandā. They lived on the Chanda Parvata (the mountain of the Moon). Thus the Chanda Parvata must be searched in the area of habitat of the Kinnaras. The fact that the Kinnaras are found occupying the same geographical tract continuously since they were first located, according to the Indian Buddhist literature, as we have seen above, compels us also to locate the Chanda-parvata in the same geographical location.

Today no mountain or mountain peak is known in whole of the Himalayas as 'Chanda' which could help us to identify with the above mountain. But in the same territory of the traditional habitat of the Kinnaras there abound some permanent geographical marks which rebound with the name Chanda or Chandra, either independently or as a prefix to a name. These are Chandra-tal (the Moon lake), the river Chandra (Moon river) and lastly the Chandrabhaga. These are not disparate names assembled here as mere collection of homonyms, but all are very well interconnected with each other. The river Chandra originates at some distance above lake Chandratal and passes close to it in Lahul and after joining with Bhaga at Tandi, also in Lahul, forms the united Chandrabhaga. The river Chandra and substantial section of the Chandrabhaga meander among the high mountains having peaks covered with silvery white snow sheets, through the whole of their course in the region. Therefore, it is not impossible to presume that one of the mountains among them on the routes of the rivers or around the lake, certainly hoisted the sublime name Chanda. Of course, Chandra and Chanda are synonyms. The Chanda-Parvata, the mountain named Chanda, existed once there in the same vicvinity in around the Chandratal or along the valleys of the Chandra or the Chandrabhaga, the catchment areas of the Chandra and Chandrabhaga somewhere in Lahul. The name of the mountain perhaps became disused and slowly it became obsolete while the names of the lake and the rivers remained alive.

Chanda-parvata is name of a real mountain. Its identification has been lost in the long historical course. Monier-Williams, quoting the same term Chandra-parvata, from a different source, translates as 'Moon-mountain', and he also means by it a 'name of a mountain' which is more important from our point of view (Monier-Williams, 1981: 386-387). This corroborates the above sources confirming the existence of the mountain named Chanda or Chandra, both of which signify the same meaning.

The Kinnaras too are not mythical beings or the celestial beings as have been described in many of the holy works. They were a class of real human beings, a race living in the High Himalayas, who came down from their habitat in the high mountains to the lower regions only occasionally. They possessed some unique traits which attracted numerous authors and hence they found place in many prominent literary works. The Kinnara of the story carries the characteristics of the existing Kinaurás in the annual transmigratory character due to economic compulsions. The mountain Chanda of the story may be identified with the existing Drilbu Ri, Ghanta Parvata or Gandhala, standing between the two rivers Chandra and Bhaga at their confluence which form the Chandrabhaga. At the middle of the height is situated the ancient temple, now monastery, of Gandhala, opposite to Tandi. We have also seen in a previous chapter that as given in the ancient Pali work Apadana, Kinnaras lived on the banks of Chandrabaga.

Thus the Lord, Tathagata Buddha, alongwith his mate Yashodhara, lived in one of his early births, as a member of the Kinnara family in Lahul Himalaya in the Western High Himalayan region.

4

Asoka's Mission to Suvaṇṇa-bhūmi An Ancient State in the High Central Himalaya

Two ancient works of Sri Lanka — Dipvamsa (CE middle 4th century) and Mahavamsa (CE middle 5th century) — narrate that on the conclusion of the third Council held under the aegis of Priyadarśī, Emperor Asoka (BCE 241), *mahathera* Moggaliputta, looking into founding of the religion in the future, advised the theras, to go each taking with them four theras, making themselves as leader, to different countries on the border for the propagation of the Doctrine. A team was sent to the Himalaya. Then notably a small team of two theras was sent to a country named Suvaṇṇabhūmi (Suvarṇabhūmi), Gold Country. Scholars have attempted to identify the country named Suvaṇṇabhūmi, all pointing to the east in Bengal in India or Burma. But there appears to exist lack of consensus among the scholars on the issue.

Mahavamsa provides that the party headed by Majjhantika went to Gandhar and Kashmir. Besides the area assigned to the theras they also preached in some part of the Himalaya. "The thera preached the doctrine, and thereupon the naga king came unto the three refuges and the precepts of duty, and this likewise did eighty four thousand serpents and many gandhabhas, yakhas and kumbhāṇḍakas in the Himalaya. But a yakkha named Pandaka with his wife the yakkhini Harita and his five hundred sons obtained the first fruit of sanctification," (Geiger 1912: 83). This latter position regarding the works by Majjhantika and his party in the Himalaya is not found mentioned in the Dipvamsa, the earlier work. It is important to note that there appear at places differences in the descriptions in the latter work from those of the earlier work. Notably they make great difference in our understanding of some of the important facts.

The Mahavamsa further provides that the party going to the Himalaya was headed by the wise Majjhima. He had gone with four other theras. The five theras separately converted five kingdoms. Eighty kotis of living beings attained to the reward of the path of salvation, (Geiger, 1812: 86). The work does not assign any name to the people of the Himalaya or the regions where they lived and also it does not name the other four theras.

Dipvamsa, the earlier work, provides that, for preaching among the Yaksha-gaṇa in the Himalaya, Majjhima went with the theras Kassapagotta, Durāsada, Sahadeva and Mūlakadeva, (Shastri, 1996, 8:10-11). Oldenberg names in place of Durāsada as Durabhisara; and Geiger, in a note, gives for Durāsada and Mūlakadeva as Dundubhisara and Mūladeva (Alakadeva), (Geiger, 1912, note-7: 85). Alexander Cunningham reports that the relics of Majjhima and Kassapa were discovered in no. 2 Tope at Sanchi, (Cunningham, 1854b: 118), corroborating the literary sources.

In both the works the term used for Himalaya is found as Himavanta which has been identified readily. Presently this name is used in Tibetan literature for Tibet itself as kha-va-can (Himvant, Himavat or Himvān).

Dipvamsa describes another relationship of Asoka with the Himalaya. It says that after the Emperor's reign spread over the whole of Jambudvipa the devas began to bring daily a pitcher of auspicious water (solah-kumbhī jal) from the Anotatta (Mansarovar) lake situated at the top of the Himalaya, mixed with life-saving drugs from the medicinal herbs, (Shastri, 1996, 6: 2-3).

Then immediately it is provided in the Mahavamsa that Soṇa and Uttara went to Suvaṇṇabhūmi. There lived a Rākshsī, female demon, who used to come forth out of the sea and devour the male child born of the king of the country and disappear.

This narrative is given in the Dipvamsa in the manner that Soṇa and Uttara in Suvaṇṇabhūmi brought under the influence of the Dharma and liberated many Piśāchas by creating faith in them. In simple statement the two missionaries worked in Suvaṇṇabhūmi among the people named Piśācha. Notably, in the latter work Mahavamsa, this fact has become slightly modified, as seen above.

About the identification of Suvaṇṇabhūmi or Suvanrṇabhūmi Geiger, the translator of Mahavamsa, in a note writes that: the general opinion was, until recently, that Suvaṇṇabhūmi 'the goldland' is lower Burma with adjacent districts. But this is very doubtful, since it is a fact that Buddhism reached Burma from China in the Mahayana form and not before the fourth century A.D. Fleet suggests that Suvaṇṇabhūmi might be the country in Bengal called by Hiuen-tsang Ka-lo-na-su-fa-la-na = Karṇasuvarṇa, or else the country along the river Son, a river in Central India, and tributary of Ganges on its right bank, which is also called Hiranayavāha, 'the gold bearer', (Geiger, 1912-Note 2: 86; Panda, 2010-I: 184).

Cunningham's view on Suvanrṇabhūmi is that, "As this land was at the sea coast, it may be identified either with Ava, the Aurea Regio, or with Siam, the Aurea Chersonesus," (Cunningham, 1854b: 118). B.C. Law maintains that Suvaṇṇabhūmi is identical with Lower Burma (Pegu and Moulmein Districts). According to Sāsanavamsa it is Sudhammanagore, that is Thaton at the mouth of the Sittaung river, (Law, 1932: 70). From all these it appears that the matter is not still quite clear.

Brahmapura: Hiuen-tsang, a great Chinese pilgrim-scholar, visited India in the first half of seventh century CE. After crossing the region of Mathura and going towards the north or north-east i.e. the hills he enters the kingdom named Brahmapura. While describing the location of Brahmpura he writes that on its north lies a country named Suvarṇagotra. Then he describes this country saying that Brahmpura is bounded on the north by the great Snowy mountains, in the midst of which is the country called Suvarṇagotra. From this country comes a superior sort of gold, and hence the name. It is extended from east to west and contracted from north to south. The land produces winter wheat and much cattle, sheep, and horses. The climate is extremely cold (icy). On the eastern side this country is bordered by the Fan kingdom (Tibet), on the west by San-po-ho, on the north by Khotan, (Beal, 1884. 198-199). Alexander Cunnigham identifies Brahampura with the regions of Garhwal and Kumaon (Cunningham, 1924: 408) which coincide with the existing state of Uttrakhand. The only country lying immediately on the northern side of Brahmpura, or Uttrakhand, befitting the above description, is the region which was known in the past as Guge and is presently popular as Western Tibet.

Western Tibet: The various geographical features of Suvarṇagotra viz. location, shape, climate, various kinds of production like the kinds of cattle, winter wheat i.e. one crop in a year in the summer, and specially the production of the superior kind of gold which came to India, all agree with that of Western Tibet or Guge. The rectangular shaped Guge lies longitudinally north-east to north-west roughly along the valleys of headwaters of Sindhu and Satluj. On its east lies Nepal, on the east and north-east the mainland Tibet and on the Indian side on the west lie Ladakh, Spiti and Kinnaur and southwards Uttrakhand.

In its earliest known history the region was known in the Tibetan history as Zhang-zhung. Srong-btsan sGampo (617-650), the king of Tibet, was the first who conquered the region and annexed it with Tibet. Srong-btsan sGampo married princess Li-mig-dman, daughter of Li-mig-skya, the king of Zhang-zhung, who came to be known as Zhang-Zhung bz'a, i.e. Queen of Zhang-zhung.

When Nyima-mgon (CE 10th century), a prince, moved from Central Tibet to this region to establish his kingdom, it was known as mNgaris. After the division of the kingdom among his three sons it came to be known as mNgaris skor-gsum, mNgari consisting of three circles or divisions.

This word mNgaris, literally meaning 'subjects of a state', is an equivalent of Sanskrit term nīvṛit (Vidyabhusan, 1911-1: 74) which the Sanskrit lexicons explain as 'any inhabited area' and Amarkosh equates it also with Janapada i.e. a district or a state, (Abhimanyu, 1999: 56). The term thus appears to carry a relationship with some ancient Indian name may be one denoting a region.

When Indrabodhi Namgyal, son of Sing-ge Namgyal (1616-1642) - king of Ladakh, was made king of this area it was known as Guge.

H. Strachey (1848) calls this area Nari (mNgari) and describes its three parts from the traditional folk knowledge in the manner: Rudok, encircled by lakes; Guge, by rocks; and Purang by glaciers or snowy mountains. Rudok was also known as sTod mNgari, Upper mNgari. The inhabitants of Uttrakhand knew the area as Hundesh (country of Huns) and its inhabitants as Huniya. Moorcroft calls it Undesh, country of wool. It was also known on the Indian side as Hiundesh, Land of Snow, and Goggadesh, Country of Guge or Goga. Today after the European scholars it is known as Western Tibet.

The name mNgaris continued to be in use with varying connotations. Zhang-zhung is found used only rarely but the name did not die. Zhang-zhung has now become a subject of much interest among the modern scholars.

(A) Gold-fields of Guge under the Regime of the Dalai Lamas: Guge, which comprises the settled part and the adjoining region, surrounding Lake Mansarovar and mount Kailash, is known to Hiuen-tsang as Suvarṇagotra from where a superior sort of gold used to come to India. Vast gold fields exist in the region even in the modern times which were being worked extensively since long past. The workers on the precious metal had become famed as 'ant' and their produce as 'ant-gold'to the world aquainted with the kind of gold since ancient times perhaps from the way of their working in the gold fields. Travellers and explorers have researched the area thoroughly during the pre-Independence period. However, the product had stopped coming to India not known since when. They also investigated the geography of the world's two great geographical monuments Kailash and Mansarovar. It is interesting to read the records of some important observers which contain valuable iinformation about the gold fields in the area and the process of its extraction. This gold was known in the past far and wide in the world and has a very long history.

Moorcroft (1812) while going from Daba to Gartok, in Guge, saw hills rich in gold. He writes, "This plain is full of shallow pits made by persons who have dug for gold-dust, and left heaps of stones by the sides of the excavations. At 306 paces ascend to another flat which has likewise been dug. At 1835 paces reach a small flat, where there has been cultivation; caves of gold miners is in the rock to the left, now deserted. At 5975 paces reach a house, near which are two gold mines with tunnels under the surface. Heretofore the excavations were perpendicular. The earth is dug out and carried to the brook to be washed. The gold here is separated by washing, there being no fuel, in the neighbourhood; or rather no wood", (Moorcroft, 1818: 440-441).

Svin Hedin mentions the gold diggers at several places in Jang-thang, extracting and procuring gold in a very simple way. 'Men come every summer, dig up the land, throw it into the air, and collect the grains of gold on a cloth spread out in the ground'. As in one year the output was abundant, the number of gold diggers doubled the following summer. 'In Jangthang the gold diggers come in the summer and the gold is washed out on flat stones in a flume 100 yards long,' (Svin Hedin, 1909-II: 279, 287, ff.). He adds, the gold fields in the Nari Khorsum Province especially at Thok Jhalung, even today represent one of the principal revenues of the Dalai Lama. The miners are still nicknamed 'ants'.

Sherring writes that there are miles and miles of rich gold-fields, of which perhaps, Thock Jalung is the best known, (Sherring, 1916:45-46). He also writes that the gold-mining industry has declined lately.

Tarikh-i-Rashidi of Mirza Muhammad Haidar Dughlat (1500-1551), of Central Asia, writing about the Goldmines of Tibet says: In most of Champa [=Jang-pa, but Jang-thang] district gold mines are found. In the level ground are pits (or caves) large enough for a man to enter. There are number of these holes and most of them terminate by running into one another. It is said that three hundred heads of families live permanently in those caves.

Alexander Gerard (1841), while writing about Kinnaur, Himachal Pradesh, also refers to the goldmines of Western Tibet and says that all the rivers abound in gold dust, and this precious metal is sometimes found in large pieces. There is a gold mine at Dango Bookpa, twelve days journey S.E. of Mansurowur, and very lately they say one has been discovered between Goongeoo and Mansurowur, which was immediately shut up by orders from Lahassa. The people told me that after the sand of the river is washed so as to be free from all the lighter particles, it is mixed with quicksilver, and the gold is detected by observing the pieces tinged by that metal, which is afterwards evaporated by heat.

Henry Strachey gives the following description of the unique phenomenon, "The principal Gold Mines, Sar Chaka, are ten days journey beyond the Salt Mines [east of Rudok] in a district otherwise uninhabited, named Sar-bachyad. These are farmed by a Sarpun [gser-dpon = gold officer], on triennial contract direct from Lhassa, independent of the authorities in Gnari. Deba Chakwa however held this contract for the last 3 years in which he was Garpan Urku-wa at Gartokh. He paid to the Lhassa Treasury 17,000 rupees per annum, and had 170 miners at work, for whose subsistence he used to send supplies of Satu, Ghiu [flour of roasted barley and butter], Tea, etc. from Pruang [Purang]. These mines are worked in shafts and galleries under ground, the gold is found in the pure native state, it undergoes no other process than washing and sifting before it enters the market, and after that requires little or no refining. The metal is sometimes found in large masses, the Lama of Gangri is said to have one weighing 5 Nega, i.e. near seer," (Henry Strachey, 1848: 548-549).

Swami Parnavanand writes, "Almost parallel to the Ganga Chhu (the stream linking Manas Tal and Rakshas Tal) at a distance of about a mile on the south there is a vein of gold deposit extending from the shores of the Manas right up to the Rakshas." "There are some gold mines in the district of Songkora or Sankora situated at a distance of a week's march on the north-east of Manasarovar. Mining is done here mostly in winter. It is reported that gold is collected at depths ranging from 18 to 24 feet and that one collects 3 to 6 tolas of gold in the course of a season." "Some 15 day's march northwards from the shores of the Manas leads one to the extensive and richer goldfields at Thok-jalung, Munakthok, Rungmar-thok, Thok-daurakpa, and to several other places where they are being worked by the most primitive methods, Gold is found in nuggets and spangles in mine and dust in rivers", (Swami Paranavananda, 1949: 49-50).

Some writers report that there was a Serpon, gold-officer, appointed from Lhasa, who superintended the goldfields which lay in the district of Rudok and collected taxes from the gold diggers.

Thus we see the extent of prevalence of the precious metal in the vicinity of high Central Himalaya or Guge in the modern times. For these reasons the area was renowned as Suvaraṇabhuūmi or Gold Land in the history since long past and is worthy to be called so even today. From the descriptions above it appears that gold in Tibet was procured in two forms in lumps and in the form of dust. But it appears that it was procured mostly in the form of dust. We generally find that gold in Tibet was measured in bre (a measuring pot) like grains. In the lower regions, on the Indian side, it is learnt that it was extracted from the rivers like Satluj, Chandarbhaga, etc. and was obtained in grains mixed with sand.

The region also produces wool, pasham (shawl wool), salt, borax, medicinal herbs and animal products of rare kind. Till sometime after the independence of India the traders from Ladak, Zanskar, Lahul, Spiti, Kinnaur and Garhwal converged in Rudok, Gartok and other market places in the area for procuring these goods which were then carried to be sent to the markets to be dispersed all over northern India.

However, trading in gold from this area is neither known nor has been heard. The traders from Lahul were regular visitors to the region who brought salt, borax, pasham, byang-bal (long stapled wool of the sheep of Jangthang), etc. But gold did not form item of their import. On this point Shuttleworth informs, "It is interesting to recall that, while a constant stream of Indian silver enters Western Tibet annually, another stream, one of gold, some of it from Thok Jalung in the Chang Tang, flows out of Eastern Tibet into China. In the year before the Great War in Tibetan gold entered Tachienlu alone. But none of this gold enters Lahul." "Tibetan government has a monopoly of gold," (Shuttleworth, 1023: 557-558).

Role of Gold in the propagation and development of Buddhism in Tibet

This gold of Suvarṇabhūmi has played great role in the propagation of Buddhism in Tibet. In Guge, Rinchhen Zangpo, in the 10th-11th century CE, was instrumental in initiating the second propagation of the Doctrine in Tibet. His patron king Ye-she 'Od, was captured and imprisoned by his antagonist king of Garlog

(Garhwal?) and in ransom gold was demanded equal to the size of his body. Gold was collected equal to his body reaching upto the neck. Then the king ordered his officers to spend the gold in bringing the most learned of the Panditas from India instead of wasting it for his release which he reasoned not fruitful. As a result Acharya Atisha was invited from the monastery of Udantpuri (or a different institution) in Zahor i.e. Bengal. Lha bla-ma Ye-shes 'Od died martyr for Buddhism. Gold was utilized by the Tibetan students and pilgrims going to India for meeting their expenses, for offering to their teachers and as presents for inviting the learned panditas from here. Gotshang-pa in thirteenth century CE while he was on pilgrimage in Jalandhar was stripped naked for snatching gold from him. Thus this gold played important role in the spread and development of Buddhism in Tibet.

These descriptions relate to the period when the ownership of the wealth belonged to the Dalai Lamas of Tibet. Its movement, use and renown during this period was confined within the nation.

(B) Pipīlika-gold: We learn from Hiuen-tsiang, as above, that gold of superior quality was produced in Suvarṇagotra or Suvarṇabhūmi or the area of Kailash-Mansarovar and came to India in his time. This fact is found mentioned in ancient Indian literature much early like in Kadambari of Banabhatta and Mahabharata and it was known as Pipīlika-gold i.e. ant-gold as the miners were identified as ants or ant-like.

Suvarṇabhū: There is a vague reference in the renowned work of Varahmihira (6th century CE) to a region named Suvarṇabhū, Gold Land, which he places in the north-east (14/31) of India. This information strengthens the tradition of knowledge on the subject.

Suvarṇapura — the Gold City: Banabhatta (middle of seventh century CE), a great Sanskrit author, appears to possess much clearer knowledge about the geography of the region of Kailash-Mansarovar and the source of gold existing there - its kind and the process of mining. In his famous literary work, Kadambari, he locates a city named Suvarṇapura situated south of Kailash. It narrates from hearsay that gold is found near the foot of Kailash in the form of dust dug out by mice, a more realistic agent than ants as stated elsewhere. Suvarṇapura is city of the Kirātas who live in Hemakūṭa where also lived Kinnaras and Gandharbas.

According to the story in Kadambari, Tārāpīd, king of Ujjain, had a son named Candrapīd. In due course Candrapīd became crown prince and embarked on an expedition of world-conquest. At the end he reached Kailash. Bana informs, 'He once conquered and seized the city called Suvarṇapura, which was not very far away from the Eastern ocean, and was the residence of the Kirātas who dwelt on the Hemakūṭa mountain and who prowled about in the vicinity of Mount Kailaṣa,' (Kale, 1924: 164). The location of the city of Suvarṇapura is described in the words of Candrapīd as, "I have heard it said frequently that to the north of Suvarṇapura is the boundary line of all the countries of this world, beyond that lies a tenantless forest, and beyond that the Kailaṣa mountain", (Kale, 1924:165). Candrapīd also describes that at the foot of the Kailash, "It had gold-dust scattered about the holes dug out by rats with their claws," (Kale, 1924:166).

Ancient Geography of Kailash: There appears a minor gap in the knowledge of the ancient geographers about the geography of Kailash. In the opinion of Bana, Suvaraṇapura or the region of Kailash is not far away from the Eastern ocean. The same fact is found in Mahavansa also. Although the fact is indicative in the Mahavansa it is explicit in the text of Banabhatta. This fact appears to have somewhat confused the modern scholars in locating Suvaraṇabhumi which they were searching near sea coasts in the east. Their search was based on the statement in Mahavansa.

Pipīlika gold and the gold-digging ants: We find a much older and more numerous references to the place and the kind of the precious metal obtained from the region of the Himalaya. Moti Chandra quoting from the great Indian epic Mahabharata says that the Himalayan tribes named "Khaśas, Jyohas, Dīghaveṇus, Paśupas, Kuṇindas, Taṅgaṇas and the Parataṅgṇas presented to Yudhishthira heaps of pipīlika gold measured in droṇas (jar) — the gold which was presented to them by Pipīlikas," (Moti Chandra, 1945: 80-81). He further adds that it was dug from the earth by the pipīlika, ants. This pipīlika-gold was sent to far away countries in the west and was famous as ant-gold among the Greeks, Romans, Turks, Arabs, etc. It may be presumed from this that this gold was worked since much earlier than this.

It appears that the inhabitants of the vast region of the Himalaya and even of the highest region, as they have been identified by different tribal names, were communicative between the highest point of the Himalaya with the plains of India even with the countries beyond.

Ancient Greek Scholars and Ant-gold: This gold mined at the high Central Himalaya was sent out to western countries and was known to the earliest Greek authors writing about India as ant-gold, a transformation of the term Pipīlika-gold of Mahabharata. They mention that the people named Darada who lived along the Indus bought the metal from the gold-diggers, famous as ants, and traded with the other Indians and Persians. Similar references, as found in the Mahabharata, are found in more detail in the descriptions of the early Greek authors.

McCrindle, elucidating the descriptions of the Greek historians on India, writes that the Dardas 'inhabited the north-west frontier of Kashmir along the Indus. This was the region made so famous by the story of the gold digging ants first published to the west by Herodotus and afterwards repeated by Megasthenes, and in Arrian's Indika and also in Pliny.' McCrindle continues further saying, 'As the regions along the banks of the Upper Indus produced gold of a good quality, which found its way to India and Persia, and other countries farther west, it has been supposed that the Indus was one of the four rivers of Paradise mentioned in the book of Genesis,' (McCrindle, 1927:107).

Megasthenes describes the source of the precious metal: 'Among the Dardai, a great tribe of Indians, who inhabit the mountains on the eastern borders, there is an elevated plateau about 3000 stadia in circuit. Beneath the surface there are mines of gold, and here accordingly are found the ants which dig for the metal,' (McCrindle, 1926: 94-95). "They dig holes in the earth like other ants. The heap which they throw up consists of gold, the purest and brightest in all the world. The mounds are piled up close to each other in regular order like hillocks of gold dust, whereby all the plain is made effulgent," (McCrindle, 1926: 96). The geographical description given here is the same as that of Suvarṇabhūmi. Thus the Daradas bought the gold from the miners of the high Central Himalaya and traded internationally.

At places the terms like 'gold-digging ants and Dardais' given by early Greek scholars are found explained differently, (Puri, 1971: 114).

The Himalayan Gold: Hiuen-tsang's remark praising the superiority of the Himalayan gold is noteworthy. We read similar praiseworthy words about the precious metal in the writings of the Greek authors also. It is a geological marvel. From the accounts of the various writers as seen above we understand that the ore too was of superior quality. The miners only did the primary task of separating rough material to extract the precious metal. It did not need any kind of treatment thereafter. Above all the volume of the metal in the mines is unestimable. They were being worked continuously from, perhaps, even before the time of composition of Mahabharata and the references in the works of the Greek authors.

Daradas and Piśāchas: Grierson writes that the Dards have a long history and they are an ancient tribe. They are mentioned by Herodotus and the Greek writers. In the Sanskrit literature they are spoken of as Dārda or Darda. Under the name of Dard country is included the whole mountainous tract between the Hindukush and the frontiers of India proper. Accordinly the tract is known as Dardistan. All the Aryan languages spoken in the area is called as 'Dardic'. To the Sansktit writers they were known as Pisacha. Therefore in the earlier volumes of the Survey this name has been applied. But for some reasons the name has been replaced Dardic in the latter volumes, (Grierson, 1919:1). Grierson treats the two languages designated as Daradic and Piśācha as synonyms, therefore their speakers also as the same. Grierson, a great linguist, thus identifies the Daradas with the Piśācha of the ancient Indian Sanskrit literature.

Evaluating the language Grierson writes that the languages spoken on the North Western Frontier of India, in Laghman, Kafiristan, the Indus Kohistan, Chitral, Gilgit, and Kashmir have been put together in a group under the name of 'Modern Piśācha', for a third independent branch of the great Aryan family which separated from the parent stream after the branching forth of the original of the Indian languages, but before the Eranian languages had developed all their peculiar characteristics. After the separation, the inaccessible home in which their speakers settled, and the inhospitality alike of the country and of its inhabitants kept them apart, and very fairly preserved the languages from contamination by those of allied origin, (Grierson, 1906: 4).

According to Dipvansa the inhabitants of the Himalaya are identified with one designation of Yaksha and those of Suvarṇabhūmi, which lay in Transhimalaya, as Piśācha, which may be identified as the same as the Daradas of the Greek historians and of Grierson.

Piśācha — Some explanations: In one of the Tibetan lexicons Paiśāci, the language of the Piśāca, is considered as one of the four great languages of India.

Piśācha is literally understood as a malignant non-being spirit. Following the Sanskrit literature a Tibetan lexicon places Piśācha along with kumbhāṇḍa, bhūt, rākshasa, skandha, etc. and some harmful planets, in the class of Preta, the beings who roam about in the air. Yet some authors have different view about the Preta and Piśācha. Amar Singh, an eminent Sanskrit lexicographer, in his well known work Amarkosh, places Piśācha under the chapter svargavarga, the division of Heaven. Piśāca is a class among the ten different classes of beings viz.: Vidyādhar, Apasarās, Yaksh, Rākshas, Gandharva, Kinnar, Piśācha, Guhyak, Siddha and Bhūta.

Daradas in Modern History: Leitner, who has worked on the subject extensively, writes that the name 'Dard' itself was not claimed by any of the race that he met, "but," the author says, "I include in it all the countries lying between the Hindu Kush and Kaghan. In a restricted sense the Dards are the race inhabiting the mountainous country of Shinkhi, but I include under that designation not only the Chilasis, Asthris, Gilgitis, Dareylis, etc. but also the people of Hunza, Nagyr, Yasin, Chitral and Kafiristan," (Leitner, 1893:59, 58).

It appears that the habitations of the Daradas in the ancient times extended farther to east and south-east including Ladakh in the Indus valley and some other adjoining areas reaching nearer to the Kailash Mansarovar. Petech writes that in the 6th century CE Ladakh, which lies in Indus valley, was inhabited by Daradas. Francke identifies the skulls excavated in the graves in Ladakk with Darada inhabitants. There is a small cultural island within Ladakh known as Da-Hanu and they are identified with Daradas.

Rahul Sankrityayan from the study of the skulls excavated at Lippa, in Kinnaur, not scientifically, considers resembling Aryan features. The skeletons accidently excavated in Lahul by the people and immediately destroyed at two places in two different valleys are said each to have been nearly six feet long, apparently longer than those of the present inhabitants.

Conclusion: Bana identifies the region of the high Central Himalaya as Hemakūṭa which may be translated as gold-mound or mountain. Hemakūṭa also formed one of the nine countries of Jambudvipa whose first ruler was named Kimpurṣa (Ali, 1966:10) therefore also known as Kimpuruṣa, the country of Kimpuruṣas or Kinnars. Rahul Sankrityayan locates the region of Kimpuruṣvarṣa in Western Himalaya. There lived in Hemakūṭa, as per the work of Bana, Kiratas, Kinnars or Kimpurusas and Gandharbas. Mount Meru, the pivot of the world of the Hindus, Buddhists and Jains, which lies at the centre of Jambudvipa which itself is situated in the centre of the seven continents of the world, is supposed to be composed of gold, (Ali, 1966: 48; Sangpo, 2012-II: 1049). It is possible that Suvarṇabhūmi, Suvarṇapura, Suvarṇabhū or Suvarṇagotra of the real geography had been one of the sources of inspiration to the earliest geographers of India who had intimate geographical knowledge of the Himalaya. They also tell some other features of the region like that four great rivers originate from the region.

Thus Soṇa and Uttara, the two greatly dedicated missionaries of Priyadarshi Asoka, reached the great heights of the Himalaya in Suvaṇṇabhūmi and worked among the inhabitants the Daradas, who on the Indian side were known as Piśācha and brought them under the influence of the Dharma and liberated many of them by creating faith in them.

5

Lha-rgyas : The Song of Auspiciousness

Introduction

The song from sTod called Lha-rgyas (great god) is an ancient ceremonial song. It is sung by a group of elderly men in the auspicious ceremonies and is the principal prayer song of Losar, the New year festival, which is celebrated for seven days. The traditional song is still in active practice. There are some singers who sing on the occasions of social importance like marriage, Losar, etc. While all such singers are known as lurpon (glu-dpon = song-officer), this term is particularly applied for the leaders of the parties of such singers. Their role is sought most during the marriages. These leading singers keep some songs in their memory. A few of them also have kept some songs in writing. The singers are generally kya-o (skye-bo = layman), but there are also a few lamas among them. They wear the local traditional dress during the sessions and it is associated with the offerings of chhang, (local beer) (Pl. 4).

In the word Lhargyas all the letters are pronounced appropriately. The term may be translated literally as 'great god'. Besides, the song is known by several other titles: kra-shi (bkra-shis, but pronounced as kra-shi = auspiciousness, throughout the song), chhags-rabs (song of settlement), dang-po'i glu (song of the beginning), lha spab-ce (bringing down of god) and gral-glu (= song of sittings). These names display the importance of the song. The song has been handed down through the oral tradition but there is no ancient manuscript of any kind supposed to exist. Some of the singers are in possession of some manuscripts copied by themselves for the purpose of singing. These are all written down from traditional oral singings recently and are generally much corrupted.

The song, of purely folk tradition, belongs to the period before the advent of Tibetan Buddhism in the area. It shows contact with Indian Buddhism. As may be seen from section V there is a reference to some monks who wear robe of single cloth length and eat white rice. These are the monks of Indian Buddhism of very early time who had come from the lower regions.

Here an attempt has been made firstly to record the song and secondly to restore some lost words meaningfully. Its traditional structure and form has not been disturbed. No attempt has been made to bind it in any metrical frame. Its flow has been maintained as it is sung and as found in the writings. However the lines repeated in some form and the redundant words introduced to fill the lyrical gaps have been dropped.

The principal theme of the song is bringing down of the deity from the high above and settle him in the community. Here the god has no name and form. He is a spirit of the firmament of the high sky above. The song linguistically is an inheritance of the ancient sTodpa and there is not much variation from the existing language. It retains old pronunciations in several words: in the title lha-rgyas, bkra-shis, dbu-rmog, etc. It retains a typical word of sTodpa language: 'a-'o in the form of a-bo which means we two, i.e. I and you.

It appears that the composition is retained almost complete in seven sections. If some stanzas are missing somewhere it cannot be detected. But the words and constructions have suffered distortions and some parts have become unrecognizable. But it is a matter of great satisfaction that it remained surviving in practice in oral tradition and written in some form. From this we also gather that the society remained almost static since long past.

The Thakurs of Khangsar played important role in preserving some important cultural practices. They encouraged the people to participate in the festivals and to come with full preparation for singing the traditional songs. They had got the songs collected and written. There were two major collections: bag-glu, marriage songs, and gral-glu, gathering songs. After the disintegration of the family of Khangsar Khar all the important articles in the household were dispersed and the books were also taken away by some unknown seekers never to be seen. Abi Shema, the Lady Thakur, wife of Thankur Sangey Dawa, Pratap Chand, was very adept in singing these songs. She had many songs in her memory.

The worst affected part in whole of the composition is section-vi which gives description of the local geography. Here the poet intends to capture the attractive scenery of the short summer giving variety to the things described. The wild flowering plants grow at different heights, they have different perspectives and there are numerous sources through which water is received. The first kind of plant grows at the highest point near the snowline and the last one on the banks of the river. The traditional practice has summarised the distinctions in the two words for various descriptions: dmar, red, and dngar, sweet.

Transcription (Original Annexure-I)

Lhar-rgyas

I. dang-po la bkra-shis

dang-po la bkra-shis yong shig. la dgung la phebs song.
yong shig. la yong shig dgung la. dgung la ma bkra shis yong shig.
la mi de nang du yong shig. la yong shig mi de.
khri ru dkyil la bzhugs sa. yong shig la dgung stod dkyil du.
yong shig. la yong shig. dgung stod dkyil la bzhugs-sa la phebs song.
yong shig. la bkra-shis brjod...1

dang-po la bkra-shis yong shig. la gangs la phebs song.
yong shig. la yong shig gangs la. gangs la ma bkra-shis yong shig.
la mi de nang du. yong shig. la yong shig mi de.
seng-chhen gyi la bzhugs-sa. yong shig la gangs stod dkyil du.
yong shig. la yong shig. gangs stod dkyil la bzhugs-sa la phebs song. yong .. brjod ...2
dang-po la bkra-shis yong shig. la nags la phebs song.

yong shig. la yong shig nags la. nags la ma bkra-shis yong shig.
la mi de. nang du. yong shig. la yong shig mi de.
stag-chhen gyi la bzhugs-sa. yong shig la nags stod dkyil du.
yong shig. la yong shig. nags stod kyil la bzhugs-sa la phebs song. yong .. brjod ...3

dang-po la bkra-shis yong shig. la mtsho la phebs song.
yong shig. la yong shig mtsho la. mtsho la ma bkra-shis yong shig.
la mi de nang du yong shig. la yong shig mi de.
nya-chhen gyi la bzhugs-sa. yong shig la mtsho stod dkyil du.
yong shig la yong shig. mtsho stod dkyil-la bzhugs-sa la phebs song. yong .. brjod ... 4

dang-po la bkra-shis yong shig. la mkhar la phebs song.
yong shig. la yong shig mkhar la. mkhar la ma bkris yong shig.
la mi de nang du yong shig. la yong shig mi de.
mi-chhen gyi la bzhugs-sa. yong shig la mkhar stod dkyil du.
yong shig. la yong shig. mkhar stod dkyil la bzhugs-sa la phebs song. yong .. brjod ..5

dang-po la bkra-shis yong shig. la dpal-khang la phebs song.
yong shig. la yong shig dpal-khang la. dpal-khang la ma bkra-shis yong shig.
la mi de nang du yong shig. la yong shig mi de.
yab yum gyi la bzhugs-sa. yong shig la dpal-khang stod dkyil du.
yong shig. la yong shig. dpal-khang stod dkyil la bzhugs-sa phebs song.
yong shig la bkra-shis brjod...6

II. gnyis-pa 'dsom glu

dgung stod du bzhugs-pa'i. khri-gdugs nyi-ma bde.
dgung smad du bzhugs-pa'i. dkar-gsal dsla-ba bde.
dgung stod dkyil du 'dsoms-pa'i. rgyu-skar 'dsom-po bde.
de nas gchig dang gnyis gsum. 'dsoms-pa'i chha gchig dgos.
ta li lang la la. la li bkra shis brjod...1
gangs stod du bzhugs-pa'i. seng-chhen dkar-mo bde.

gangs smad du bzhugs-pa'i. g-yu-ral legs-mo bde.
gangs stod dkyil du 'dsoms-pa'i. seng-phrug 'dsom-po bde.
de nas gchig dang gnyis gsum. 'dsoms-pa'i chha gchig dgos. ta li ...brjod...2

nags stod du bzhugs-pa'i. stag-chhen khra-bo bde.
nags smad du bzhugs-pa'i. ri-mo legs-mo bde.
nags stod dkyil du 'dsoms-pa'i. stag-phrug 'dsom-po bde.
de nas gchig dang gnyis gsum. 'dsoms-pai'i chha gchig dgos. ta li ...brjod...3

mtsho stod du bzhugs-pa'i. nya-chhen nyul-mo bde.
mtsho smad du bzhugs-pa'i. gser-mig legs-mo bde.
mtsho stod dkyil du 'dsoms-pa'i. nya-phrug 'dsom-po bde.
de nas gchig dang gnyis gsum. 'dsom-pa'i chha gchig dgos. ta li...brjod...4

mkhar stod du bzhugs-pa'i. mi-chhen gong-ma bde.
mkhar smad du bzhugs-pa'i. rgyud-ris mthon-po bde.
mkhar stod dkyil du 'dsoms-pa'i. grong 'khor 'dsom-po bde.
de nas gchig dang gnyis gsum. 'dsoms-pa'i chha gchig dgos. Ta li...brjod...5

dpal-khang stod du bzhugs-pa'i. yab yum pha ma bde.
dpal-khang smad du bzhugs pa'i. bu nor mod po bde.
dpal-khang stod dkyil du 'dsoms-pa'i. gnyen-drung 'dsom-po bde.
de nas gchig dang gnyis gsum. 'dsoms-pa'i chha gchig dgos. ta li...brjod...6

III. gsum gur spub che

dgung stod dkyil-du gur zhig spub song. chi dang chi-yi gur de spub song.
ser-po dar gyi. gur de spub song.
su dang su yis tshugs-shing btsugs song.
khri-gdugs nyi-mas tshugs-shing btsugs song.
su dang su yis mtshams-thag stsal song.
rgyu-skar mang gis mtshams-thag stsal song.
mtshams-thag stsal ba'i bkra-shis 'ang brjod...1

gangs stod dkyil du gur zhig spub song.
chi dang chi-yi. gur de spub song.
dkar-po dar gyi gur de spub song.
su dang su yis tshugs-shing btsugs song.
seng-chhen dkar-mos. tshugs-shing btsugs song.
su dang su yis mtshams-thag stsal song.
seng-khrug mang gyis mtshams-thag stsal song.
mtshams-thag stsal ba'i bkra-shis 'ang brjod...2

nags stod dkyil du. gur zhig spub song.
chi dang chi yi. gur de spub song.
khra-bo dar gyi. gur de spub song.
su dang su yis. tshugs-shing btsugs song.
stag-chhen khra-bos. tshugs-shing btsugs song.
su dang dang su yis. mtshams-thag stsal song.
stag-phrug mang gis mtshams-thag stsal song.
mtshams-thag stsal-ba'i. bkra-shis 'ang brjod...3

mtsho stod dkyil du. gur zhig spub song.
chi dang chi yi. gur de spub song.
sngon-po dar gyi. gur de spub song.
su dang su yis. tshugs-shing btsugs song.
nya-chhen nyul-mos. tshugs-shing btsugs song.
su dang su yis. mtshams-thag stsal song.
nya-phrug mang gyis. mtshams-thag stsal song.
mtshams-thag stsal-ba'i. bkra-shis 'ang brjod...4

mkhar stod dkyil du. gur zhig spub song.
chi dang chi yi. gur de spub song.
se-bo dar gi. gur de spub song.
su dang su yis. tshugs-shing btsugs song.
mi-chhen gong mas tshugs-shing btsugs song.
su dang su yis. mtshams-thag stsal song.
grong-'khor mang gyis. mtshams-thag stsal song.
mtshams-thag stsal-ba'i. bkra-shis 'ang brjod...5

dpal-khang stod dkyil du. gur zhig spub song.

chi dang chi yi. gur de spub song.
smug-po dar-gi. gur de spub song.
su dang su yis. tshugs-shing btsugs song.
yab yum pha mas tshugs-shing btsugs song.
su dang su yis. mtshams-thag stsal song.
gnyen-drung mang gyis mtshams-thag stsal song.
mtshams-thag stsal-ba'i. bkra-shis 'ang brjod...6

IV. bzhi pa khri bzhangs che

sngon tshe bskal-pa bzang-po la. khri zhig bzhangs song.
chi dang chi yi. khri de bzhangs song.
ser-pho gser-gyi. khri zhig bzhangs song.
de ru su dang. su mi bzhugs song.
de ru steng gi. lha yang bzhugs song.
dbu-rmog tho-ba'i lha. de la bkra-shis 'ang brjod...1

sngon tshe bskal-pa bzang-po la. khri zhig bzhangs song.
chi dang chi yi. khri de bzhangs song.
dkar-pho dngul gyi khri zhig bzhangs song.
de ru su dang su mi bzhugs song.
de ru bar gyi btsan yang bzhugs song.
gangs-ri bzang-po'i btsan. de la bkra-shis 'ang brjod...2

sngon tshe bskal-pa bzang-po la. khri zhig bzhangs song.
chi dang chi-yi. khri de bzhangs song.
sngon-po g-yu yi. khri de bzhangs song.
de ru su dang su mi bzhugs song.
de ru 'og gi klu yang bzhugs song.
g-yu mtsho sdings-po'i klu gnyan. de la bkra-shis 'ang brjod...3

sngon tshe bskal-pa bzang-po la. khri zhig bzhangs song.
chi dang chi yi. khri de bzhangs song.
khra-bo shel gyi khri zhig bzhangs song.
de ru su dang su mi bzhugs song.
de ru mi-chhen gong-ma bzhugs song. rgyud-ris mthon-po'i mi de la bkra-shis 'ang brjod...4

sngon tshe bskal-pa bzang-po la. khri zhig bzhangs song.

chi dang chi yi. khri de bzhangs song.
smug-po dung-gyi khri zhig bzhangs song.
de ru su dang su mi bzhugs song.
de ru yab-yum pha-ma bzhugs song.
bu nor 'dsom-po pha-ma. de la. bkra-shis 'ang brjod...5

V. lnga-pa ni na-bz'a spul-che

mtho-ba ri sum rtse na. bzhugs-pa bya rgod-po spun gsum de bzhugs.
snam me snam la chi snam. snam me snam la bya-spu sna-tshogs snam.
'don ne 'don la chi 'don. 'don ne 'don la rgyu-skar skar-chhung 'don.
skyem me skyem la chi skyem.
skyem me skyem la seng-'brug rang chhang skyem.
ta li lang la la. la ta li bkra shis brjod. ..1

shal-ma dkar gyi 'dabs su bzhugs-pa'i. shva-ba spun gsum de.
snam me snam la chi snam. snam me snam la sprin-chung lang-ling snam.
'don ne 'don la chi 'don. 'don ne 'don la men-tog sna-tshogs 'don.
skyem me skyem la chi skyem.
skyem me skyem la gangs-chhu khral khrol skyem...2

brag dmar 'dabs su bzhugs-pa'i. btsun-pa spun gsum de.
snam me snam la chi snam. snam me snam la ras-gzan rkyang gchig snam.
'don ne 'don la chi 'don. 'don ne 'don la 'bras-dkar sro-lo 'don.
skyem me skyem la chi skyem.
skyem me skyem la sing-chhang sing-ma skyem. ..3

dpal-khang stod du bzhugs-pa'i. rgyal-bu spun gsum de.
snam me snam la chi snam. snam me snam la dar-men gos-shen snam.
'don ne 'don la chi 'don. 'don ne 'don la zhim-zag mngar-bchud 'don.

skyem me skyem la chi skyem. skyem me skyem la a-rag bdud-rtsi skyem. ...4

VI. drug-pa dbu-thod spul-che

sro-lo ser-thod bsnams-pa de. su dang su yi drin.
spang-ma dmar gyi drin. de'i drin-lan gangs-chhu brjod.
la ta li la lang la la. la ta li bkra shis brjod...1

nya-lo dbu-thod snams-pa de. su dang su yi drin.
shal-ma dkar gyi drin. de'i drin lan chhar-chhu brjod. la.ta ... brjod...2

glang-ma bal-thod bsnams-pa de. su dang su yi drin.
chhu-mig mngar gyi drin. de-yi drin-lan thang-chhu brjod. la.ta ...brjod...3

'om-bug dar-thod bsnams-pa de. su dang su yi drin.
gtsang-chhab sngon-mo'i drin. de'i drin lan dslar-chhu brjod. la.ta ...brjod...4

rgyal-bu dbu-thod bsnams-pa de. su dang su yi drin.
yab dang yum gyi drin. de 'i drin-lan dkar-chhu brjod. la.ta... brjod...5

VII. bdun-pa men-tog spul-che

rgya-gar gyi rgyal-po. bde-'o sku khams bzang.
rgyal-mo'is tshig legs gsungs. men-tog tsam zam 'khrungs.
shis ha-lo tsam zam 'khrungs.
men-tog brgyad zam 'khrungs. ha-lo brgyad zam 'khrungs. ..1

gchig ni yang men-tog. gchig ni ha-lo.
bde-bo su-la spul. shis ha-lo su la spul.
steng phyogs lha la spul. shis lha la spul ba'i. bde-bo bkra shis brjod. ..2

gnyis ni yang men-tog. gnyis ni ha-lo.
bde-bo su la spul. shis ha-lo su la spul.
bar phyogs btsan la spul. shis btsan la spul ba'i. bde bo... brjod..3

gsum ni yang mem-tog. gsum ni ha-lo.
bde-bo su la spul. shis ha-lo su la spul.
'og phyogs klu la spul.

shis klu la 'bul ba'i. bde-bo bkra-shis brjod. bde-bo... brjod...4

bzhi ni yang men-tog. bzhi ni ha-lo.
bde-bo su la spul. shis ha-lo su la spul.
a-ba yab la spul. shis yab la spul-ba'i. bde-bo... brjod...5

lnga ni yang men-tog. lnga ni ha-lo.
bde-bo su la spul. shis ha-lo su la spul.
a-ma yum la spul. shis yum la 'bul ba'i. bde-bo...brjod...6

drug ni yang men-tog. drug ni ha-lo.
bde-bo su la spul. shis ha-lo su la spul.
a-cho sras la spul. shis a-cho sras la 'bul ba'i. bde-bo...brjod...7

bdun ni yang men-tog. bdun ni ha-lo.
bde bo su la spul. shis ha-lo su la spul.
a-chi lcham la spul. a-chi lcham la 'bul ba'i. bde-bo...brjod...8

brgyad ni yang men-tog. brgyad ni ha-lo.
bde-bo su la spul. shis ha-lo su la spul.
a-bo rang la spul. shis a-bo rang la spul ba'i. bde bo...brjod...9

Manuscripts consulted

1. Tashi Lhargyal, Khangsar.
2. Tashi Karingpa, Karing.
3. Gyaltshan, Tinno.
4. Old Song Lyrics in Bhoti Culture Lahaul from Dartse.
5. sTod Ghati Kalyan Sabha, Kyelang.
6. Tashi Phuntshog Zhabzhepa, Karing.
7. Roerich, George De. (1934: 126-147).

Notes: Below are given the variations occurring in different sources from those as given here above.

Title: *lha-rgyas* = This word may be pronounced as *'lhar-gyas'*, pronouncing all the letters.

Verbs: The verbs used in this composition are honorific.

In section 1, there are six stanzas. When the song is sung at mkhar (House of Thakur) the stanza 6 is not sung. In the house of a villager the stanza 5 is not sung.

Section-I

Stanza-1/Line-1 and at all places in the composition: *bkra-shis* = This word may be pronounced throughout as *kra-shi*.

Stanza-1/line-1, and in all other sections: *shig* = All the sources write *she*, *shes* or *shis*.

Stanza-1/line-2. dgung la ma = Most of the sources write dgung bla ma.

Stanza-1/line-4. khri ru dkyil la bzhugs sa. = In place of bzhugs some sources write lhab-sa, lab-sa, shar-sa. Tashi Lhagyal writes: dkyil bzhugs sa la lag sa. Roerich writes bslebs = reached.

Stanza-1/line-6 and other sections. brjod = The sources write: mdsod, dsod, zo-sto, bzod, etc.

Stanza-6/Line-2 and other sections. dpal-khang. = At places it is dpal and at places it is dpal-khang. All have been changed to dpal-khang throughout.

Section-II

Stanza-1 to 6/line-1 to 3. *bde* = All the sources write de.

Stanza-1/line-3 = *sgyu-skar* = All the sources write gab-ral.

Stanza-1/Line-5. *ta-li lang-la-la. la-li.* = These words, here, and also found in many songs, are words meaningless. They help to complete or expand the lyrics of the stanza.

Section-III

Stanza-1/line-6. *sgyu-skar* = All the sources write gab-ral.

Stanza-4/Line-5. *nya chhen nyul-mo* = The sources write yur-mo, myur mo, etc.

Section-IV

Stanza-1/Line-6. *dbu-rmog* = All the sources write *a-ur-mong*. This indicates that letter '*r*' in the word *rmog* was also pronounced.

Stanza-2/Line-6. *gangs-ri* = All sources write *rgyab-ri*.

Section-V

Stanza-1/Line-2, etc. *snam-me-snam*. = Roerich in place of me at all the places for this word has mi. The term mi has negative connotation. The term me is a particle placed between a verb used twice to give emphasis.

Stanza-1/Line-3. *sgyu skar skar-chhung* = All sources write *chag dkar dkar chung/chhung.*

Stanza-2/Line-1. *shal-ma dkar gyi 'dabs-su.* = All sources write *shal-ma dmar.*

Stanza-2/Line-2: *sprin-chung* = The sources write *phin-chung or pin-chung.*

Stanza-3/Line-3: *sro-lo* = Others: *'o-lo. hro-lo. sro-lo from srol-srol* (= bulky but comparatively light in weight, like hay).

Stanza-3/Line-4. *chhang sing-ma skem.* = Roerich: gser mig gsum kyang skem. Source E, Kalyan Sabha, Kyelang, gives three current forms of this sentence like: "la ser-gi sumchhang kyem (singchhang singma) la sermi sumchhang kyem." Sonam Tashi, a lurpon, explains "ser-mig sum-chhang" as the chhang contained in a chhap-kyen, a vessel for chhodpa, sacred offering, on the mouth of which three pieces of ghee are placed at three places, as sacred symbol.

Stanza-4/Line-1: rgyal-bu = The sources write: rgyal-lu or rgya-lu. These are vernacular forms.

Section-VI

Stanza-2 /Line-2. shal-ma dkar = sources have shal-ma dmar. chhar-chhu = sources have dngar-chhu.

Stanza-3/Line-2. chhu-mig dngar = souces have dmar.

Stanza- 1 to 5/Line-2. gangs-chhu, chhar-chhu, thang-chhu, dslar-chhu and dkar-chhu. = All sources give dngar-chhu for all these words.

Stanza-2/line-2. shal-ma dkar = Roerich: shal-ma mang. Similarly in all the stanzas he uses the word mang. The sentence containing the word drin-lan is found only in one source.

Section-VII

Stanza-1/Line-1: rgya-gar gyi rgyal-po = All the sources write: rgya-gar nge rgyalpo.

Stanza-1/Line-3: shis = Sources shes. All sources.

Stanza-1/Line-2: rgyal-mo'is tshigs legs gsungs. = Sources rgyal—mo de/nge tshigs legs su.

Stanza-2/Line-2: bde-bo = Sources de-bo.

Stanza-2/Line-3. shis = Sources gyis. shis = Sources shes de-bo.

Translation: The Great god

I. In the beginning Auspiciousness

In the beginning may there come auspiciousness!
Yes. He has reached there in the firmament.
May he come. May he come in the firmament.
May auspiciousness come in the firmament.
May the man come in. May the man come.
There is place for sitting on the throne in the middle.
May he come in the middle of the firmament above.
May he come. May he come.
He has reached at the place of sitting in the middle in the firmament above,
May he come. Pronounce auspiciousness!...1

In the beginning may there come auspiciousness!
Yes. He has reached there over the glacier.
May he come. May he come over the glacier.
May auspiciousness come over the glacier.
May the man come in. May the man come.
This is the place of sitting for the Great Lion.
May he come in the middle over the glacier above.
May he come. May he come.
He has reached at the place of sitting in the middle over the glacier above.
May he come. Pronounce auspiciousness!...2

In the beginning may there come auspiciousness!
Yes. He has reached there in the forest.
May he come. May he come in the forest.
May auspiciousness come in the forest.
May the man come in. May the man come.

This is the place of sitting for the Great Tiger.
May he come in the middle of the forest above.
May he come. May he come.
He has reached at the place of sitting in the middle of the forest above.
May he come. Pronounce auspiciousness!...3

In the beginning may there come auspiciousness!
Yes. He has reached there in the lake.
May he come. May he come in the lake.
May auspiciousness come in the lake.
May the man come in. May the man come.
This is the place of sitting for the Great Fish.
May he come in the middle of the lake above.
May he come. May he come.
He has reached at the place of sitting in the middle of the Lake above.
May he come, Pronounce auspiciousness!...4

In the beginning may there come auspiciousness!
Yes. He has reached at the castle.
May he come. May he come in the castle.
May auspiciousness come in the castle.
May the man come in. May the man come.
This is the place of sitting for the Great Man.
May he come in the middle in the castle above.
May he come. May he come.
He has reached at the place of sitting in the middle in the castle above.
May he come. Pronounce auspiciousness!...5

In the beginning may there come auspiciousness!
Yes. He has reached at the prosperous house.
May he come. May he come in the prosperous house.
May the auspiciousness come in the prosperous house.
May the man come in. May the man come.
This is the place of sitting for the honourable Father and Mother.

May he come in the middle in the prosperous house above.

May he come. May he come.

He has reached at the place of sitting in the middle in the prosperous house above.

May he come. Pronounce auspiciousness!...6

II. Second, Song of Gathering

Sitting in the firmament above, the Sun, on the throne with parasol, looks admirable.

Sitting in the firmament below, the white shining Moon, looks admirable.

Assembled in the middle of the firmament above, the stars, who are happy to assemble, look admirable. Then one, two, three...

There is need of a companion for assembling. Pronounce Auspiciousness! ..1

Sitting on the glacier above, the Great white Lion looks admirable.

Sitting over the glacier below, his beautiful manes look admirable.

Assembled in the middle over the glacier above, the lion cubs, who are happy to assemble, look admirable. Then one, two, three....

There is need of a companion for assembling. Pronounce Auspiciousness! 2

Sitting in the forest above, the Great Tiger with variegated colours, looks admirable.

Sitting in the forest below, his beautiful stripes look admirable.

Assembled in the middle of the forest above, the little tiger cubs, who are happy to assemble, look admirable. Then one, two, three...

There is need of a companion for assembling. Pronounce Auspiciousness! 3

Sitting in the lake above, the Great wavering Fish, looks admirable.

Sitting in the lake below, his beautiful golden eyes look admirable.

Assembled in the middle of the lake above, the little fishes, who are happy to assemble, look admirable. Then one, two, three,...
There is need of a companion for assembling. Pronounce Auspiciousness! 4.

Sitting in the castle above, the Great Man, uppermost in the row, looks admirable.
Sitting in the castle below, his high lineage looks admirable.
Assembled in the middle of the castle above, the householders, who are happy to assemble, look admirable. Then one, two, three...
There is need of a companion for assembling. Pronounce Auspiciousness! 5.

Sitting in the prosperous house above, the honourable Father and Mother look admirable.
Sitting in the prosperous house below, abudance of the wealth of offsprings, looks admirable.
Assembled in the middle of the prosperous house above, the kinsmen, who are happy to assemble, look admirable. Then one, two, three...
There is need of a companion for assembling. Pronounce Auspiciousness!...6

III. Third, Pitching the Tent

In the middle of the firmament above, a tent was pitched.
Of what material it is made of, the tent that was pitched?
Is of yellow silk, the tent that was pitched.
Who were those, pitching the tent-poles?
The Sun, sitting over the throne with parasol, pitched the tent-poles.
Who were those tying the tent with stitching-ropes?
The multitude of stars stitched the tent with stitching-ropes.
Pronounce auspiciousness for stitching the tent with stitching-ropes...1

In the middle of the glacier above, a tent was pitched.
Of what material it is made of, the tent that was pitched?
Is of white silk, the tent that was pitched.

Who were those, pitching the tent-poles?
The Great white Lion pitched the tent-poles.
Who were those stitching the tent with stitching-ropes?
There were many lion cubs who stitched the tent with stitching-ropes.
Pronounce auspiciousness for stitching the tent with stitching-ropes...2

In the middle of the forest above, a tent was pitched.
Of what material is it made of, the tent that was pitched?
Is of particolour silk, the tent that was pitched.
Who were those pitching the tent-poles?
The Great Tiger of variegated colours pitched the tent.
Who were those stitching the tent with stitching-ropes?
There were many tiger cubs who stitched the tent with stitching-ropes.
Pronounce auspicious for stitching the tent with stitching-ropes...3

In the middle of the lake above, a tent was pitched.
Of what material is it made of, the tent that was pitched?
Is of green silk, the tent that was pitched.
Who were those pitching the tent-poles?
The Great wavering Fish pitched the tent-poles.
Who were those stitching the tent with stitching-ropes?
There were many little fishes stitching the tent with stitching-ropes.
Pronounce auspiciousness for stitching the tent with stitching-ropes...4

In the middle, on the castle above, a tent was pitched.
Of what material is it made of, the tent that was pitched?
Is of grey silk, the tent that was pitched.
Who were those pitching the tent-poles?
The Great Man, uppermost in the row, pitched the tent-poles.
Who were those stitching the tent with stitching-ropes?
There were many householders who stitched the tent with the stitching-ropes.

Pronounce auspicious for stitching the tent with stitching-ropes...5

In the middle, on the prosperous house above, a tent was pitched.
Of what material is it made of, the tent that was pitched?
Is of blue silk, the tent that was pitched.
Who were those pitching the tent-poles?
The honourable Father and Mother pitched the tent-poles.
Who were those stitching the tent with stitching-ropes?
There were many kinsmen who stitched the tent with stitching-ropes.
Pronounce auspiciousness for stitching the tent with stitching-ropes...6

IV. Fourth, Raising of Throne

In the former times, in the bhadra-kalpa, the blessed kalpa, a throne was raised.
Of what material, the throne that was raised, is made of?
Of yellow colour, of Gold, the throne was raised.
Who are the persons those who sit on the throne?
Thereon sits the god of the above.
For the god whose head is held high, pronounce auspicious...1

In the former times, in the blessed kalpa, a throne was raised.
Of what material, the throne that was raised, is made of?
Of white colour, of silver, the throne was raised.
Who are the persons those who sit on the throne?
Thereon sits bTsan (the god named) of the middle region (the region between the earth and the firmament).
For bTsan, (god) of the good 'Gangs-ri' (Kailash mountain), pronounce auspiciousness. ...2

In the former times, in the blessed kalpa, a throne was raised.
Of what material, the throne that was raised, is made of?
Of green colour, of turquoise, the throne was raised.
Who are the persons those who sit on the throne?
Thereon sits the Naga, the Serpent god, of the nether world.

For the powerful and fearful Naga of the blue and deep Turquise Lake (Mansarovar), pronounce auspiciousness...3

In the former times, in the blessed kalpa, a throne was raised.
Of what material, the throne that was raised, is made of?
Of grey colour, of crystal, the throne was raised.
Who are the persons those who sit on the throne?
There sits the Great Man, the uppermost in the row.
For the Great Man of high lineage, pronounce auspicious....4

In the former times, in the blessed kalpa, a throne was raised.
Of what material, the throne that was raised, is made of?
Of Purple colour, of Conch-shell, the throne was raised.
Who are the persons those who sit on the throne?
There sit the honourable Father and Mother.
For the honourable Father and Mother, blessed with the wealth of offsprings, pronounce auspicious 5

V. Fifth, Offering of Garment

Sitting on three peaks of the high mountain, there live three wild eagle brothers.
They wear, but what do they wear? They wear various kinds of feathers.
They eat, but what do they eat? For meal, they eat little stars.
They drink, but what do they drink?
For drinking, they take the very own beer of the White Lion and the Dragon.
Pronounce auspiciousness...1

Sitting beside the white gravels, there live three stag brothers.
They wear, but what do they wear? They wear the small slices of light cloud.
They eat, but what do they eat? They eat numerous kinds of flowers.
They drink, but what do they drink? They drink the gurgling water of the glaciers.
Pronounce auspiciousness...2

Sitting beside the red rock, there live three monk brothers.
They wear, but what do they wear? They wear robes of a single length of cloth.
They eat, but what do they eat? They eat white rice, each grain separated.
They drink, but what do they drink? They drink pure kind of thin beer.
Pronounce auspiciousness. ...3

Sitting in the prosperous house above, there live three prince brothers.
They wear, but what do they wear? They wear costly silken clothes.
They eat, but what do they eat? They eat delicious healthy meal.
They drink, but what do they drink? They drink arag (wine) that is like ambrosia.
Pronounce auspiciousness...4

VI. Sixth, Offering of Turban

'Srolo' (a grass), wearing yellow turban (flower), due to whose kindness is it?
This is due to the kindness of the red spongy grass-land.
The cause of its kindness, is said, is the water from the glacier.
Pronounce auspiciousness....1

'Nyalo', wearing a turban, due to whose kindness is it?
This is due to the kindness of the white gravels.
The cause of its kindness, is said, is the rain water (washes the gravels).
Pronounce...2

gLang-ma, wearing woolly turban, due to whose kindness is it?
This is due to the kindness of the sweet water from the spring.
The cause of its kindness, is said, is water from the ground. Pronounce ...3

'Om-bug, wearing silky crown, due to whose kindness is it?
This is due to the kindness of blue water of the river.

The cause of the kindness, is said, is the water from the ice. Pronounce ...4

The Prince wearing turban, due to whose kindness is it?
This is due to the kindness of the honourable Father and Mother.
The cause of this kindness is the white water (milk). Pronounce ...5

VII. Seventh, Offering of Flowers

King of India, may he be happy and healthy. Oh, Queen, say some good words.
How many flowers have grown? How many auspicious flowers of *ha-lo* (a wild flower) have grown?
About eight flowers have grown.
About eight auspicious flowers of ha-lo have grown...1

Firstly the flower, firstly the auspicious flower of *ha-lo*,
Well, to whom should it be offered? To whom the auspiciousness ha-lo should be offered?
Offer it to the god above.
For auspiciously offering to the god,
well, Pronounce auspiciousness...2

Secondly offer the auspicious flower to ....
bTsan, the god of the middle region 3

Thirdly offer the auspicious flower to ....
The Naga god (of Nether region)....4

Fourthly offer the auspicious flower to ... Father....5

Fifthly offer the auspicious flower to .... Mother 6

Sixthly offer the auspicious flower to .... Brother ... 7

Seventhly offer the auspicious flower to ....Sister....8

Eighthly offer the auspicious flower to ..
us, ourselves (you and we)...9

6

Chhodpa Festival :
An Ancient Mask Dance of Folk Tradition

The festival of Chhodpa (mchhod-pa = Worship) is held at village Khangsar in sTod in the Khar (mKhar = palace) of the Thakurs of Khangsar, twice in a year in the summer and winter called Yar-chhod (dbyar-mchhod = Summer Worship) held on 15th of 7th month and Gun-chhod (dgun-mchhod = Winter Prayer) on the 15th of 2nd month of the Tibetan calendar (Plates 5 & 6). These two dates are full moon days and come approximately in July-August and Feb-March. It is a festival for entertainment of the people and is connected with important seasonal agricultural operations. The mowing of grass and harvesting of crops starts immediately after the Yarchhod and the operations connected with sowing starts sometime after the Gunchhod. In Lahul one crop is grown and all the operations are done in stages by all the farmers almost at the same time, differing slightly from area to area, according to height. The season is short.

Summer Worship: In this part of the play there are three scenes. Firstly there appears a pair of a male, a monkey, and a female, his spouse, masked persons. Then there is the dance of Snow Lion and lastly there appear five female players all dressed similarly but over the head they wear a thin cover of cloth of different colours.

The Lion dance: The mask and the form of the lion is unlike those seen elsewhere. The festival remained abandoned for about twenty-five years and was restarted in 2016. The dance of the Snow Lion is the main attraction of the drama both from the angle of story and from the point of view of the audience. There are some stories about it as to how it started. Thille Namgyal tells that long ago some person from the house of the Thakurs of Khangsar went on hunting expedition to Larang at the top of the mountain on the opposite side of Khangsar across the river Bhaga. There at Larang he saw a lion dancing. Imitating this the dance was started at Khangsar.

Sonam Phuntsog of Tinno tells that once a hunter went up the mountain opposite Khangsar. There he found a lion dancing. He himself fell down from the cliff and died. From there started the Chhodpa. He names the two kinds of lions: Gangs Sing (Snow Lion) and Dam Sing (Forest Lion). Bokar Nawang Tobdan tells that once a gaddi shepherd saw above the Romkhang-za, the rock sprinkled bank of Bhaga opposite to Khangsar, a lion dancing. He told it to the Thakurs in Khangsar. Then began this festival of Lion Dance. All these stories point to the origin of the play locally and that the festival began with the Lion Dance. Here the real story is eclipsed. These stories become relevant and reliable only if we presume that the Lion Dance was incorporated later in the drama, because for the beginning of the drama there is a different story. All these stories appear to have been composed in the present social set up looking at the signs of Khangsar Khar and the gaddi shepherds. As we would soon see one of the story tellers himself narrates that the festival was formerly held at Jispa and from there it was shifted to another place and from there to Khangsar. This fact is corroborated by other people also. However, we don't know about the proper origin of the drama.

The well accepted story is that earlier this festival was held in Jispa at the place called Thotang. The Thakurs used to go to see the festival there riding horses. When the village was merged in water the play was shifted to Te-thab, about one kilometer from Gemur towards Jispa. Then it was brought to Khangsar in the palace of the Thakurs. But the story does approach the origin of the play.

Tshom chhedmo - Big Hall (Dancing Hall): The play is enacted in a hall in the palace situated on the second floor called Tshom-chhedmo (Plate 7). It is about fifty by fifty feet in dimension. There are two thick and high pillars in the middle of the floor spanning two floors up. The roof of the tshomkhang or the floor of its upper floor is left open around these two pillars which allows light to come in from the sky. The dancers dance between the walls and the four pillars. There also sit the spectators around. Some others sit on the upper floor who watch the show down through a wide opening in the upper floor.

The Play: The Onpo, astrologer, from the village of Sarang, house of Sarang Yogma, used to come to open the door of Srungma, the room of the guardian deity, where also the masks are kept, on the day of Chhodpa. Then came the Onpo from Karing Hayar. Now Lama Rigzin of Phyima Yogma of Tinno comes to open the door as the field connected with the Khar named go-zhing in Tinno has been sold to them. Before starting the dance the lamas, the one from Tinno and the priest of the monastery of Khangsar Khar recite prayers. Beyond this lamas have no role in the festival.

Masks: All the dancers wear wooden mask. They all give impressive antique look. The mask of monkey is said to have been made by Meme Kasse, an old man named Kasse, of the house of Yarzhi from the village of Jispa, belonging to second half of the nineteenth century. There is said to be an old broken mask of monkey lying in the store and another one unfinished. It is presumed that the mask of the lion also may have been constructed by him. But from the standard of workmanship it appears it may be much older. The mask of the lion has also two short horns. Nawang Tobdan Bokarpa, an aged lama from Tinno, told in around 1980, that the old mask of the lion is lying there in Srungma. But presently it is not seen and none has been heard ever talking about it other than him which might have disappeared silently. (Plate 8).

Phu Chhodpa: It is noteworthy that the players before moving out to enter the stage offer prayer to dGra-lha. In the beginning there appear the monkey and his spouse who is also named as Karmakar or pha-spre'u and Brag-srinmo (demoness of the rock). The pair is termed as Phu Khyad and the play as Phu Chhod. They appear wearing masks amid the sound of drums saluting the audience in the tshomkhang. The monkey holds a stick in his right hand. Karmakar appears holding a stick in the left hand and a small gormo, cup, named na-li, of mixed metal in her right hand. The symbolic meaning of the cup cannot be explained. They take twelve rounds of the tshomkhang.

After three rounds Tangrag-tsugche, a dance, is offered. The labdag, priest of folk gods, wearing serthod (gser-thod = golden turban, a turban of white cotton cloth over it a strip of gold) and holding a sword on the waist dances with a group of dancers holding hands of each other in circle behind the two masked dancers. The song is named Tongrog.

Tongrog: Singing of this song now a days has become a mere ritual because its meaning is not known to anybody. It is a sacred song sung on ceremonial occasions of the community or village. This singing of the song is termed as 'tongrog tsug-che'. The song is sung by a single person or a group and it may accompany a dance or not. In the chhodpa it is done twice, in the first occasion the song is sung and at the other it is not sung but only dance is performed. Following are some of the initial lines of the song.

tho-re tho-re jo-to jo-to
kho-re ra-ṇu bab-re ra-ṇu
re-to ra-ṇu kho-re ra- ṇu bab-re ra-ṇu

Then they sit and they are offered kalchhod (bskal-mchhod, folk Kal-chhor = auspicious offering). Datsag, beer prepared from buckwheat, is offered for drinking. Firstly the monkey makes offerings to the gods in the customary manner by dipping the stick in the pot and sprinkling. Then they are given straw pipes for drinking. First they are given a piece of ḍal, stem of mushutsi, pipe of stalk of a grass. They try to drink. It has no hollow. They break it doing indecent gestures and throw away. Then they are given don, pipe of a different grass. It is proper pipe.

In the last three rounds the monkey throws a walnut on the ground before himself and crushes under his feet.

The dance of Snow Lion and Monkey: Then in the second scene there come the lion and again the monkey. Monkey leads the lion to show him path till he reaches about the middle of the stage and intermitently throughout the scene. They dance and the monkey sometimes acts to take hold of the mane of the lion in joke.

The lion has a heavy mask of wood. There enter three strong young men to form the body of the lion. He dances by taking steps lifting up the legs coinciding with the music of the drum. At the same time he shakes head left and right, creating sound by striking the lower jaw, which is light, with the upper heavy jaw, coinciding with the music of the drums. In this manner he takes three frantic steps right and three steps left and then goes further jumping five steps. Then again he repeats the performance. He completes one round in five stages. After three rounds he is offered kalchhod. He completes twelve rounds and departs.

'bag chong-chong and tshomo kug-kug (Thin faced masked dancers and Tshomo, having face curved inward): In the third scene there appear seven mask dancers. Firstly comes the 'bag-gadpo, the old masked-man. After him comes a gaddi. He represents the gaddi shepherds of the Bharmaour in Chamba who have been coming to Lahul since long. He is called chhos-log, heterodox. While dancing he dances separately alone, separate from the row. He is in full dress of gaddi. He wears a woolen cloak with heavy waist band of woolen rope. He holds an axe high in his right hand, a hookah tied at the waist and a sug-tse, forepart of leg of a goat in the bossom. After them come five mask dancers: 'chhodpe lamong' worshipable goddesses of chhodpa. They are five female dressed in white, red, yellow, green and blue or pink light covers over their usual cloaks.

They dance for three rounds. Then tongrog is offered where they run briskly dancing in the style called shono. After three rounds they take rest. They beg money during this time. The last dancer Koko tshomo receives much of the money collected. They dance again to complete 12 rounds and disperse from the stage saluting the audience. After the dance the dancers of the lion and those taking part in the Phu chhodpa were given meal and drink by the Thakurs in the palace.

On this occasion all the khangcungpas (small households, a class of the householders) from Tinno to Meh bring datsag and serve to the spectators. In the summer festival the villagers of Tinno bring chhang and serve the spectators. They also bring a dangye, a four cornered effigy of about a foot high, made of rtsampa measuring three de.

This effigy is then offered in the name of the honourable audience of the show who are sitting on the upper floor of the dancing hall, by offering small pieces and throwing up and pronouncing the following mantra, in the customary method of offerings made in the worships:

gyalpo dang gyalmo hurmo gsum
dponpo dang chhag-shi do-khri thamschad la mchhod.

Translation: Offerings to the king, queen and Hurmo(?), the three; to the Minister and the collaterals of (of king i.e. Thakur) first stage and of the second stage, we offer! The remainder is offered to the drummers. Now the Tinnopas don't bring anything and this part of the Act is not played.

Three days after the chhodpa the festival of Namchim is held where again the gser-thod-pa is present and sangrag, horse race, is held. Then starts the mowing of the grass and thereafter the cutting of the crops begins. These rules are not relevant now.

Srungma, the guardian deity: The guardian deity of Chhodpa is Tshe-bdag-mo, a goddess. She is said to have been brought from Jispa. She is represented in a statue of stucco which is simple, without any ornaments or symbols sitting in meditative posture. Presently a new statue has been done. The earlier one got missing some years back. There are three older statues of the deity.

Gunchhod: The lion dance which is exhibited in summer is not shown in the winter. In the winter one pair is of the Gyapho Pekar and Bon-nag (Black Bonpo). Both are kings. In place of lion there is one called lamshagpa, opener of path (as on fresh snow) also known as nyil-da-pa (nyi-zla-pa?) who carries an arrow and bow.

7

Gepang : The Spiritual King of Lahul

Gepang: Gepang, a god of folk religion, is the spiritual leader of Lahul. He is revered principally in Tinan valley. Gepang came to Lahul, with a group of deities, from northern direction across Baralacha pass according to the story. Except Tangjar all of them are resident in Tinan valley. Drabla (dgra-lha) was earlier the spiritual king of Lahul. Perhaps he inhabited the place before the advent of Gepang. The two deities went at the Raja of Chamba, to ask for the right over the land. Gepang, a clever one, went into the palace to meet the king, and kept Drabla waiting outside at the gate of the palace with the rein of the horse in his hands. Latter Gepang introduced Drabla to the Raja as his groom. Since then Gepang became the Raja of Lahul.

The original place of residence of Gepang is at Yangling, slightly above Khwagling (Sissu, on the left side of the Sissu stream towards Khoksar) and there is situated the old temple of the deity. Presently his temple is situated at Sra-srin (Sissu on the side of Gondhla) on the upper side of highway. It was here at this place at the time of visit of Moorcroft. There are two stories told about their advent into Lahul: Lha-rabs and Mi-rabs, the Story of gods and the Story of men. The greatest obligation Lahul owes to Gepang and his group is that he was able to bring into Lahul, saving from the clutches of the demons who obstructed their way and seized all the articles the gods were carrying, two grains of cereals, one white and one black, from which spread the crops of huskless barley and buckwheat, respectively, the principal cereals of Lahul, only till sometime back,

According to the story the first char, a beam of wood, the rath or vehicle of Gepang, was brought from Malana in Kullu. Two persons, Milang and Ghyap, went to sTeng Malana i.e. up above to Malana to bring char, a long wooden beam of juniper tree, of about nine feet long. Milang became priest of Gepang and Ghyap that of Boti in Ropsang. They are settled in the villages of Yangling and Ropsang respectively, where there reside the two gods, with the same name of their households. Ghyap however shifted lately to Khwagling.

Gepang visits Malana periodically say after about five-six or more years. The two, Gepang and Jamlu, are considered as brothers. The tradition is that whenever he goes on a trip to Malana only his chhatra, umbrella, fixed on a stick, is carried. A new char is brought prepared from Malana. There he has a large jungle from where the tree is selected. It is prepared to the finish by the people of Malana. This is dressed with pieces of cloths of different colours with the umbrella of silver at its head. The dressed vehicle is carried by the young men of Malana upwards upto the top of Chandrakhani Pass.

In the biannial trip in the valley, it is not necessary that the new or the latest char should be taken. Presently there are about eight or nine such chars. Any one of them can be taken. But it is told that whichever beam shakes itself is taken for the trip.

Following are the names of the gods and goddesses who accompanied Gepang while coming to Lahul and the names of the villages where they reside. Alternative names of the deities and the villages are also given therewith:

	Name of Deity	**Name of Village**
1.	Tangjar	Chugṭa , Pyukar
2.	Milang tete	Guley, Gundhla
3.	Gyungdul, Nag devta	Sakar, Margyad
4.	Melakar, Boṭi, Tangjar dong, Pha-la Mekar	Ropsang
5.	Tinglogur	Srasrin
6.	Gepang	Yangling & Srasrin
7.	Lungkhorball, Nyunglabar	Jāgle
8.	Drabla	Rāling
9.	Mogg, Pha-la Mogar, Mokab	Shooling
10.	Shelābar, devi Shelbar	Ṭīling

The villages of Thorang and Khyinang are said to have no deities in their villages. These are the names of the deities considered to have accompanied Gepang while coming to Lahul.

According to Gopi Ram only the first six are the gods who came Others are local deities. Gopi Ram appears to be quite reliable. Drabla (dgra-lha=god of enemy, god who helps to empower enemy) was the king god of Lahul before the advent of Gepang.

In the rath of Gepang, to give it life, a small article called Khyung is attached whenever it is dressed. It is its srog, life. Once, around 1980s, it was stolen. It was told to be a piece of iron.

Earlier people used to offer to Gepang white ram of silver. Mardanzi, ghee, is offered every month. Earlier there was a pujari with long beards and he wore white shawl at the time of worship. Phaah (Phāh) is Pujari, priest, in the journey to Malana. He carries the big incense holder and offers mardanzi to the deity on the way wherever they take rest. He was astrologer. He did astrology in every village. He earlier resided at Kholagmurti (literally a place where there is water and the travelers take kholag, rtsampa with tea or chhang) now known as Kholagmur near Karing in sTod. Whenever Gepang came out for journey two persons went to bring the Phaah. They went wearing Pula, straw shoes, and clad very lightly. They avoided mdong-thug, meeting any person on the way.

Gyungdul (elder) and Melakar (younger) are daughters of Tsishag. Zangdulma is mother of Gepang who lives at Kewag. When Gepang is on the move she joins him on his rath. Thus we understand that Gyungdul and Melakar are goddesses. But Gyundul is also considered as Nagaraj, a god. According to Gopi Ram Tangjar is a devi and she is sister of Nagaraj Gyungdul. But at Chugta, the village of his residence, Tangjar is revered as a god. They cannot be properly distinguished in practice whether one is devi or otherwise.

Among the deities Milang Tete of Gundhla is considered as the eldest. Tinglogur of Srasrin Bazir, Minister. Melakar of Ropsang is designated as Boti (Hindi) i.e. cook and is also known generally by name as Boti. She remains always with Gepang because she is considered as cook of Gepang. Tangjar earlier used to come to Sissu through Rangtsa pass, the pass between Kardang and Gundhla.

A festival called Kyesumdor of these deities is held every third year at a place called Guntsaling above Gundhla, Gule (dgu lha = nine gods) for three days in the winter. Offerings to Gepang is made of only ghee.

Tangjar is said to have come to Chugta from Sarang, in sTod. At Sarang there is a sacred grove of trees of seabuckthorn dedicated to Tangjar. Like this, although there are some other evidences of relationship of Gepang with sTod but in his stories there is no reference to sTod or any place in sTod. Earlier Gepang did not visit sTod.

Advent of Gepang to Lahul — The story

There is a custom in which the priest of Gepang narrates the story of his coming and of the other gods, into Lahul, on a day in the winter, to the villagers, in his shrine. There are two stories: Lha-rabs (Story of gods) and Mi-rabs (Story of men). The first story tells the story of the gods coming to Lahul. The second story tells the story about founding of a tsug-lag khang, a Vihar, but this is not revealed from its title. The first story belongs purely to folk religion. In the second story a touch is given to Buddhsim. Thus the story may be a later addition. In the history of Buddhism in the area it belongs to quite early period. The application of the term tsug-lag-khang belongs perhaps to the period of First Spread of Buddhism in Tibet.

We have another version of the first story from Sakar which appears to possess little more archaic characteristic. We learn that the story was narrated at three different places: Yangling (Gepang), Ropsang (Boti) and Sakar (Gyungdul). It could have been more.

Below are given the translations of the three stories. First two are Lha-rabs related to Gyungdul and Gepang and the third is Mi-rabs from Gepang.

a. La-ra (lha-rabs) - The Story of gods

Formerly there were no gods in Ling. Gyungdul said, "Let us go to reign over Ling." All the gods proceeded from India. They brought everything with them. These, Gyungdul took with himself.

From there they reached Baralacha pass. Gyungdul seated himself there on the snow. Then the others reached Naphen Nuphen. There they were overtaken by a demoness. She threatened them saying, "Why did you bring my property?"

As soon as she said so Gepang disrobed himself and placed all their belongings in a heap there. He thereafter took three grains of Ne (huskless barley) and buckwheat each and concealed them in a bamboo stick which he stuck on the ground above the pathway.

Then they recommenced their journey. At Zemug the same demoness appeared, stretching her legs over the path and blocking their way. She ordered them to pass through beneath her.

They then counted themselves. All were present except Gyungdul who was missing. They enquired each other where to search him. Tangjar volunteered himself, "If nobody is ready, I will go." So he set out.

Meanwhile he noticed Gyungdul sitting perched on the snow. Tangjar bending down before him, saluted thrice and prayed to stand up. Rising out of the snow Gyungdul asked Tangjar the reason for his coming. Tangjar replied, "We are going to take over Ling."

At Zemug the same demoness was seen obstructing their way. Brandishing a weapon, Gyungdul struck at her. Mutilating her with the weapon to pieces, he threw the demoness away across nine hills and nine passes. From there they set out again. They then heard human voices at Pyukar. They asked among themselves as to who were settled there.

Tangjar stayed back to rule over this land. Others went crossing Rangtsa pass and heard human voice at Guley (Gundhla). Milang Te-Te stopped there to rule over this land. Then they arrived at Srinpo Thoyar from where human voice could be heard at Margyaling (Margyad). "I will settle down here to rule over the land," said Gyungdul. The others reached at Rogal and Melakar settled down at Ropsang. Tinglogur (Bazir) settled down at Srasrin. The rest reached at Yangling. Gepang stayed there. On that day there was none who could supply them food. During those days only Mons lived in Srasrin.

They consulted among themselves. They invited Gyungdul. He advised, "Give these Mons chhang made of cannabis for drinking and mattress of nettle." Gyungdul then served them with chhang and provided mattress of nettle and made them mad. All the Mons then ran away.

Gyungdyul suggested, "Why should we sit over here idle?" We have nothing to eat." Addressing Bazir (Tinglogur) said, "We two shall go to enquire about the welfare of our mother," He got prepared a ring of gold, threw it up towards the sky, saying, "If you are really a powerful mother this ring will fall in the lap of Hor (?)". It actually fell in the lap of Hor.

Mother was in deplorable condition, her nose was flowing and water coming out from the mouth. Gyungdul saluted her. He bathed her with saffron, milk of red cow and white goat, and made her look as if a goddess had descended from heaven.

Mother said, "You are the eldest among the nine gods. After three years nine gods will come to salute you." Addressing Milang Te-te, "You are younger by one year, you will have to come to greet him (annually)."

"You are Minister," told to Tinglogur. "You will have to go to collect lari lathang (lha-ri lha-thang = hills and lands of deities) from the king of Chamba". "You are the youngest, you will open the doors (of temples) of the nine gods every year," she told Melakar.

Tinglogur prepared a whirl of turquise, a spindle of gold and made a silver ball of wool and set out towards Chamba for demanding lari lathang. Then at the mountain pass leading to Chamba he met with the shepherd of the king of that country. He enquired from Tinglogur, where he was going. "I have come to collect lari lathing from your king." Tionglogur further suggested, "Why should we wait in idle, why not play dice?"

The shepherd questioned, "What items will you put in stake?"

The Bazir answered, "I have whirl of turquoise, golden spindle and thread ball of silver. I will put them as stake." Then in turn he asked the shepherd the articles he had to put in stake.

"I have nine suits of dress and nine kinds of meals. Those I will put in stake." The two then started playing. Bazir lost the whirl of turquise, golden spindle and thread ball of silver to the shepherd. Bazir proposed to play another game. "This time the stake will be like this. He who loses the game, his body will be split into two parts, starting from the tip of the hand to the tip of the toe."

This time Bazir won. He started displaying his knife again and again. The shepherd appealed, "Whether you are god or human being, kindly forgive me. You may even take back the whirl of turquoise, golden spindle and thread ball of silver, nine suits of clothes and nine kinds of meal."

"I don't want your nine suits and nine meals. You deliver my message to your king that he should give my lari lathang."

Next time when he met with the shepherd, he enquired, "Did you deliver the message to the king of Chamba or not?"

"I forgot," replied the shepherd.

"Today I will send with you a remembrance," said Bazir. He took a small round stone and tied it to the horns of a goat. The shepherd drove the cattle home in the evening.

The queen went with a golden vessel to milk the goats. The goat hit the bucket with the stone and overturned it and spilled out the milk.

The king ordered to produce the shepherd before him. He also ordered to fetch a sword in order to execute the shepherd. The shepherd appeared before the king and petitioned.

ral-dri shub nang la bzhugs.
rGya-pho khri stog la bzhugs.

"May the sword remain in the sheath,
The king be seated on his throne.

'I make an appeal. This is not my contrivance. It was the plan of Bhotdeva (Bazir)."

The Bazir was sitting over the water tap belonging to the palace. Water-women from the palace came and warned him. Be away from this water."

He replied, "I am not Bhot. I am Bhotdeva." The water-women then went in, carrying water. The Bazir sent message with them asking them to tell the king to come out.

The Bazir transformed himself into the shape of a ram and went in piercing seven sheets (walls) of iron. He asked, "Tell the king of Chamba to come out." The king said, "This must be a beggar. Give him some drink of chhang and rtsampa, and turn him out."

The Bazir retorted, "I haven't come for your rtsampa. Nor do I want your worn out clothes." And repeated, "Tell the king to come out. If he does not, I will laugh."

"Tell him to laugh as much as he can," said the king.

As soon as the Bazir started laughing, there appeared seven suns. All the plants in the courtyard of the palace and jungles were burnt down. "Be kind, don't do like this. I pray you. I know you," said the king.

Then Bazir eclipsed six suns and left only one. The king did not pay any heed to him even then. The Bazir sent in message, whether he should cry.

The king retorted, "Cry as much as you like."

The Bazir then started crying. No sooner had he started crying than started heavy hailstorm and flood. Trees in the jungles were uprooted. King's courtyard was damaged. The king sent message to tell him that he should not cry. " I honour him."

Still the king took no care of him. The Bazir posed, "Should I roll from side to side.?"

"You may even turn upside down," replied the king.

The Bazir rolled over the ground and turned the king's courtyard topsy turvy.

The king finally showed up and said, "Why not?"

Gyungdul, the eldest will get eighteen shares. You (Tinglogur) too will have eighteen shares. Others will get three, four, five shares each."

The king then reached at Guley on way to mTsho (Riswalsar). There Gyungdul caused snowfall nine yards deep and prevented the king from moving further.

The king enquired from the people, "Who is this, who has caused snowfall?" The people told this is Gyungdul. Only he has power to make it melt."

"Where does he live?"

"He lives at Sakar," the people told the king.

Then the king came there and entreated, "Make the snow melt within nine days and nine nights. I will give you half of my estate."

The earth became visible within nine days and nine nights. The king while returning from Rewalsar paid obeisance to Gyungdul saying, "You are really a powerful god. You have miraculous powers. I offer you half share in my estate," (The story was narrated by Gopi Ram). (Tobdan, 1979: 52-61).

b-i. Larab — Story of the gods —

Raja Gepang came with many devi and devatas from the northern direction. They were carrying seeds of number of kinds of grains. When they reached at Naphen-Nuphen they came to know that the demons were also following them. The demons compelled them to throw away the seeds there.

Gepang took vow that he will not take anything except ghee. Then devi Melakar became angry. She expelled fire from her mouth and smoke from her nose and with a rod of iron compelled the demons to go crossing nine valleys and mountain ranges. After this the devi and devatas started their journey towards their destination. On the way in the crevices of glacier were stuck up Melakar, devi Boti, and devi Gyungdul (Sakar Devi), and mother Chishag (Tsishag). Then the devis Brogma, Mogar, etc. reached there. While going across her they spat and passed on instead of helping her in bringing her out.

After sometime devi Boti and Gyungdul reached. They saw that their mother had fallen in the snow. They brought her out and cleaned her. Then they thought how to bring her. They thought if they bring her on their back it will be like showing back to their mother. So how it should be done. After considering for sometime they decided that they will carry her face to face. So the two sisters walked carrying their mother both facing their mother. In this manner they were feeling much difficulty. On the way the two started laughing. Chishag then said, "man laughs when he is in pleasure, but it is good that one should laugh in the distress also". Mother Chishag also said that Brogma Mogar will be worshipped only with lashel pug (roasted grains of buckwheat). To Chishag she told that you are Chhunpun (younger sister, says narrator), you will have to bow before the nine devi and devtas, and will have to perform the task of mahang altsi, opening of the doors of the nine temples. After three years with her rath, vehicle, she will have to welcome them all.

Thus they all reached in Lahul. Gepang told them to stay at different places and he himself stayed at Yangling above Sissu. In Shashin village stayed Tinglogur presently known as Lonpo, Bazir. Here it is clarified that the rath as known to be that of Gepang which comes out after every third year, is actually that of Bazir. He goes on tour of whole Lahul. Gepang comes out only rarely.

At that time there lived at Shashin, Srasrin, only montsa (Mon). They did not worship Bazir. On this Tinglogur applied his power for expelling the montsa from there. Then the montsa slowly went away from there.

During those days these areas were ruled by the Raja of Chamba. Tinglogur wanted to demand his right. Therefore one day he started to go towards Chamba for demanding his right. On the pass towards Chamba he rested there. Raja's shepherd used to come daily to graze the sheep. He sent message through the shepherd to the Raja that there has come a Bhotdev to demand his right. But the shepherd forgot daily to deliver the message.

One day as a rememberance he tied a stone with the horn of a goat. After putting the sheep and goat in the bar the shepherd sat to take rest. As the queen started milking the goats the stone fell in her goldern pot and spilled over the milk. The queen went running to the king and told him either to expel the shepherd immediately or to kill him. He had tied a stone with the horn of a goat which fell in my milk pot and turned over the pot and spilled over the milk.

On asking the shepherd he said, "You may punish me any way you like. But I have to make a petition". The Raja asked to tell. He told, "Your honour used to send seven meals every day earlier. Now it remains only for one day". The king asked how it happened. The shepherd told, there has come a Bhotdev on the pass. He is asking for his share. He sends this message every day but I forgot every day. Therefore I had tied this stone to the horns of the goat. For this reason only one share remains out of seven.

Now I am at your mercy whether you kill me or do any way you may like. It is acceptable to me any way. On this the king told him to call him in the palace the next day.

Next day the shepherd started again towards the pass as usual. There the Bhotdev asked about the message from the king. Or has he forgotten. The shepherd replied that the Raja has called him in his palace the next day. On this he accompanied the shepherd. But there he did not go straight into the palace. At slight distance from the palace there was a water spring. There he sent message with the persons coming there to convey to the Raja that Bhotdev has come to demand his right. The Raja heard the message, but ignored it.

In this manner many days passed away. But there was no message from the side of the king. Women came at the water source for worship but whatever they offered fell into the mouth of Bhotdev. On this one day he asked the women that whatever you offer in worship all fall in my mouth. Some women extracted the offerings from his mouth. In this manner several days passed on.

One day Bhotdev sent a message to tell the king whether I should laugh. The king sent message you can laugh as much as you like. Bhotdev told that he will not laugh to the extent that mouth may get torn, but only to a small extent. He laughed a little. Soon there appeared seven suns in the sky. Jungle, fields, orchards all started burning. Then the Raja sent message to tell Bhotdev that he will get his right.

Then he hid the seven suns. Then again some days passed. But no information came from the side of the Raja. Then Bhotdev sent a message asking whether I should cry. The Raja sent message, yes, you can cry. You can cry as much as you like, till your eyes become swelled.

Bhotdev started crying. Soon it started raining. There was flood in all the directions. People started crying. Water even reached upto the palace of the king.

Then the king sent his men with the message to tell him that he will get his right. On hearing this Bhotdev stopped crying. Rain also stopped and there was no flood. The Raja again forgot his promise. Bhotdeva kept on waiting for the answer but there was coming no indication. Then Bhotdev decided that he will use his power to create massive destruction.

Bhotdev sent a message with the men of the Raja whether I should take turns. The king sent message in the same manner as he had done earlier. He said, yes you can take turns as much as you like, even till your neck breaks. Bhotdev started taking turns on the ground. The earth began trembling. The palace also started shaking.

Then this time the Raja himself came to see Bhotdev and took him with honour into his palace. In the palace Bhotdev introduced himself to the Raja. The Raja gave all the lands above the road to Bhotdev Tinglogur and then gave him farewell with great regard.

Tinglogur then came back to Shashin. Now it was necessary to build a rath, vehicle, for the deity. For this there was need of a long staff which is called char. It was decided that char should be brought from sTeng Malana. Two persons Milangpa and Ghyap were the two persons selected for the work. When they reached with the char at Gufa Hotel, a place below the village of Teling, there they were required to cross the river, from left side to the right side of the river.

Firstly Milangpa crossed the river. Now the two were on either side of the river. Both of them had bow and arrows with them. They thought although we have brought char, but now who will be the real priest of Tinglogur.

Before crossing the river they decided as to who will be the murpa (pujari). Firstrly they had competition with bow and arrow. Then they decided that the one who crosses the river without falling will become the pujari. Ghyap entered the water and fell down in the water even though it was shallow. Milangpa was able to cross the river easily. The two then reached Shashin with char. From this time onwards Milangpa became pujara of the deity.

Thus time passed on. Everyone was happy in his place. Once it was the month of Shailik (July). The people had not yet sowed the summer crop because there was heavy rain and snowfall during that time. Farmers were worried. At this time Erich and Thengkuts were sent to Gudumts Apa (grandmother). At that time she was in ferocious form. She had extended one of her udders outside the door and she was herself sitting on the other. Erich and Thengkuts sucked milk from the udder of Gudumts. Gudumts dragged both of them in and said, O you are children, otherwise I would have taken you as morning meal. Then she asked from them the cause of their coming. They told that the month Shailik has come but people have not yet sowed their crop. Apa said at this moment I am impure. You come tomorrow. Next day the two came again. Gudumts told that a goddess has been driven down in the river from Kyuling in Spiti. Presently she is lying either below Shooling or Mooling.

Kyuling gi lha Shooling gi leh, yang na Mooling gi leh (leh = below, in folk).

(Kyuling lha ki Shooling ley, yang ki Mooling ley yang).

It means that Kyuling devi will be found either below Shooling or Mooling. As suggested by Gudumts the people searched the deity below Mooling and Shooling. They found her below Shooling. Now the deity was installed. But the goddess demanded human sacrifice. There was none ready from that area. The man was offered a de of silver and a de of gold. Lastly two men were given the responsibility to find such a person. They set out with the silver and gold towards Pangi. They met with a woman in a house. They gave the gold and silver to the members of the family and brought the woman. On reaching Shooling preparations were made.

Firstly she was taken to the water spring. There she said you are offering me to a great devi, it is not proper to bathe me here. Take me to a rivulet. People did as she told. After reaching the rivulet she again told them to take her to the main river. Then they took her to the main river. While going there the woman put her cloak over a red churi (yak-cross cow). Then all the men went with her to the river. As she started bathing she crossed the river swimming. The people were surprised. Then the woman said, 'Miganga, Miganga, what are you seeing towards me, look there at Shooling Jiganga'.

The meaning is that why are you looking at me, see there in the ground in Shooling. All the people came there and saw that the woman had kept her cloak on a red churi.

Then they offered the churi to the devi. As the sacrifice was given the sky became clear. People sowed crop. In that year there was an excellent crop. (This story was narrated by Sher Singh).

b-ii. Mirabs: The story of Man

Gangchen (Gangs-chhen) and Gangchung (Gangs-chhung) were two fairy sisters. One day the two went to jungle to collect flowers. When they had finished collecting flowers they sat to take rest. They began picking lice from the hair of each other's head. As they were doing so the elder sister fell asleep. While she was sleeping the younger sister looked into the elder sister's basket and saw that her elder sister had gathered more flowers than she had. So she picked up some from there and put into her own basket.

As a cause for the sin she had committed, the younger sister had to visit the human world. There she was married to a man called Mirzi (mi-rdsi = a person grazing men). With him she gave birth to a son. He was named Mitsa (Mi-btsa'). After three years her husband died. Then she was married to Khyirzi, who grazed dogs. She had a son with him too. He was named Khyitsa. Again after three years her husband died. Thereafter she was married to Tarzi, a person who grazed horses. With him also she had a boy who was named Tatsa. After three years her husband died. In this manner she passed nine years among the men. Then she returned to join her sister whom she found still sleeping. She pulled her sister gently and asked her to get up. The elder sister woke up, with a long breath saying, "Oh! I fell asleep. The younger sister said No, it is not sleep, but it is as a result of my sinful actions."

The younger sister narrated whole of her story. The elder sister told that the Mitsa will become king; Khyitsa will become Lonpo (blon-po), Minister, and the Tatsa will be Chhodne (mchhod-gnas = priest), also say servant. All this happened as was predicted.

In this manner some years passed by. One day the king called Lonpo. The two kept talking for long. Then Lonpo requested for the King's orders. The king told that he should construct a bridge of sand. The Minister became silent. He could not say anything and came home without saying anything.

At home he lay himself on the ground, behind the door, head resting on one of his arms and the other arm lying over the legs. As his wife came she saw her husband very sad. She asked, "O, Lonpo, what happened? Why are you so sad today?" "Please get up, wash your hands and mouth and come have your meal." The Lonpo sat for meal. During the meal his wife asked again for the cause of his grief. He told the whole story. Then she asked, "What reply did you give?" Lonpo replied that he said nothing.

Then his wife suggested, "Tomorrow when you go to the king, you ask for grains for construction of the bridge. For measuring the grain you take a bottomless 'de'," a measuring pot. Lonpo did as his wife had advised. Then he asked for grains from the king. The king ordered the servants to give grain to Lonpo. When the pot was filled with grain the servants raised it up but all the grain fell down on the ground. The servants asked Lonpo with such a bottomless pot how can we measure the grain? Lonpo replied if a bridge of sand can be constructed why not grain can be measured with a bottomless pot? In this manner the Raja received answer.

Time passed on. One day the King again called Lonpo. They kept on talking for long. Then Lonpo asked the king for orders. The king told, "You have to build a Culekhang (gtsuglag-khang = Vihar). It will be built not on the ground but it will be hanging in the air." Lonpo became silent. He came home with his head bowing down.

At home he lied down in the same manner behind the door. As his wife came she asked from her husband. He told that this time the Raja told to build a Vihar which should be hanging in the sky. Then she asked, "What did you reply?" He told that he said nothing.

Then the wife suggested, "Tomorrow you go to jungle and bring catching a red bird. Tie its feet with a string and train it for some days to stay in the air for some time and then come down only at your call." Lonpo did as his wife had suggested. Then he again went to the Raja. He asked the Raja to allow him to construct the Vihar. The Raja gave orders for construction of the Vihar.

Lonpo sent the bird to sky. Then it started chirping like pidik, pidik. Lonpo told the labourers to hand over stones and mud to the bird for construction of the tsuglag-khang.

The men asked how can we give stones and mud up towards the sky? The Lonpo replied then how can gtsuglag-khang be built in the sky. In this manner the king again received reply.

After some days the Raja again called Lonpo. They kept talking for long time. Then Lonpo asked the Raja to give him orders. The Raja told, this time you have to construct a tsuglang-khang over the ground. Lonpo had knowledge about this. He told, "Yes, I will construct." Lonpo today came home very much delighted.

By the time he reached at home, his wife also reached from the work in the fields. After washing hands and face he sat down for meal. The wife said, "Today you look happy." He told, "Today the Raja has told me to construct a tsuglag-khang over the ground. I have knowledge about this. So I have told the Raja positively".

Lonpo started his work from the next day. He was reciting a mantra;

mdung-ma brgya dang brgya-tsa bzo bar shog
sgo brgya dang brgya-tsa bzo bar shog
kar-khung brgya dang brgya-tsa bzo bar shog.
ka-ba brgya dang brgya-tsa bzo bar shog.
ka-zhu brgya dang brgya-tsa bzo bar shog.
khrol brgya dang brgya-tsa bzo bar shog.
(dungma gya dang gyarsa zo bar shog
go gya dang gyar-sa zo bar shog
kar khung gya dang gyarsa zo bar shog.
ka gya dang gyarsa zo bar shog.
ka gya dang gyarsa zo bar shog.
tro-lu gya dang gyarsa zo bar shog).
Translation: May there be built one hundred beams.
May there be built one hundred doors.

May there be built one hundred windows.
May there be built one hundred pillars.
May there be built one hundred capitals.
May there be built one hundred carvings and engravings.

As he was reciting this mantra, the Vihar was coming up as if the whole work was being done by the gods and goddesses.

The work was in progress. But a block of stone was not being fitted properly over the lintel of the main door. Lonpo was busy working on the stone, striking the stone with a small hammer. Meanwhile the prince came to see the progress of the work. After seeing all the works he reached at the gate. He was standing under the beam of the gate. Then the Minister lost control over the stone and it fell down and hit just on the head of the prince. The prince fell down instantly on the ground and after some time he was dead. Lonpo dug up a pit near the gate and put the dead body in it. Then he came home.

As he came home he again kept lying behind the door with his head on one of the arms and the other arm over his legs. When his wife came and saw Lonpo again in sad mood, She imagined something unpleasant has happened again. She asked Lonpo to get up, wash his hands and face and sit for meal. As they were taking meal, the wife asked from Lonpo, as to what had happened. Lonpo told that this time very sad incident has occurred. "You should not tell it to anybody. Today the prince came to see the Vihar. I was dressing a stone sitting over the lintel of the main door. When the prince came under the door the stone fell down slipping from my hands. It hit the prince and he died".

Then his wife asked, "Presently where is the body?" He told that he had buried it under the ground under the gate. On this the wife could not say anything. Both of them became silent and as it was midnight they went to sleep. But the sleep had vanished from the eyes of the Lonpo. He thought he had done a mistake by telling the secret to his wife. He thought:

pu-gu bdun-ne a-ma la snying-gtam ma-bshad,
la-la skyid-du 'gro, la-la dga' ru 'gro.

(pu dun ne ama la snying tam ma-shad.
la-la kid-du do, la-la ga-ru do.)

Meaning: It is not proper to tell the secrets of your heart to the mother of seven children. Sometimes it is good, but one cannot say what will happen at another. Therefore the Minister thought that he must move from here, it will be better. Then he set out towards the jungle in the mid night.

In this manner the Vihar of the Raja remained incomplete. Meantime there was a rumour that the prince is missing. Search began. Men were sent in all the directions. Even after the search for several days there was no news about the prince. The Raja made an announcement declaring prize to the person who brings any news about the prince. He will be rewarded with half of the kingdom and if it is a woman she will be made queen of the kingdom.

The Minister's wife thought that it is better to be a queen than a wife of a minister and this is the opportune time. So she went to the king and told, "O, Raja, listen to a secret news. Your son has been killed by the Minister." Then the king asked, "Where is he now?" The Minister's wife told that it is burried in the ground near the gate.

On this the king ordered his servants to dig near the gate. They started digging. As they were digging they struck with horns. The servants asked from the king, did your son had horns? The king said, no, no. Then the servants dug up into more deep. They found legs of a goat. They asked from the king did your son had legs of goat. The king replied no, no. Lastly they found the body of a goat.

The Minister had dug up the grave and extracting the dead body had thrown it into the river. In its place he had put a body of a goat.

The king punished the wife of the Minister. He ordered to cut the hair of her head on one side, and blackening her face on the other side, to expel her from the kingdom.

Then the king asked the astrologers, where is my son? They said, Oh, king your son has been washed away in the river.

The king became very angry. The king started fighting with the river. Then the river told, O Raja, don't be angry. The water carrying your son has passed farther away. The king then became silent.

The construction of gtsuglag-khang remained unfinished. The Raja was worried. But he was determined that it must be completed.

The king prepared two persons and asked them to search an expert craftsman who could complete the work of the construction. He gave them one de of silver and one de of gold. They started towards a direction in the morning from where they expected they would be able to find a suitable person. They kept on moving and enquiring from the people.

One day they saw from distance two men ploughing in the field. The two ploughmen, father and son, also saw the two persons coming from afar. The son asked his father, before the two persons reach here, hide me somewhere. The father asked where can I hide you. The son told, hide me here in the row. The father did in the same manner.

When the two persons reached there they saw that earlier there were two persons now there is only one. They asked the ploughman:

O rolpa mi (me), rolpa mi, rol gtul-de rgyob.

O ploughman, plough the land deep. After saying this the two moved forward. Then the boy asked, O father have the two persons arrived. If they have come and passed on, then take me out. The father told that the two have gone passed further. The boy asked did they ask anything? The father told whatever they had said.

Then what did you say? I said nothing, said the father. Then the boy told his father to go and tell the travelers the following message:

bzang-po mi bzang-po mi gompa gtul de rgyob.

(zompo mi, zompo mi, gompa tul de gyob).

O gentlemen, put your steps carefully. The father went running behind the two and said the above sentence and came back and engaged himself in his work.

The two thought that there must be a second person also with him. So they returned and met the father and son. They kept on talking for long time. It was going to be night. Therefore the two had to stay there for the night.

As it became dark, the father and mother went out from the house. The two then asked from the boy, "Where have your father and mother gone?" The boy replied: "a-ba gtam tsal-la-la song". Father has gone to search for gossiping. "a-ma mig tsal-la-la song." Mother has gone to search eyes. Then he said further:

> brang-khog zhig gshag-ga yod, rgyu-ma zhig rgyang-nga yod,
> khang-pa dbu-'i (u-i') nyi-ma brgya-shar stong-shar yod.

I am tearing the breast and am filling intestines. From above the house there appear hundred and thousand suns.

After some time the father and mother of the boy came. The mother lighted fire and cooked meal. The father came carrying chhang. They started drinking chhang and talking. Then they took meal and kept on talking.

Then the men asked the boy that when we asked you where has your father gone and where has gone mother, you replied that father has gone to search gossiping and mother has gone to search eyes. The boy replied: Mother has lighted fire. With the light I can see my father and you can see me. This is the meaning of the term that mother has gone to search eyes. Then mother gave us meal and father gave us chhang, we are talking after having meal. This is the meaning of the term that father has gone to search talk.

Now after having meal we are getting warmed near the fire. rGyu-ma zhig rgyang-nga yod, brang-gog zhig gshag-ga yod, means the same that we are eating meal and are baring our chest for warming. nyi-ma brgya shar dang stong shar, you will know the meaning of this term in the morning. Then after gossiping for long time they went to sleep.

When they got up in the morning the guests again asked from the boy the meaning of the term nyi-ma..... The boy replied I cannot tell you now. I can tell you only after the sun has risen. When the sun appeared, they saw that there were small holes in the roof as the house was old and the layer of mud on the roof had become thin. Therefore sun rays were coming in the room through the holes from here and there. So the boy told that this is the meaning of the term.

After all these the two guests were impressed from the boy and thought that he is the right person. We should take him.

They gave the silver and gold to the parents of the boy and they took him with them. On the way they saw signs of hoofs of a bri-mo, yak-cow. The boy asked from the two, "Whose hoof's signs are these?"

O mgron-po mi mgron-po mi 'di rzhes chi-si yin dag shod bar mdsad. O guests, of what kind of cattle are these with such signs of hoofs, please tell me. They replied O, nga-rang ni mi-shes nyo-rang shes-na-ni gzigs par mdsad. We don't know. If you know please tell us. Then the boy told, a little further from here you will meet a bri-mo, yak-cow, with one eye healthy and the other one blind, and having crooked horns. These are the signs of that bri-mo. On going ahead they actually found a bri-mo with crooked horns.

Then going further they found the signs of feet of men. The boy asked 'O mgron-po mi, O mgron-po mi di rzhes chi yis yin dag bshad par bya." The two replied, "nga-rang ni mi-shes nyo-rang she na ni gzigs par bya". Then the boy told, on going further we will meet a woman, with one eye right and one eye missing, and carrying a child on her back and with a spindle in her hands. These are the signs of her feet. On going further they actually met a woman with a spindle in her hands and a child on her back. On this the two men became more impressed and thought this boy is very clever. He recognizes the animals and men by the signs of their feet.

They kept on going. In the evening they halted for stay in the night, they selected a place and halted. They slaughtered a sheep. They filled intestines and started eating. Meanwhile they felt thirst. The two men were going to fetch water. They told the boy, "the-tse bzang-po la lag-pa ma-thug, rtsig-pe gseb la shor yong." Don't touch your hands at the good mark, it may fall amid the stones of the wall. On saying this, the two went to drink water to the nearby spring. As the two disappeared the boy ate the thick part of the rgyuma, the cooked intestine, and he held a small piece of it on the mouth of a hole in the stone wall. As the two came in and saw him in this manner, the boy said, ya rgyuma shor song. the-tse bzangpo la lag pa thug song, sig pe gseb la shor song. Look, gyuma is lost.

I touched the good the-tse. It has missed in the wall. So saying, he cried out.

The two men thought, Oh this was our idea which this boy copied and acted.

After sometime the boy started playing with paaz, the bone of the joint of the hind leg of sheep. As he was playing a crow came and flew away snatching the paaz. He said this time the crow has won. See how he is defeated the next time.

Next time he took the urine bladder of the sheep, filled in it some hay and a bit of fire, and started playing with it. After sometime a crow came and took the bladder away and put it in his nest. As wind became strong the fire became stronger and it burnt the crow's nest. The chicks of the crow fell down. Then the boy said, see how the crow won first then now I have won. The two men thought this man is so clever and intelligent. He can defeat even the bird in the sky. Then they moved further and reached their destination. They made arrangement for the stay of the boy.

Next day the boy went to see the vihar. He checked all around the Vihar. Meanwhile an old woman was passing through there. On seeing the boy she asked, O, boy what are you seeing? You have been brought to construct this tsuglag-khang by giving a de of silver and a de of gold. Then the boy asked, O grandmother, O grandmother, tell me, who constructed originally this vihar.

The old lady told, sometimes back there lived here a Lonpo Rigpakhan, an intelligent Minister. He constructed the Vihar. Then the boy again asked, where does he live now? The old woman told, he now lives in lung-phug (cave) with his seven sons. After this the boy went to his residence. He had prepared chhang. It was of excellent grade. He put it in a tsoli, a small pitcher. He prepared mar-zan (porridge of tsampa eaten with ghee) and put it in a polkhud, a bag made of lamb skin for carrying lunch, generally by the shepherds. Carrying these articles he started riding a horse towards the lung-phug. Soon he reached at the residence of Lonpo.

By this time the Lonpo had become quite old and was blind. Presently he was sitting alone. His seven sons had all gone to jungle for hunting. The boy started talking with the Lonpo. Meanwhile the boy opened the mouth of the polkhud and took it nearer to the nose of the Lonpo.

Lonpo said sgon la ni za mnyong thung mnyong, da-lan dri-ma zhim-po zhig byung. Earlier I have eaten and drunk, this time the smell is very pleasant.

The boy said meme this is like rang-zan (rang-byung) (the meal I prepared myself) will you have it? Lonpo said, su re gter-mkhan yong na ni, lem za, lem thung. If there is somebody who can give, I will have just now. Then the boy gave the marzan. The old man ate all the marzan. After having it the Lonpo felt thirst. The boy then opened the mouth of the tsoli and took near the nose of the old man. He said sngon la za mnyong, thung mnyong dalan drima zhimpo zhig byung. Earlier I have eaten and drunk this kind of food. This time the smell is appealing.

The boy said Oh meme, this is bang chhu (weak kind of chhang). Will you have it? Lonpo replied, su yis gter mkhan yong na ni lem za, lem thung. The boy gave him the chhang and the old man started to feel the impact of the chhang.

Then the boy started talking with the Lonpo. He said, Meme at a distant place from here there is a tsuglag-khang, is it that you constructed it? He replied, yes I constructed. Then the boy asked, how is it constructed?

Lonpo told, it is very easy. The boy asked again, How is it constructed and kept on serving chhang. The Lonpo went on saying, it is very easy.

Now Lonpo was under heavy impression of the drink. Then he started narrating :

sgo brgya dang brgya-tsa bzo rgyu
kar-khung brgya dang brgya-tsa bzo rgyu.
mdung-ma brgya dang brgya-tsa bzo rgyu
ka-ba brgya dang brgya-tsa bzo rgyu
ka-zhu brgya dang brgya-tsa bzo rgyu.
khrol brgya dang brgya-tsa bzo rgyu.
(go gya dang gyarsa zo kyad
kar-khung gya dang gyarsa zo kyad.

dungma gya dang gyarsa zo kyad
ka gya dang gyarsa zo gyad
ka-zhu gya dang gyarsa gyad
Tro-lu gya dang gyarsa zo gyad.)
May there be built one hundred doors.
May there be built one hundred windows.
May there be built one hundred beams.
May there be built one hundred pillars.
May there be built one hundred capitals
May there be built one hundred carvings and engravings

In this manner by chanting this mantra the tsuglag-khang is constructed by itself. Then the boy asked, O meme Lonpo, is this the only mantra.

Lonpo replied, yes this is the only mantra. After he had learnt this he started to go home. As he started moving out he told the me-me, "lo of my horse has broken, do you have thag-dum?" Lonpo with great difficulty searched the thagdum and gave it to the boy. (Lo = rope for leading the horse. blo = intelligence) (thagdum = piece of rope).

The boy said again, meme tradpa of my horse has broken. Could you please give me snyung (thick needle of shoemakers). The Lonpo again searched the snyung with great difficulty and gave it to the boy. The boy went home taking the two articles.

In the evening when the seven children reached back home, Lonpo told them that his blo (= knowledge) has been stolen. On this they chased the boy and caught him on the way.

They asked him, so you are the man who stole the knowledge of our father. The boy replied, avo, mi-chhen ma-rab bzhin-'dra, Oh, the great man is a bad man. The lo (rope) of my horse had broken, so I brought a piece of rope which you can take back. The boys came back with the thagdum. They gave it to their father and said here take it.

On this the Lonpo said, 'i ta man. nga'i snying rkus song. It is not that, My heart has been stolen. On hearing this the seven boys again went after the boy and caught him on the way. They asked, you stole the heart of our father. Avo mi-chhen ma-rab min-na. (Is not the great man bad?) Who can steal the heart of such a man. The tadpa of my horse had broken so I had brought snyung. You can take it back. The boys came back with the snyung and giving it to their father said take it. On this Lonpo said, it is not that. Anyway, leave it now.

The boy now reached his residence. On the next day he started construction of the tsuglagkhang. He started reciting the mantra as told by the old man.

In this manner the work was completed and a beautiful tsulagkhang was constructed. (The story was narrated by Sher Singh).

The tradition of Human Sacrifice in Lahul

The story of the tradition of human sacrifice in Lahul is also connected with this story of the gods. The deity Mogg of Shooling earlier used to take human sacrifice. It is supposed to have been given in turn by each household. Once there came turn of a household in which there were only mother and her daughter. The family was prosperous. On the day their turn had come the two were querrelling with each other. In the night there came two thievcs. They looked in through the window. They saw that there were two women both were decorated in new dress. And they were eating nice meals. At the same time they were weeping. One was insisting that she will go, the other was insisting that she will go.

The two thieves talked among themselves saying they are eating nice meals but why they are weeping. The two decided that before making theft we should know the reason for this. The two went in. They asked, you are taking so nice meal but why are you weeping? They told, we have a deity. He takes human sacrifice. This time it is our turn. We are crying for the same reason. The two thieves then told that they will go in their place. The two became pleased. They gave nice meals to eat in plenty of quantities. They also enjoyed the meal well. They gave chhang and arag. Under the impact of chhang and arag the two went before the devata. There was a statue of the devata. One of the thieves offered first his arms, said, it is here you take it. When nothing happened he put his head before the deity, then legs and then the whole body. When in the last they saw that nothing is happening, they broke the statue, put it in a basket and threw into the river.

Tangjar: The story of god Tangjar tells the existence of the tradition of human sacrifice in sTod. Urgyan Chhering of Chugta, Pyukar, tells that Tangjar formerly resided at Sarang in sTod. He took sacrifice of a human being after every twelve years. Once it came turn of a family in which there were only a man and an old lady, son and his old mother. The lady was very much aggrieved. She had only her son as support. There arrived a lama and asked the reason for her weeping. Then he offered himself in place of the old woman's son. They agree. The lama presented himself before the god and said, Oh god, you take my life instead of that of the only son of this old lady. You can take my arms, head, legs and all. He offered one by one and then the whole body. When nothing happened the lama threw the statue of the deity in the river. The lama suggested to stop the tradition of giving human sacrifice. The villagers agreed to him.

As the statue flowed down in the river it stuck with a rock at a place called Samen-dumen, (sa-man rdo-man = a place neither earth nor stone) in the mid of the river, a place between the villages of Pyukar and Stingri. There people saw from distance a flickering light. When it continued for a long time an old man of the household of Thwas of Stingri went there to see. He saw a statue stuck between rocks in the river. He recognized the deity as Tangjar of Sarang who used to take human sacrifice. The man took promise from the deity that if he is prepared to abandon taking sacrifice of human beings and instead is ready to take offerings of brangs and markentsi, a ball of tsampa and ghee, he will be honoured and established as god in the village of Stringri. Tangjar agreed. Then the deity was established in this manner in Stringri and the custom continued for many years. Occasionally sheep and goat were also offered. The place of the deity was below the road. Then the people thought this is not appropriate. People walk above and the deity resides below the road. So the villagers decided to shift his place to Pyukar to keep with the local deity Srwag. On the request of the villagers the deity Srwag agreed to the point on the condition that all the offerings will first be made to him and his position will always be first, and that of Tangjar second. Urgyan also tells a slight different version of the story. He says once a lady, who had no offsprings, went before the deity appealing for grant of two children and then she took vow that she will offer one of them to the deity. The lady had two sons as promised by the deity, but due to love for her offsprings she backed up from her commitment. Due to the curse of the deity she remained always upset and sad. Then there came a lama and the rest of the story is as told above.

The story of human sacrifice in Lahul also spread to Pangi and Chamba. About the story in Pangi, the Gazetteer of Chamba records that at Kilar, 'Near the rest house in a grovc of cedar trees, is the temple of Det Nag, who, it is believed, was originally enshrined in Lahul enjoying human sacrifice. Once, the legend goes, in the series of sacrifice, it was the turn of the only remaining son of a poor widow, and the time of sacrifice having drawn fast, she was bewailing her misforture when a Gaddi happened to pass by and after knowing about the tale of woe volunteered to replace her son. He, however, stipulated that the Nag should be allowed to devour him alive, and on his presenting several parts of his body in succession without any result, he got angry and threw the Nag into the Chander Bhaga. It got out of the river at Kilar and being found by a cowherd was carried upto the site of the present temple, when it fell from his back with the face on the ground. A shrine was erected and the image set up with its face looking inwards, and a clump of cedar trees at once grew up around the shrine. Previously a buffalo used to be sacrificed every third year,, fifth, or seventh year in the month of Katik at this temple of the Nag. The expenditure for the purchase of the victim was borne, during the State regime by the erstwhile Chamba State. After the merger of the State the inhabitants of the area contributed but once for the purchase of a buffalo. Subsequently the sacrifice was discontinued for the lack of funds, (Gazetteer, 1963: 439-440).

In Chamba, Bharmour, where the Kailing devata is enshrined, it is told that the devata came from Kyelang in Lahul where he used to take human sacfrice and then the statue was thrown into the river and the devata reached here.

The Story of Gepang — some explanations: Presently the living members of the two families of Milangpa and Ghyap (Ghyapa) and that of the priest of Gyungdul at Sakar relate the story of coming of the deities to Lahul regularly in the winter in custom. Gopi Ram, priest of Gyungdul (khyung+'brul = Eagle and serpent) (Nag devata) was of 80 years of age in 1974. Presently his grandson is in charge of the task in his place. Sher Singh is Milangpa and Gyaltshan, who also tells the story, is Ghyap.

To both the original stories of the Lha-rabs additions have been made in the last. In the story of Gopi Ram there is a very short addenda about the visit of the Raja of Chamba to Riwalsar. The stories added in the second story are different and are longer.

Apparently the direction from which the gods are shown to have come by the composer of the story is from the northern direction, the direction of high Central Asia as all the sources relate them coming through Baralacha pass. Dondub Pankharpa tells that Gepang came from Hor.

The two stories of Lha-rabs and Mi-rabs appear to be compositions of two different authors and also belonging to two different periods. The first is purely folk in content unaffected by any great religious faith. The second story is set up in a different cultural setting of Lahul. The culture is in contact with Buddhism, as the main theme of the story is construction of tsuglagkhang, Vihar. But this is at a very early stage in the development of Tibetan Buddhism in the area.

It is told that there was a book of the stories of Gepang. It was lost in a glacier and only the wooden covers have been left. Thakur Duni Chand recites a sentence from the book: 'dre mi (me) lha la mchhod, 'Offerings to the demons, men and gods'. This is like a group of spirits revered in the folk custom. Here in the middle is me which we may presume is mi, man. We cannot say whether this word me or mi is right or not. The order in which they are placed, as the three spirits should be ranked according to the honour they are to be conferred in our present culture, is uncommon, rather it is in reverse. The usual names and the sequence which comes in the pre Buddhist folk religion is: lha, klu, 'dre (god, naga and an evil spirit). But this is not a mchhodpa, prayer.

We presume that this may be its usual form. Although Gepang has very few ritual performances and there are no prayers for it, in its single ritual performance Gepang takes notably circumambulations in anticlockwise direction as against the usual practice of clockwise in Buddhism. We also know that the same ritualistic rule is said to be followed by Drabla also.

Tangjar is named in all the three stories. In the story of Gopi Ram Tangjar stayed at Chugta. But we observe that Tangjar was settled at Sarang, near Kolong. From there he went to Tingrig (Stingri) and then moved on to Chugta. In the two stories of Gepang there is no reference to sTod although their route from Baralacha lay all through the valley of sTod. At Sarang there is a small grove of trees of seabuckthorns which tell the age of the history. There are other much stronger instances of Gepang's relationship with sTod. In fact the larger contribution in the origination of the system appears to have come from sTod.

From the first story we get some hint on the history of Lahul. Here we observe that the reference is to only the king of Chamba. It indicates that the valley of Chandra and Pattan is under the rule of Chamba. The history of Kullu in Lahul begins from the time of the battle between the two kingdoms when Lahul was partitioned into Kullu-Lahul and Chamba-Lahul; Lahul and Chhota Lahul; or British-Lahul and Chamba-Lahul; and now Lahul.

Visits of Gepang to Malana: Gepang has a custom to visit Jamlu at Malana periodically. In 2008, the frequency of visit being very short for it had visited only in 2005, the reason given for his visit to Malana was to express sympathy for the loss incurred to Malana and Jamlu due to the heavy fire during the year. There is also told a legendary story. Prem Lal Yotarpa narrates that once there was an invasion of an army of Asuras, demons, on Malana or Jamlu. Jamlu asked for assistance from Gepang. Gepang gave a Narsing, a long bugle. It was told that upto the distance upto which its sound reaches the Asuras cannot enter. Jamlu won the battle. But he did not return the article despite demands made. It is kept in a small temple situated below the main temple. There the people of Gepang are not allowed to go. Once the goor from Ropsang and Jagdang went to demand the article. The villagers of Malana stood in line to protect the temple. Then Gepang sent Hidimba of Jahlma. The people stood in queue and started jumping one by one down a cliff. Gepang withdrew the messenger thinking the village in this manner will become devoid of any population. Some others also tell similar story about Conch shell or bell. Some others tell that Gepang visits Malana to ask back one of his articles back from Jamlu.

Lahuda Ghaund (Lāhuṛā Ghaund) **- The Bell from Lahul:** In Parvati valley in Kullu on the right side of the river Parvati opposite to at some distance before Jari there is the village of Pini (Pīṇī) where there resides the goddess Bhaga Siddh. Every year there is held a mela named Shawni Jach, the festival of Sawan. It starts on 31st of Sawan. Next day on the first of Bhadra is Sankranti, the day of Saza. It comes in about the month of August. The devi is in possession of a bell which is named as 'Lahuda Ghond' 'Bell from Lahul'. This is brought out from the temple store and displayed to the public and kept for about four days. On the days of Shaanu and Punu it is taken out for one day each. The bell is wrapped in chains said to be of silver. The Bell is said to be made of eight metals. But understandably it is of gold. Gepang possesses another heavy article made of gold. Till the bell remains outside the temple the people remain in strict discipline. They discard drink and smoke. In the mela a half Patha of sattu, rtsampa, is given to every person who attends the mela even today. It is considered as sacred and is considered to have come from Lahul. It had been so in tradition. Presently it is procured locally. It is also told that there is an image of four armed deity made of silver. From hearsay, all this came from the Thakur of Gundhla from Lahul.

Several distracting stories are told about it. The bell has become somewhat damaged and its sound is defective. Raja Siddh Singh of Kullu fought with the Thakur of Gundhla whose name was Nagartnu. Siddh Singh got defeated. Then he went to Mandi. He was a joking man. He used to play jokes with the devatas. At Mandi he got respect. Once in Lahul there was no rain in the summer. The Thakur of Gundhla asked who is powerful devata in Kullu who can cause to fall rain. It came to be known that devi Bhaga Siddh is such a powerful devi. The devi caused to bring rain and there was a good crop in Lahul. This bell and the statue were given as present at that time to Kullu. Then revenue of eighty or eighty four khar of barley as kaur, tax, was also gathered. Firstly the Thakur thought that it may of gold so he did not give. When he came to know that it is of silver then he gave it.

The goor, priest, of the devi, aged 70 in 2010, tells that his lineage has sixteen families. He tells that the Seri, the fields of Gundhla, belonged to Bhaga Siddh. He further tells that there lived about 60 families of Bhot in Pini. On conflict with devi all were killed. There was a Rani named Sunni who went to Spiti. The external gate of the temple is built simply by raising two big and long stone slabs of about nine feet high above the ground and another slab is put above to span the two. It belonged to them. There are six carved miniature stone temples placed around the courtyard. They are attributed to Bhot. The remnants belong to Indian Buddhism.

The tradition leads to an important point of junction in the history of Kullu, Chamba and Lahul. The whole incident belongs to the period of Raja Siddh Singh who founded the new dynasty of Singh of the Rajas of Kullu. It might have been Siddh Singh who defeated the Raja of Chamba and annexed Lahul to Kullu. The fact stated above that fields of Gundhla belonged to Bhaga Siddh is reliable. Lyall tells that the Vaziri of Gundhla was held by the Thakur as half share of some Rani of Kullu. The bell might be of gold and most probably belongs to Gepang. The bell and the statue are sacred articles. The kaur, tax, collected from Lahul is said to be of 84 khar (khar = 20 patha, of barley).

Travel of Gepang in Lahul in 2008

Gepang goes on the round of Lahul after every three years. Gepang appeared on Saturday on October 18, 2008. The Committee proposed that this year visit to Pattan may be cancelled and will go after three years in 2011 and consent was received from the deity. Gepang will travel with his mother and other six deities in the valley of Tinan. On Saturday Gepang reached at Srasrin from Kewag. Met his mother and then he will travel with devi Boti for two months. There were with him 30 Harook, Goors of Gepang and Tangjar, Bhatt and Haaryan (Hāryān). On Saturday the deities joined

Gepang: Mogar of Shooling, Drabla of Shaling and Lungkhorball of Jagla. Eight deities gathered in Sakar in the evening. They reached back on third December, 2008 on Tuesday. Gepang and other deities travel whole of Lahul for three months after every three years. This time it was finished in about one month. They travelled through Sakar, Teeling, Thorang, Dalang, Yangley, Gundhla, Khangsar, Raling, Jagla, Shooling, Ropsang and Gompathang and then reached Khoksar. On 16 November they came from Khoksar back to Teeling, Chhokhor, Kewag, Shoorthang, Retill and Jagdang, and on Tuesday reached at Srasrin. They dispersed from there.

List of Officials: Below is given a list of the officials accompanying Gepang on his visit to Malana in July, 2008, prepared on July 18, 2008 at Khoksar.

There were three umbrellas or parasols made of silver fixed on sticks representing the rath of Gepang, devi Hidimba of Jahlma and Thara Nag of Marbal, the two from Pattan. These are counterparts of the deities of the same name in Kullu. Names of the persons, age, village from which he belongs and the designation he holds with his concerned deity or the function he was assigned during the visit are given. The names of the valleys Pattan (Pt.), Gahar (Ga.) and Tinan (Ti.) are indicated with each entry. There was none from sTod.

i. Devi Hidimba, village Jahlma

1. Ranbir — 35, Goor: Jasrath (Pt.).
2. Amar Lal — 40, Pujara: Jahlma (Pt.). He carries incense holder.
3. Surendra — 25, Harook: Haling, Jahlma. Carries rath.
4. Subhash — 25, Harook: Gorma (Pt.). Carries rath.

The articles carried with the deity are: Narsing, Shangli (chain), Katari, trishul (trident) and sword.

ii. Thara Nag, Marbal

1. Suresh — 40, Pujara: Marbal (Pt.). Holds incense holder.
2. Vivek — 25, Harook: Sumnam (Pt). Carries rath.

iii. Gepang, Sissu

1. Sonam Angrup — 73, Pujara: Sissu (Ti.).
2. Sonam Tashi — 48, Goor: Jagdang (Ti.)
3. Prakash - 40, Phaah: Jagla (Ti.). Carries incense holder and offers markemtsi.
4. Kishannath - 40, Bhaat/Bhatt: Junda (Pt.). Works like goor.
5. Gyaltshan — 51, Goor of Tangjar: Pyukar (Ga.).
6. Chhering Tashi — 60, Goor of Milang tete: Gundhla (Ti.).
7. Sher Singh — 54, Pujara of Gepang: Yangling (Ti.).
8. Govind — 42, Chief (Pradhan) Harook: Labrang (Ti.).
9. Surendra - 22, Harook: Jagdang.
10. Rahul — 23, Harook: Sissu.
11. Vijay — 26, Harook: Yangling.
12. Khushal — 48, Harook: Jagdang.
13. Ankush — 22, Harook: Kathal (Ti.).
14. Ram Lal — 35, Harook: Shooling (Ti.).
15. Rajeev — 27, Harook: Shansha (Pt.).
16. Ashok — 25, Harook: Shooling.
17. Shivlal — 30, Shepherd (Puuaal): Shooling. Accompanied 14 sheep.
18. Vijay — 31, Shepherd: Shooling.
19. Ram Lal — 47, Musician (Dragdi): Jagdang. Plays drum, nagara.
20. Phuntshog — 62, Dragdi: Jagdang. Plays nagara.
21. Subhash — 32, Dragdi: Jagdang. Plays nagara.
22. Norbu — 56, Harook: Yobrang (Pt.).
23. Motilal — 34,. Harook: Shooling.
24. Ram Lal — 44, Harook: Yangrang, above Lote (Pt.).
25. Pawan — 25, Harook: Malang (Pt.).
26. Rohit — 25, Harook: Malang.

27. Surendra — 30, Harook: Yurnad (Ga.).
28. Chane Ram — 52, Harook: Shipting (Ti.).

Articles carried

Katari (small dagger) 2 with Gepang
Katari 2 with Hidimba
Narsing 2 with Gepang of silver
Narsing 1 with Hidimba of copper

Word Explanations

Ghyap: Ghyap means one belonging to Ghya or Gya. There is a village of this name which we meet first as soon as we enter Ladak going from Lahul. There was also a family of the Thakurs at Gya as Tashi tells, "During the times of Kings the pastures of the hills and valleys of Gya-Miru, and Shang were under the control of Gyapa Cho (rGya-pa jo, Chief of Gya) and the cattle were kept there," (Tashi sTobdan,2005: 181). This indicates that our Ghyapa has possible relationship with the Gya of Ladak. The village also falls on the route of travel of Gepang.

Milang: Milang is a name of a village in sTod, but it does not exist presently. It is situated on the right bank of Bhaga just at the point of junction of the three rivers of Yotse, Bhaga coming from Baralacha and Rarig. The village was covered under a fall of hill, but not known when and presently it is known as Zemug, a plain covered with split boulders. This Milang has possible relation with Milangpa, the family of the priests of Gepang, and the deity Milang Tete of Gundhla. There is also a dokpo, stream, named Milang, forming one of the two tributaries of Yotse.

Naphen-Nuphen: Naphen-Nuphen is a place on the other side of Baralacha Pass towards Ladak. There are small heaps of stones and earth on level plains. It is also named as Lha-phug klu-phug, the caves of gods and nagas. Koels gives description of the place, "We reached at Sarchu, the boundary between Lahul and Rupshu. Just below Kinlung and extending for about two miles are scattered on the plain conical mounds of glacial rubble 15 to 60 feet high. These are called Gephan's grain piles. Gephan came from Tibet and camped at this spot. It seems he brought immense stores of grain with him, which the people back home decided to recover. When they came, however, the grain was turned into earth and Gephan went to Lahul taking with him a few seeds of each kind, concealed in this headgear. Buckwheat was thus introduced into Lahul. Gephan now resides on one of the most magnificent peaks in Lahul and is an object of worship. There is a serai at Sarchu built on a green meadow with nice streams full now of fish from the river". (Koels, 1932: 97).

Harook (Hārūk) — There are some traditionally identified families who are required to provide service to the deity as and when required. They are not provided any kind of remuneration for their services. Gepang has Harooks from Tinan, Pattan and Gahar but none from sTod. The term although not heard in Kullu, apears to be of origin from there.

Haryaan (Hāryān) - This term is used in Kullu. It means the subjects of the deity, the whole population of the area submitting to the deity.

Phaah (Phāh) — The term is of unknown origin. Practically it means an astrologer. During the visit of Gepang to Malana he carries his incense holder and offers mar-kemzi to the deity wherever he takes rest. Earlier Phaah used to live at Kholagmur (Kholagmurti) near Karing in sTod and two persons used to go to bring him whenever Gepang was out for long visits.

Pujara or Pujari — Priest. The term Pujari is used in Kullu and the same in Lahul is called Pujara.

Tradpa — (Ṭadpā) - Tradpa is a tubular pad of leather of about eight inches long placed under the tail of the pony. Through it passes the thick rope connecting the two sides of the horse cloth over the back of the horse under the wooden saddle.

8

Temples and Monasteries of Lahul

There are three systems of faith followed in Lahul and all of them have their separate worship places. Nearly whole of the population practices two faiths simultaneously. The religion of the folk deities is universal throughout Lahul and is oldest of the three traditions. The spirit worshipped differs from area to area and may be even from village to village. The great religions of Hinduism and Buddhism are latter adoptions, or we may say they came later on.

1. Temples of folk deities: The temples of folk deities, throughout Lahul, are of one storey high and of small one room size. There may not be any object of worship placed in the room or there may be a very simple symbol.

Presently in Pattan in some temples there are kept masks of brass in shape like those of the devatas in Kullu. Roofs in Pattan are slanting, made earlier of wooden planks and now of iron sheets. At some places they are flat like those of the traditional residential houses. There is a small temple of Khordev at Lindoor and of Buhari Devata at Sidhwari near Thirot. There are similar temples at other places. In village Mooling on the left side of Chandra there is a small temple dedicated to a goddess named Le-be A-pa (grandmother Le-be). (Plate 9). A deity named similarly as A-pa-tsi is worshipped during the time of New Year festival in the villages of Chhokhor and Thorang in Tinan valley. They have masks of clay. At Chhokor the mask is kept in the monastery of Dolma. It is told that earlier there was a figure of a full size man which was carried away in an avalanche and the mask, which is like that of the Buddhist temple mask, was prepared later on. There is also an image of horse alongside. At Thorang there is a similar figure with a householder which is said to be omplete figure of a man. These two figures of A-pa-tsi can be seen only on the day of New Year festival.

Gepang, called Raja, has a temple at Sissu. Earlier it was a simple room structure. Now it has a head of horse as symbol of the deity. Its real symbol is a long wooden pole decorated with cloth pieces and silver canopy at its head. Original temple of Gepang is at Yangling, above Khwagling. Its associate deities, numbering more than half a dozen, similarly have temples in various villages in Tinan valley and at Pyukar in Punan. Some of them also have moving symbols like that of Gepang.

At Jispa there is a small hut under a big juniper tree dedicated to Ting-ting-tsi or Dorje-legpa (rdo-rje legs-pa), known as a tutelary deity in Buddhism. It has a carved stone representing the deity. Presently a new temple has been constructed above the highway. On the Rarig stream at the right angled curve there is a miniature monastery dedicated to the goddess Paldan Lhamo a guardian deity in Buddhism, greatly revered in sTod.

In sTod every household has two three or more small cairns of stones of about a foot high and about a foot by foot in area, called lha-tho, (god-pillar). A bunch of shugpa, juniper, branches is placed standing in the centre. These are dedicated to different deities. The deities are worshipped every year in the summer before the cutting of crops and new twigs of juniper are placed. Over it are also placed small strips of cotton cloth of different colours which are called re-kha (ras-kha = cotton strips). (Plate 10). bTsan is represented by a conical stone block about a foot or more high. The stone is usually red or otherwise it is painted red and is placed on the roof. bTsan is an indifferent deity. (Plate 11). Nothing is demanded from him. But his place should not be polluted. It is kept clean. Otherwise it may harm in the form of disease, etc. Dogmo (brog-mo) resides on natural boulder which also is a similarly neutral deity. But the two can harm if their sites or their symbolic objects are polluted by anybody. There is a tradition with some houses to worship the goddess annually in the summer time by the landlady of the household. In this tradition the lady dresses herself with good clothes and ornaments and on a big fire she prepares roasted grains of buckwheat. In the process she takes names of all the fields of the household in a traditional lyric.

In Punan there is a deity named Srwag (Ṣ-vāg) in village Pyukar (Chugṭa). At Kyelang there is the Kyeling devata. The deity has a room in a house. In the room there hangs a big bunch of strips of cotton cloth of different colours from the roof which symbolizes the deity. Similary there is a room allotted to Tangjar in a house at Karing in sTod where also the symbol of the god is similar. This room is called lha-khang, room of the deity. At both these places the households are recognized as Lhabdag (lha-bdag), priest. But they are mild kind of priests. They don't possess the spirit. They perform the worship with some simple mantras at their own house and at the houses of others in the village. There are only few such families and only the families belonging to certain particular clan can become lhabdag.

There was a lha-khang, perhaps a separate temple, according to the settlement report of 1868, in village Kyelad, near Kolong which also possessed land. A Lhabdag is prohibited from serving as robdag (ro-bdag), to serve in funeral ceremony. Lhabdag has a special dress. He wears a cloak and a white shawl is put over the shoulder. A cap called baltib (cap from Baltistan) and also called Uggar (Uigur in Central Asia) is also worn.

2. Temples of Hindu faith: The temples of Hindu faith may be classified as. i. Temples of Early period. ii. Temples established during the period of Kullu Raj. iii. Temples of Nath sect. iv. Temples founded in modern times.

i. Temples of Early Period

Mrikula Devi temple, Margul: The village or town of Udaipur had been a very small village of about half a dozen households known as Margul. Raja Uday Singh of Chamba, (1690-1720) renamed the place as Udaipur. Today Udaipur is a popular and official name.

The ancient temple of Markula or Mrikula devi stands on the slopes, above the village. The temple is made of wood and stone having slanting roof of wood planks. The interior is richly carved with scenes from Mahabharata, Ramayan and others. The panel on the northern side in the ceiling depicts the scene of Mara-daman, Assault of Mara, an event from the life of the Buddha. Goetz writes that it is not different in style, technique, etc. from the others. The temple has been studied thoroughly by numerous scholars. The main statue is of Mahisasurmardini in folk tradition called Kali. There is a wooden idol of the deity, which perhaps occupied the place of the present metal image. It is now in the State Museum, Shimla.

On the pedestal of the present idol is an inscription in late Sarda script, which states that it was cast by one Panjamanaka Jinak from Bhadravah in the shastra year corresponding to year 1645 C.E. and was dedicated by Thakur Himapala (Vogel, 1911- I: 249-251). The deity is named Markula devi. The statue was stolen on August 14, 1972 but fortunately was recovered soon.

The Buddhists venerate the deity as rDo-rje Phag-mo, Vajravarahi. The place is called Maru or Marul. It is considered as one of the twenty-four Buddhist tantric Pithas, corresponding to the thumbs of Vajrakaya, thus called the-boṅ ma-ru i.e. Maru, the thumb.

Markula Devi temple, Tindi: The temple at Tindi is also dedicated to a deity named Markula Devi also known as Bhawani or Mahakali. She is said to have come from Margul, Udaipur, and is related to the deity of Margul. The newly constructed temple is situated in the middle of the village. The temple has no signs of any ancient structure. But there is enough evidence to show that there existed a temple in the village since ancient times.

The temple is in possession of some important artefacts of archaeological interest. A ḍhol, drum, made of sand gold, has an inscription in Sarda, is said to have been donated by Musa Varman, Raja of Bhramour, 9th century, and a bell was granted to it by Sahilvarman, the founder of Chamba state, early tenth century C.E. The inscription is not readable due to its being old and rubbed.

Mahadeva temple, Mayling: The temple of Mayling village is named as Mahadeva temple dedicated to Shiva. In the temple a ling is worshipped. Some carved wooden shafts are lying in the outer room indicating to the existence of a grand temple structure in the past of which people have no knowledge. A three-faced stone statue of Shiva, somewhat damaged, is kept outside, in the compound. (Pl. XII). Goetz based on the carvings on the wood says that it belongs to the Gupta period, (Goetz, 1955: 66). But other specialists based on the study of the idol have a slightly different view. Mankodi (co-author of Antiquities of Himachal) tells that this 'form of Siva was current from Kashmir to HP for centuries'. Christian Luczanits, an art historian, says, 'it shows a lot of comparisons to 8th century art from Kashmir', (personal communications.). A celebration known as Jagra (= to remain awaken like in the night) is held by the people here in the summer every year.

ii. Temples established during Kullu Raj

Hidimba Devi Temple, Jahlma: The temple dedicated to devi Hidimba is situated in village Jahlma, about a kilometer away from the village. She is said to be sister of the deity of the same name residing at Dunghri in Manali, Kullu. The temple was founded in the time of Raja Man Singh (1688-1719 C.E.) of Kullu. An annual sacrifice of a yak, collected from different kothi each year, called Mālī, was performed here earlier.

Thara Nag, Marbal: At Marbal there is the temple of Tharah Nag (Thārāh Nāg). The temple was erected during the reign of Kullu Rajas. This has connection with the temple of Tharah Nag of Gushal, near Manali. The priests of Tharah Nag and Hidimba accompany the party of Gepang when he visits Jamlu at Malana and enroute they all visit the temples of Tharah Nag and Hidimba in Kullu while going to Malana. The two deities remain associated with Gepang in many of his functions.

iii. Temples of Natha Sect

Naunath temple, Rwaling: In Rwaling village there is a small temple of one room of one storey high built in local style of flat roof, devoted to the deity named Naunath also called Virnath. The deity is said to have migrated from village Shalang, Lag valley, in Kullu. It was accompanied by a goor, a priest, or some say a sadhu, who was given land in the village. It was actually a goor because in a document from the area a reference to the family of goor from Rwaling is found. It has a rath, a vehicle, and nine metal mohras, masks, all like those of the devatas in Kullu. The masks and the rath are comparatively smaller in size than those ordinarily seen in Kullu. Three of the mohras are inscribed in Tankri script and one of them reads the name of Raja Tedhi Singh of Kullu, of the middle of eighteenth century. The devata was taken out in procession annually in the summer to some villages like Jahlma, etc. The custom continued till around 1960s and then it was stopped.

To this sect also belongs the small temple of Tilo devi in village Rwaling with slanting roof of wood planks. Similar temples are situated at some other villages also in Pattan. There was also a temple dedicated to Nār Singh in village Gushal.

iv. Temples founded in Modern times

Sanatan Dharam temple, Gushal: Gushal is perhaps the largest village in Lahul and it had been culturally one of the most dynamic villages in the history of Lahul.

There is a temple named Vasudev Kutumkabam, full name: 'Brahm Prakash ji Maharaj ka Vasudev Kutumb'. The Asharm was founded on July 8, 1941, by Rishi Brahm Prakash ji Mahaharaj on the land measuring 2 bisva donated by Chhering Tandup. The temple is affiliated to Sanatan Dharm. A sadhu named Jayavant came from Ratnagiri, Maharashtra, twice in 1939 and 1940. He founded the temple and the new tradtion of Sanatan Dharam was founded here. (Plate 13). At that time the celebration of annual Yor festival of ancient folk tradition was stopped. The masks used in the dance were either buried under the earth or cast away into the river nearby. There is also a modern temple in the village dedicated to Shiva.

Shiva temple, Thorang: There is a temple dedicated to Shiva in village Thorang in Tinan valley which was founded c. middle of the twentieth century. It was founded by the villagers themselves.

3. Temples and monasteries of Buddhism: These may be divided into: i. Temples of Indian Buddhism and ii. Monasteries of Tibetan Buddhism.

Temples of Indian Buddhism

Indian Buddhism arrived in Lahul quite early and it has left a number of evidences. As the practice of the Doctrine declined in the lower regions it came from the northern direction in the form of Tibetan Buddhism and the tradition continued unbroken as it is seen even today.

Gandhala: Gandhala is the most ancient temple in Lahul. In the modern literature the name is written as Gandhola and also as Guru Ghantal. In sTod it is pronounced as Gandhala. In Pattani it is called Ghandhāhṛ. In the writings about the monastery in Bhoti from the area they write Gandhala. (Plate 14). Some scholars trace its origin from the Sanskrit word Gandhalaya from Bodhgaya. From some archaeological artefacts discovered from the area like the engraved copper loṭa, and marble bust of Bodhisattva, it is learnt that there existed a temple in ancient times, certainly belonging to Indian Buddhism. Due to the fact that the area is prone to snow avalanche there exists no structural remain. The lota was dated originally to second-third century CE but later on revised to 1st century BCE. The area above the site is named as Drilbu Ri (dril-bu ri), Bell Mountain, and it is presumed that the famous Indian siddha Ghantapad, one of the 84 siddhas, stayed here. There also exists an ancient carving of a female deity on a boulder nearby the site of the monastery, belonging to the period of Indian Buddhism, which in the tradition here is named as Dolma Chhudong, image of 'Tara, below which is supposed flowing a stream of water'.

On the spread of Tibetan Buddhism in the area it became affliated to Tibetan Buddhism. Some early renowned Tibetan siddhas related to the place are Gozangpa (rGod tshangpa, 1189-1258), Urgyanpa (Dharmsinge Namgyal, 1223-1303), etc. Lately the monastery was reconstructed by Tashi Tamphel of Ladak in around 1870-1880. The site has now been abandoned and the monastery shifted to Tubchiling. However a structure exists there.

Lyall in his report writes about the temple, 'The big monastery of Guru Ghantal, with its chapels of ease at Koksar and Sansa holds a good deal of land in different kothis rent free as endowment. More than half is held of the Gonpa by kang chumpa tenants, who by way of rent only present annually some shoulders of mutton, pots of whisky, and plaited sandals, but are bound to perform certain fixed services, such as the cultivation of the rest of the monastery land, the sweeping of snow off the roof of the monastery in winter, the bringing in to many fagots for winter fuel, etc.' (Lyall, 1874: para. 138).

Snellgrove visited the monastery in 1953 and writes, 'In 1953 it presents itself as one of the smallest and certainly the most neglected of Lahauli monasteries. Being in the charge of one solitary monk. There are remains of ancient wood work without, and inside standing amongst images of recent workmanship on the altar is the head of a bodhisattva, which had been dug up in the valley below. Is this a possible example preserved from the time when Kulu was a Buddhist land. It shows a striking rsemblance to some Central Asian models', (Snellgrove, 1957: 293, Note-39). Madanjeet Singh identifies the image with Avalokitesvara and states that it belongs to 8th century, (Madanjeet, 1971:105-6). Some of his important remarks and statements like that the image was consecrated by Padmasambhava are not possible to be verified from any source.

Tubchiling Gonpa: Tubchiling is name of a place, a plateau, situated near the river bed, at the confluence of Bhaga and Chandra. There are cultivable fields which belong to Gandhala monastery. Earlier there was a Labrang (bLa-brang), a resting station for the lamas visiting the monastery of Gandhala and going on pilgrimage. The whole monastery of Gandhala has now been shifted to Tubchiling. The process started from about 1960s. A three storey high building of undressed black sandstone in local style has been constructed. It has been kept unplastered. The idols have also been shifted and arranged. The most valuable statue, the marble bust of a Bodhisattva has been lost and replaced by a fake model. There are other small idols of wood and metal. Among them some were received from the householders who no longer found their utility in their houses. A few old wooden idols have been left unpainted and they show their real age.

Lamas come here from Wardan Gonpa, Zanskar. Among the three of them, one is Nyerpa, manager. The monastery serves the area from Sumnam to Lote and the four villages on left bank of Chandra. There were large stock of wood blocks for printing books which have been taken away to Ladak. It adheres to Lho Dug.

Triloknath: The famous temple of Triloknath is situated in the village of the same name, locally known as Tundye. The temple structure has been studied comprehensively by Widorn and Kozicz (Widorn-Kozicz, 2012: 15-35) and the idol by the renowned arcaheologist and epigraphist J. Ph. Vogel (Vogel, 1902: 35-40). The temple was earlier known as Vihar. In Tundye and the villages nearby the temple and the place is still known as Vihar, also noted by Vogel. All others in whole of Lahul know the temple as well as the village as Rebag (Rebāg, Ras-'phags). In religious literature the deity is known as Ras-'phags 'phags-pa (Phagspa, Avalokitesvara, of Rebag).

The sacred shrine is today revered both by the Buddhist and Hindu devotees. The ancient structure of the temple is built in Nagar style. There are similar miniature-temples around. On the wall on the front side, there is an inscription in Sarda script which has been dated to c. early ninth century C.E. (Plate 13). It enshrines a marble statue of Avalokitesvara, with six arms and an image of Amitabha on the crown. The earlier statue made of black stone is similar with six arms but the figure of Adibuddha is not present on the head. This is the original standing monument of Indian Buddhism and is a rare living monument of this kind in whole of the North-West India. Thakar or Rana of Triloknath customarily had been the manager of the temple. Presently it is managed by a Committee headed by the government representative. Gandhala and Triloknath have guidebooks in Bhoti. Distinctive identity of the holy place of its being a sacred place devoted to Avalokitesvara since its origin is evidenced from the practice that here no dmar-mchhod, red sacrifice, is offered in the temple.

Tibetan Buddhism

Tibetan Buddhism reached Lahul after the tenth century CE. This came to Lahul after foundation of the movement of the second foundation of Buddhism in Tibet, i.e. in the neighbourhood of Lahul and Spiti in Guge by Rinchhen Zangpo. It gave continuation to the practice of Indian Buddhism in Lahul. Some temples lost the original structures but the artefacts inside remained intact in the form of Tibetan Buddhism. Chhokhor in Tinan is one of such monuments. Chhukutsi gonpa also has some similar articles. But it has lost its principal statue from which an establishment receives its name and recognition. No new statue was also established here. We don't have much knowledge about the establishment of the Nyingma wave of Padmasambhava's influence. Even though Tinno gonpa is devoted purely to Padmasambhava, its date cannot be determined.

a. Tinan valley

Dimphug gonpa — Khoksar: The monastery located in the cave at Khoksar is locally named as Dimphug gonpa. The village is known locally as Dimphug but in sTod it is known as Damphug ('gram-phug = beside the cave). Others in Lahul call it Gram-phug, and those from outside Lahul and officially it is called Khoksar. Actually Khoksar is name of another village, situated nearby it, which is the first village one meets while climbining down from Rohtang. The place Damphug on settlement received recognition from the cave. The cave might have been earlier used by the travelers crossing Rohtang. Above Rahla, on the side of Kullu, there is a big cave named Gyamphug (brgya-phug = cave of hundred) with a capacity where about one hundred persons can sit at a time. The travelers starting from Manali halted here and launched their journey next day in early morning and halted in the evening at Damphug. Khoksar was the most important stage for all the Lahulis in the journey between Lahul and Kullu where one had to stay compulsorily, both while coming and going.

The monastery is located in a cave above the village. Lama Tashi Tamphel from Ladakh expanded the structure of the monastery. The village derives its name from the cave. This new gonpa was built in 1996 but the temple is much older. It is partly roofed with tin. Its full name is brag-phug rdo-rje rdsong (Rock Cave Vajra Fort). The chief idol is of Tshering-ma who is also Srung-ma, protective deity of the monastery. Other statues are of the Buddha, Padmasambhava, Milarepa, etc.

The priest-lama comes from Hemis monastery, Ladak, once for three years. Therefore now it is zhung-dug. Earlier it was Nyingma. As Lyall writes earlier it was subjoined with Gandhala monastery.

Chhokhor (chhos-'khor) Gonpa: The monastery is situated in the village of Chhokhor near Sissu. The building of stone and cement concrete is one storey high and has two rooms. The main idol of Dolma, Tara, with Odpagme (Buddha Amitabh) over the crown is made of metal.

Besides, there are two more small important idols, one of stone and the other of marble. The first one contains on its backside a beautifully engraved dharṇi, sacred formula, in Sarda script alongwith a carving of a chaitya. (Pl. XV & XVI). Some scholars date this image to eighth century CE. The inscription was examined by Vogel. Francke writes that it contains nothing but mystic syllables. Francke had seen another but somewhat indistinct inscription in Sarda characters on a boulder about a mile below the present village of Tinan or Gundhla, (Francke, 1926-II: 214-Note).

Rahul Sankrityayan also visited the monastery and examinsed the inscription. He read it partly as: 'Hum phat swah!' The other figure of marble contains writing in the same script in superficial scratches. All these indicate to its being a remnant of a foundation of the period of the practice of Indian Buddhism.

Moreover the monastery also possesses a mask of clay, with three eyes, of a folk deity named Apa-tsi, grandmother, kept separately shut up in a box, considered as tutelary deity of the family of the priest. This is taken out for public exhibition once in a year during the festival of Halda, New Year. This must be the earliest of the three traditions. This, a figure of a deity of the personal deity of the family of the priest appears to be a private property like that of Thorang.

Thus this monastery carries traditions of three cultures, viz. the ancient folk culture, Indian Buddhism and Tibetan Buddhism, simultaneously and parallel to each other without disturbing one another.

Labrang Gonpa: Labrang gonpa is situated near the main road near Sissu. The present building of stone, cement and concrete was built in 1997. It was formerly known as Shelting gonpa which was situated at some distance below the present spot. The chief image, in clay, is of Paldan Lhamo. Others are Buddha and Padmasambhava.

Earlier it was being served by the Lamas from Kyi gonpa, Spiti, the followers of Gelug.

Before this it was Dugpa. One sign of earlier tradition is that even during the time of Gelugpa holding a religious ceremony of annual Tambarigya was held regularly. Such kind of ceremony is said not held in the Gelugpa gonpas. Presently the lama-priest comes from Hemis, Ladakh, each for a term of three years and belongs to gZhung-'brug sub-sect.

Khinang or Khyimnang gonpa: Khyimnang gonpa is situated on the way of Kora, circumambulation, of Dril-bu Ri, between the Rangtsa Pass and Gundhla, near Khyinang village. Those coming on Kora from the side of Kardang after crossing the pass rested here, took tea and meal. Thakur Duni Chand tells that it was constructed by the lamas. On This analogy he also tells that Silha gonpa was constructed by the villagers and that of Maane by Thakars (all of Tinan valley).

Maane Gonpa, Gundhla: Maane (Maṇi) gonpa is situated in the village of Tinan or Gundhla. Guru Rinpoche is the chief deity. Vogel visited the gonpa in 1902. Thakur Hirachand told him that he had built the monastery in 1880 C.E. A small image in this sanctuary had the inscription: Jo-Bsod-rnam-stob-rgyas-la-na-mo referring to Hirachand's deceased brother, Sonam Tobgye. But the person cannot be identified. The monastery must be quite old keeping in view the history of the household.

Earlier Chham used to be held here which is said to have been introduced by Tashi Tamphel. A photograph of a scene of the chham has been published in the Journal Urusvati, vol. I, 1931, p. 73. He had also prepared a Thanka of two storeys high. The chham is not held now and the thanka, and perhaps some idols, have been lost to thieves.

Si-lha gonpa: Si-lha gonpa, situated near Gandhala monastery and Gundhla village, was earlier known as Duphug (sgrub-phug) gonpa, monastery of meditation cave. Donyod Dorje writes that it was place of meditation of Gyalwa Gozang-pa and his pupil Urgyanpa. It is said to have been founded by a lama named Si-lha who came from Tibet. It was community monastery of the villagers of Gundhla kothi, and was founded by them. Main statue is of Padmasambhava. It is Zhung dug. Srungma is Dorje Tshedag (rDo-rje tshe-bdag). A layman from the village of Dalang serves at the monastery.

b. sTod valley

Dartse Gonpa, Darcha: Dartse gonpa, Thugdam Chhosling (thugs-dam chhos-gling), is situated in the village named Dartse Dangma, commonly known as Darcha. The place is said to have been blessed by sTagtshang Raspa who stayed in the area for sometime. The structure of the monastery was founded in the time of Tashi Tamphel, of sTagna Gonpa in about 1870-80. Guru Padmasambhava is the chief deity. There are 4-5 lamas. The chief Lama comes from Gemur gonpa, designated as Dar-se la-ma, for three years.

Yarzhi Gonpa: Yarzhi gonpa, with two rooms of one storey, is situated above the village of Jispa about half an hour's walk. A lama named Meme Kasse who belonged to village Jispa is said to have built the monastery in about the beginning of the twentieth century or slightly early. The main statue is of Padmasambhava. Dorlag (rdor-rje legs-pa) is Srungma.

Photang, Jispa: The sacred structure called Photang (pho-brang), castle, was built in 1994 when Dalai Lama visited Lahul and Kalchakra ceremony was held here, at Jispa. The building is of two storeys, has a hall and arrangement of statues like a monastery. There is a living room in the upper storey. The lama-priest is sent here from Gemur monastery, each for a term of one year.

Gemur Gonpa: It is told that the monastery, known popularly as Gemur gonpa, and in religious literature as dge-smon gsam-bstan chhos-gling, is said to have been founded by sTagtshang Raspa, in the first half of seventeenth century, and was constructed by lama Tanzin Paldan of village Gemur with the assistance of the Thakurs of Khangsar.

Earlier the gonpa was situated at a higher place. It was reconstructed in around 1870. Tashi Tamphel had done wood carving. The gonpa was washed away by the avalanche again in

1979 in the heavy snowfall. One nun who was residing there died. Some valuable articles were swept away to the river and were lost.

In an inscription c. 1700 CE discovered by Francke from a chaitya, a commemorative of the death of a Jo, chief, of Hayar household of the village of Karing in sTod, it is mentioned that a nun joined the funeral ceremony from the monastery of sMes which may be identified with the Gemur gonpa because earlier the monastery was situated below sMes village, above the present site of the monastery, (Tobdan and Dorje, 1996: 23).

The chief deities are Avalokitesvara, Kunkhyen Padma Karpo, Shamonath, Lama sTagtshang Raspa, Padmasambhava and Tanzin Paldan.

It has a statue of Vajradhara of one storey high, in the aspect of longsku, sambhogkaya. On its left is Vajrayogini. Tshechu is held on 19th of fifth month in which chham is held. Chham, it is said, was introduced by sTagtshang Raspa. The masks and dress were sent from Hemis monastery in Ladak. The monastery is associated with Hemis. About 20 lamas are associated with the monastery. Head lama is called Gondag (dgon-bdag), Owner or the Chief of the monastery. Other offices are Umzad (dbu-mdsad), Uchhung (dbu-chung), Konyer (dkon-gnyer), Nyerpha (g-nyer-pha)-2, musicians and makers of chhodpa (mchod-pa) (sacrificial effigies).

Lamas are sent from here to the gonpas of Dartse, Chhukutsi, Zong gonpa, Khangsar khar and Photang in Jispa. The lama sent to Dartse is designated as Dartse Lama and others as Kongnyer. Except the Kongnyer to Photang who is sent for one year, all others are sent for three years.

It had a big thangka of Dam-can Jagpa Me-len, srungma of the monastery, about one storey high, made of silk cloth, made in the method of tshem-hrul (sewing patches, here of silk, with hand) which was stolen alongwith other valuable articles, in the 60's of twentieth century. It used to be displayed every year on the day of Tshecu festival. The Tschecu festival is held here every year on the 19th of 5th month of Tibetan calendar in which a chham of tshe-bdag is held. Nebesky has given some photographs of the chham from the monastery in his work from a film obtained in

1952 illustrating some highly intricate movements of chham-yig, (Nebesky-Wojkowitz, 1976: 120, plates III & IV).

Chhukutsi Gonpa: Chhukutsi (chhos-sku-rtse?). The gonpa is situated in village Khangsar. There is a household known by the same name situated close by, which also looks after the monastery. Before Gemur gonpa assumed the status of the gonpa of sTodpa community it held the same position. The real form, viz. as to whom the monastery is principally dedicated or was, is not known. It is in possession of some articles belonging to both Indian and Tibetan tradition. There is a small metallic image named Ja-khyung (bya-khyung, garud, eagle). Other statues are of Chenrezig, Avalokitesvara, in the aspect of 'gro-ba-drug-sgrol (Emanscipator of the six kinds of beings), like that of Triloknath. Similar statue is seen in Tubchiling-Gandhala. Earlier it was Gelug and the lama-priest used to come from Zanskar. One of its notable possession is the small stucco statue of Urgyan Padma i.e. Urgyanpa. (Plate 17). Presently the lama comes from Gemur gonpa for a term of three years. It finds mention in the Phugtal Boyig of Zanskar, c. 1450 C.E. The monastery is attributed to Lotsaba Rinchhen Zangpo.

Khangsar Khar, Chhod-kyang: Khangsar Khar (khang-gsar mkhar), the Castle of village Khangsar, the palace of the Thakars of Khangsar, widely known as Kolong, was completed in around 1890. The people contributed great labour in the construction. The big wooden beams for pillars were brought from Mooling by the people of the same area. Wood carving was done by Meme Kasse who belonged to village of Jispa. He had constructed also some wooden masks at Khangsar Khar. There are said to be 108 rooms. In the uppermost floor there is a worship room known as chhod-kyang (mchod-khang) which is like a monastery and is maintained by the residents of whole sTod like an independent monastery. There is a clay idol of Mila-Repa whose hair is said to grow longer as natural. Lama-priest is deputed from Gemur.

Zong Gonpa of Tinno

In village Tinno there is an old monastery named Zong (rdsong) Gonpa, fort monastery, built in a rock cave. It lies above the village about a kilometer away towards north-east. According to Lama

Gyaltshan two monasteries were founded in the village which are named as Zong gonpa and Pala (Pa-la) gonpa. These were founded by two old men named Zong meme and Pala meme. Pala gonpa is situated slightly above the village on a ridge towards south east of the village, just above the fields named Rasta-tsi, and presently it is in ruins. It is said to have been destroyed in a natural calamity. The walls of the foundation of the building stand above the ground and the area is surrounded by big juniper trees. From the ruins of the structure it is observed that in the built up area of about 90 square feet there were four rooms and a passage in the middle. Earlier the houses of the households named Bokarpa and Kyelangpa of the village also were located there. Gonpapa had their house at Kho-'a.

Zong Gonpa lies in a rock cave above the fields named Tshog-dang. Earlier the building was of two storeys. Some pillars of the structure got rotten and the monastery crumbled down. Now it is of one storey. There are four statues in the temple all of clay: on the left of the viewer is that of Avalokitesvara, in the middle are two statues of Padmasambhava and on the right is of Mila Repa. Of the two statues of Guru the larger one belongs to the monastery itself and the smaller one is said to have been brought from Pala gonpa, narrates Lama Gyaltshan.

The monastery has two regular officials. dKon-gnyer, the lama priest, is appointed for a period of three years by the monastic organization of Gemur gonpa, which overlooks all the monasteries in whole of sTod valley. The regular mchhod-gnas, the lay person who lights lamps and attends to some other small chores in the monastery is appointed by the villagers for a period of three years.

Every year in the month of June white-washing of the building is done called dkar-rtsis (white-paint) in which locally obtained white earth is painted. One person comes from each household for the service. Prayer lamps are lighted everyday. There may be defaults during the period of heavy snowfall. A worship is held occasionally called gsol-ka. A big prayer called Zong Tshe-shu (bchu) is held every year on the fixed day of 10th day of 6th month of Tibetan calendar, about in August. This is celebrated as the date of birth of the Guru. But it is observed that the date of celebration of the occasion varies. While the date remains the same at all places as the tenth of the month, the month varies from place to place. Here it is held in the sixth month, at Riwalsar in Mandi it is held in the first month and at other places it is held in the fifth month of the Tibetan calendar.

The monastery is in possession of an old object called Gyam-mchhod (brgya-mchhod = hundred worship lamps, actually 108). (Plate 18). It is a round circular flat stone slab of diameter of about one and half feet. On it is carved in concentric circles ridges and drains alternately with one hundred and eight holes for lighting the worship lamps. Oil can be put in it at one place and it spreads uniformly to all the lamps itself. It is still used sometimes. Such objects are seen at very few places in Lahul. There are one big and one small gyam-chhod at Rangtsa, on the pass between Kardang and Gundhla. The slabs are square and in them there are only holes and oil has to be poured in the individual hole. In the bigger slab the holes may number 108. These are not in use presently. It is told that similar multi-lamp stone slab existed at Riwalsar in Mandi. This is one of the signs indicating antiquity of the monastery.

Earlier there used to be held the festival of Tshe-shu, in which mask dance was held. This is held as the Padmasambhava's birthday. The people of village Melang used to come to see the festival walking along the river Bhaga and stayed at Tshog-dang in the fields near the monastery. They wore a cap named Baltib. The Milang village which is now called Zemug was a village of one hundred households. Once there came an old lady in the village. In the gathering of the villagers she was not given any importance and she was placed in the last in the row in the sitting. But one of the observers sensed some importance and took her to sit at the head of the row. In the night a portion of the hill above the village fell down over the village and buried the whole village under its debris and killed all the villagers. But the man who had given place at the head of the row to the old woman was thrown away by the force of wind to the other side of the river and was saved. This house is presently known as Lumpa Champa (Lungpho byungpo = the spirit of wind). The ruins of the village situated near Dartse just below the junction of rivers on the bank on the right side of the river is wholly covered by the big boulders of split rocks and is named as Zemug. It is also told by some people that some articles like broken wood pieces sometimes become exposed near the river as it eats up the edges of the ruins. At present there is no sign of any kind in the monastery indicating the existence of the tradition of mask dance if ever it was held here.

Here there is a small source of water. It drips from the crevices of the rock and is collected below. It is told that when smoke is made below the rock the flow of the water increases. The monastery is in possession of land. This is recorded in the Settlement report of 1868.

From all the artifacts existing in the monastery it may be assumed that the monastery was originally founded in the tradition of Nyingma, ancient tradition, dedicated to the Guru, including that of Pala gonpa. Both the statues of the Guru are original. There are small old books containing prayers to the Guru like Le'u bdunma. But they are incomplete.

The title of one of the books reads: na-ra-ga dong sprugs rnal-'byor gyi spyi-khrus. The colophon at page number 27a reads: rnal-'byor gyi spyi khrus na-raga dong sprugs 'gyod tshang gyi rgyal-po'i bshags-pa glang-po-che rang 'bog gi rgyud las khol dang phyung-p'o. a-u-rgyan gyi mkhan-po padma-'byung gnas dang. kha-che'i pandita bi-mala mi-tra dang. bod kyi lo tsava snyags dsnyan ku mara dang rm-rin-chen mchog gis bsgyur cing zhus te gtan la phab p-'o. Thus it informs that the book was translated into Tibetan by four scholars: Padmasambhava, Vimala Mitra, Jnyan Kumar and Ma Rinchhen Chhog. The work, however, does not name the title of the original work and the language from which it was translated. In the Tibetan books translated from Sanskrit it is usual practice that they first give the title of the book in Sanskrit and then they give the Tibetan title. According to Rahul Sankrityayan the former three are contemporary, (Rahul: 1948: Appendix-9, sa). Another work indicates that Padmasambhava reached Tibet in 749 CE.

Karing, ancient ruins: At Karing there is a level plane. On its south-western edge there are ruins of an old building structure. Some part of the ground is covered with stones of walls of the building. Stones are placed in a block of about 8x8x6 feet. Over it are placed two carved pillar bases. This indicates that there could have been a beautiful building mostly of stone, certainly a model of Indian architecture, of good size (Plate 18). There was another important structure at Srangbar (Khangsar), at the edge of the plane, overlooking the whole valley, which was known as Dankhar. It was a stone structure built of about 8x8x15 feet. The original could have been higher. There were stones around it from which it could be understtod that the structure was higher. It is told there was a room inside it. It was perhaps a watch tower.

Gahar, Punan Valley: Pyukar Gonpa: The gonpa is situated on the upper side of the village Pyukar. Earlier it was a small cell of one room situated on a ridge, about four hundred meters away from the village, known as Gompa-ri (monastery-hill). Presently there are about six chhortens situated there. It housed a single statue of Guru Rinpoche, in clay about four feet high, according to Urgyan Chhering. Thak te-te was Komnyer who later on committed suicide there. The new monastery was founded by Kyaṭu Me-me, real name Dorje Zangpo (rdo-rje bzang-po) of Chheling village, in about middle of twentieth century. There live lamas and nuns in the monastery.

Tayul Gonpa: Tayul gonpa is situated at about one and half kilometer up from Stingri village. It's full name is Urgyan Chhoskhor Ling (u-rgyan chhos-'khor gling). Lama Serzang (gSer-bzang) Rinpoche founded the monastery whose statue is also kept in the monastery, alongwith that of Padmasambhava, the main deity worshipped here. The old statue of the Guru has been stolen. In 2016 there lived one lama priest and four nuns.

Gumrang: The ancient gonpa of Gumrang located in the house of the Thakurs is attributed to Rinchen Zangpo. The main image is of Vairocana (sNam-par snang-mdsad). Christian writes that, 'The temple contains 12 badly damaged clay sculptures mostly seated on a ledge along the main wall, together with extremely fragmentary remains of painting on the entrance wall and on the ceiling,' (Christian, 2004: 107). He further writes that the Gumrang figures have surprisingly little in common with any other sculptures known from the region. The round faces of the Gumrang scultprues are particularly uncommon, being rather reminiscent of Central

Asian clay sculptures of a comparatively small size, such as those found in Tamsuq and Shorsuq/Karashahar.

Bokar Gonpa: The new gonpa of Gumrang is known as Bokar gonpa, and in religious literature as Tashi Chhosling (bkra-shis chhos-gling). It is situated above the village of Gumrang. Gyalwa Jampa (byams-pa. Maitreya) is the main statue. Others are Tshepagmed, Avalokitesvara, etc. There is an idol named Zonkul Lama. Nothing is known about him. This is certain that the lama belonged to Zonkul monastery, Zanskar.

Zholing: The village of Zholing (zho-gling, zhol-gling) is situated on the left bank of Bhaga opposite to Gumrang. The ruined monastery is considered to have been founded during the time of Rinchen Zangpo in the eleventh century. It is said that this temple was decorated with carved wood. Two beautiful wooden idols have been found preserved in this monastery. One that of Amitabha is in the British Musuem and the other of the Buddha is in the Bhuri Singh Museum, Chamba. Rahul Sankrityayan visited this monastery and had seen both the idols. Christian remarks that the two sculptures differ from each other considerably and they are attributed to 11th-12th century, (Christian, 2004: 68).

Kardang Gonpa: The monastery of Kardang village is famous as Kardang Gonpa. The main statue of the Buddha, in clay, is about six feet high. Others are of Avalokitesvara, Amitabh, Amitayus, Tara, Heruk, and of two local lamas Norbu Rinpoche and Kunga Rinpoche. There are chaityas made of silver in honour of the two Teachers. The monastery was founded by Lama Norbu of Kardang village in 1912. Before this there was a chhorten, chaitya, named Timur says Lama Paljor. In 2016 there lived about eight lamas and fifteen nuns. There is arrangement for boarding and lodging for pilgrims. The facility is beneficial more for the pilgrims going on Kora, circumambulation, of Drilbu Ri.

Zhab-zhe Gonpa, Kardang: There is an old gonpa named Zhab-zhe (zhabs-rjes = foot-print) situated in the middle of the village of Kardang, known less, but historically important. In 1973 the building with two storeys looked new. There are rows of statues on both the floors. On the ground floor beside the main statue of the Buddha there is the statue of Gozangpa. Nearby on a rock are shown two hoof-marks which are known as zhabs-zhe from which the monastery derives its name. The monastery reveals its connection with Gozangpa and can be presumed to be of the time of Gozangpa, thirteenth century, or somewhat later.

Shashur Gonpa: Shashur Gonpa or Tashi Shugling or in the religious literature known as sha-shug bkra-shis chhos-gling is situated about five kilometers above the town of Kyelang. It is told that although the monastery existed earlier, it was founded by Deva Gyamtsho, a high lama from Wardan monastery in Zanskar in the early seventeenth century C.E. His idol is placed in the monastery. A chaitya is also said to exist containing his relic. The monastery is a tin roofed three storeys high building. Tshechu with Chham is held on 10th day of 5th month of Tibetan calendar.

Tashi Tamphel made renovations to the monastery. There reside about eight lamas. Khunu Rinpoche died here in 1977.

Yordong Gonpa: Yordong gonpa, as is locally known, is situated in a cave above the village of Beeling. Don-yod rdo-rje writes it as dYor-dsong and sTag tshang Raspa as gYur-rdsong. The last named is more appropriate. The monastery is situated in a cave and below there flows the g-yu-ra, canal, of the village.

The cave has capacity for sitting to accommodate about fifty persons at a time. The statues are of Mithugpa (Akshobhaya), etc. Dorlag is its srungma. In 2016 there lived about six lamas and previously there also lived a nun. It is believed that Gozangpa meditated here and then later it turned into a monastery. sTagtshang Raspa meditated and stayed here during the winter for six months. Nawang Tshering also is said to have meditated here.

All the monasteries in Punan belong to Lho Dug and are affiliated to sTagna gonpa in Ladak and also to Bhutan.

c. Pattan valley (Manchhad, Melogs)

Gushal: In Gushal there was a monastery dedicated to Thugje Chhedmo (thugs-rje ched-mo), Avalokitesvar. There is a cave named Jaba Phug in the rock face, where lamas used to sit in meditation. It is very difficult to go there in the normal times. But it is easy to go there in the winter when the gorge near it is filled with snow. The Lamas recognise Gushal as Ku-lu-ta and consider it a sacred place, as one of the twenty-four sacred Buddhist tantric pithas, corresponding to the knees of Vajrakaya.

Othang Gonpa: The monastery has presently been shifted to a new place, besides changing its facet. It houses image of the Buddha in the centre. Presently five lamas reside here including the priest in-charge who hails from Zanskar.

The tradition is that the lamas used to come from Karsha monastery in Zanskar. The monastery belongs to Gelug sect. It serves large part of Pattan valley. Earlier chham used to be held here. It possesses a handwritten yum in 12 volumes.

During the visit to the brief and simple looking monastery on August 26, 1973 the main statue was that of Tsong-kha-pa with his two principal disciples before him rGyal-tshab-rje (on his right) and mKha-grub-rje (on his left). Before them were the idols of the Buddha and Padmasambhava, respectively. This is the only Gelug monastery in Lahul. Perhaps it was first founded as Gelug and still continues to be under the umbrella of the same sect.

Lindoor: The village is called locally as Lindoor. The lamas transcribe the name differently as: gLing-btub by Don yod Dorje and gLing-stog by Lama Domba. In 1973 the main idol was that of the Buddha. Another one was of Padmasambhava. The monastery is now deserted. There is a Kankani chorten (chaitya) constructed of undressed stone like the walls of the residential houses in Lahul and is kept without plastering with mud. Nawang Tshering of Zanskar stayed here. Tashi Tamphel made renovations.

Yobrang Gonpa: There was a gonpa at Yobrang which was founded by Nawang Tshering of Zanskar (1657-1730).

Shansha: There was a monastery at Shansha subjoined to Gandhala. The last reference about the monastery is found in the Report of Lyall.

d. Patanam (Miyar Nala)

Urgos Gonpa: The gonpa of village Urgos is named Tashi Chhosling (bkra-shis chhos-gling). It is situated in a nallah about half kilometer from the village. Earlier it was located in a rock cave nearby and was called Wardang, said to have been founded by a lama from Wardan gonpa, Zanskar. It was shifted to the present place in around 1960. The two storeyd modern building is tin roofed. Some wooden parts with carvings have been brought from the original structure.

Main statue is of Avalokitesvara. It belongs to Lho dug. Jagmen (Jag-pa me-len) is srungma. Earlier the priest-lama was from the village itself. Now he comes from Sharabai, Kullu. It serves the Miyar valley from Shikoli to Khanjar. The old handwritten Yum in 16 volumes was brought by a lama named Pata, Lobzang Namgyal, of Urgos from Bhutan in around 1900. Earlier Chham was held.

9

Tradition of Tantric Practices in Lahul

Lahul possesses a varied and interesting tradition of the practice of Tantrism. Presently the kinds of followers of Tantrism may be given as: the Buddhist lamas, goors (priests) of the Hindu deities like Siva, Himdimba, etc.; and goors of local deities like Gepang, Tangjar, etc. Lala Kaka, a devotee of Siva, who died in around 2010, was a popular goor in Lahul. Some of them keep long hair and the goor of Gepang also wears a round black woolen cap which is folded up at the corners, as is worn by some persons of the same class, in older fashion, in Kullu and Kinnaur. This kind of cap was worn in Lahul in some areas previously by the common men. There are some other practitioners of the profession related to folk deities who keep knowledge of the profession but they dress and live like ordinary people and they don't practice any austerity.

In Bhoti tradition the name of Lahul itself has an adjective as gar-zha mkh'a-'gro gling, 'Lahul the Land of Dakinis'. Dakinis are the female deities in the Tantrik system. In Kyelang the teacher Deva Gyamtsho from Zanskar of seventeenth century restorer of the Shashur Gonpa, was known as Dubchhen, Mahasiddha, a great siddha. Some visitors from Tibet and Zanskar were great siddhas like rGyalva Gotshangpa, Urgyanpa, sTagtshang Repa, Nawang Tshering, etc. They visited Lahul taking it as an important place of Tantrism. There still exits a cave with a chaitya raised therein, called Gotshang Dubphug, the Cave of meditation of Gotshangpa, near Sila gonpa. sTagtshang Repa remained here for whole one year. He stayed at Yurzong gonpa for six months for meditation. Drilburi, Ghanta Parvat, the mountain of Ghanta, known in local tradition, is associated with the great siddha Ghantapad (c. eighth century C.E.), one of the prominent among the famous eighty four siddhas of India.

The following tradition relates to the folk tradition, unconnected with the great religions of Buddhism or Hinduism. It is presumed that as the people in Lahul celebrate the New Year ferstival — Kus or Phagli or Losar — the letsogma, the evil she-spirits, of Lahul all gather at about the same time in February-March every year at the plain of Karga, near Tandi at the confluence of the rivers Chandra and Bhaga to celebrate the New Year. Each one of them comes carrying with her some kind of contribution like a yak, etc, for the feast.

The lamas have to do necessarily meditation for a prescribed period before they enter into the order. Thereafter they continue to practice intermittently. The Goors or priests of the local deities and the brahminic deities have to attain the siddhi, accomplishment, of one's personal deity.

There is saying current in Lahul: *khyi-nang 'onpo srinmo bzung, Joling 'onpo nyi-ma bzung, sarang 'onpo sangs-rgyas gsung byon.*

It means that the Onpo, Astrologer, of Khyinang, a house in a village of the same name in Tinan valley, caught a fiendess; the Onpo of Joling (=Zholing) stopped the sun, and the Onpo of Sarang knows discourse on the scriptures of Buddha. The instance here conveys the sense of competition among the three leading professionals. The two stories, as told by Nawang Norbu, run like this.

i. Khyinang Onpo: There lived a lama in Khyinang village near Gundhla in Tinan valley. He was Onpo, astrologer. Besides his profession he was skillful in tantric practices. He used to go to the villages for various purposes like to cure diseases, remove certain kinds of unknown problems, etc. Once he had gone towards the Pattan valley with the same objective. While returning he became a little late and it was getting dark. When he reached Grango, after Tandi towards Gundhla, opposite to the village of Bargul, he stopped, got down from his horse, and went to a side to get relieved of the natural call. When he came back and took hold of the reign of the horse he sensed that there is something on the back seat. Immediately he could guess that it must be the same fiendess Lebe who lives in a cave on the other side of the river Chandra above Bargul village. As he got on the horse he threw his sacred scarf abruptly back. Then he applied the tantric power, took her in his fast grip and bound tightly with the scarf at his back.

At home he took off the clothes of the fiendess and put them under the slab of the hearth in the living room. By nature, she could not go near the hearth. She also could not go anywhere without these clothes. Now she was under the hold of the lama and she worked in the house like a servant. She was very clever at work. It was custom to discuss in the evening in the family the work to be done the next day. The fiendess would hear all carefully and by the next day she would have done all by herself. The family was very happy.

One day the Onpo went to attend the annual festival of Kesunder, held at a place nearby the village. Before going, he instructed his wife that if any woman comes and asks her for anything she should not pay any heed to her words. So saying the Onpo went away. Afterwards the fiendess taking human form came to the wife of the Onpo and requested, O mother, I am a poor woman. Lamaji had kept some of my clothes safe under the hearth, please give me my clothes. I wish to go to the festival. The old lady took pity and taking the clothes out gave them to the fiendess. As soon as she took hold of the clothes she made a shrieking noise and went straight to the place where the Onpo was heading the celebration. Suddenly he noticed a woman dancing at the front of the row with a fresh human heart held in her hand. Blood was dripping from it. The Onpo recognized the woman and sensed that the unexpected had happened. He came running to his home and found that his wife was no more. The fiendess had taken out the heart of his wife. In this manner the fiendess Lebe became free from the hold of the Tantric Lama. It is told that she still lives in a cave above Bargul. It is also told that sometimes the fiendess casts her shadow and the people have to bear its effect.

Norbu's story ends here. The villagers of Mooling, a village near Bargul, narrate the same story slightly differently. Now going into the actual position, in Mooling village, somewhat above the village, there was a small temple dedicated to the goddess Lebe. The temple, which has been lost to fire, had carved wood panels and there was an idol inside. The presiding goddess is called 'Lebe Apa'/'Grandmother Lebe.' The young boys and girls and some people were afraid to go inside the temple. The villagers tell that it is the same goddess whose story we have told above. Presently there exists a small temple with wooden slanting roof dedicated to the deity above the village of Mooling.

ii. Joling Onpo: There lived a Lama in the village of Joling, above Kyelang, across Bhaga, famous as Zholing associated with Rinchen Zangpo. He was adept in the Tantrik practices. He used to help the people and the villagers with his knowledge. In turn the people used to come to work in his fields for free. Once people had come for working in his fields and they were cutting grass. Sometime before the sun was about to set the Lama observed that the work which was to be finished that day before the sunset was not likely to be so. Therefore he started working on a plan. He stopped the sun from moving further. The villagers kept on working till the work was over. As soon as the work was finished the Lama let the sun free. The people working there were surprised that it had become night abruptly. For this reason the Joling Lama was famed as the one who could stop the sun from moving.

In tantric history Lahul is known more widely for the subject as Lahula Vir in Nathpanth and as a Tantrik Pīṭh, a seat, in Kashmir Saiv and Bhoti literature.

Pīṭh in the Tantric system: It is well known that Pith (Pīṭh), a sacred meditating place, is an important concept in all the Doctrines following the Tantric system.

D.C. Sircar traces that in early tradition in both Buddhist and Brahmanic systems regarding Pith there was the common concept of Catuṣpīṭh, four Pith. In Buddhism the four Piths were.: 1. Jālandhar, 2. Oḍiyāna or Uḍḍiyāna, 3. Pūraṇagirī and 4. Kāmarūpa, (Sircar, 1973: 12).

Abhinavgupta, a great scholar from Kashmir, states that a Pith at mountain-tops and river banks are good for meditation, although they are useful only externally. It also tells that just as there are a good number of holy spots outside, similarly they have locations inside the human body. The term Pith has the same definition in Saivism and Buddhism.

Pith in Buddhist System: Later on the number of Pithas in Buddhism became increased to twenty four or more. Among these Jalandhar is identified with Kangra in Himachal. Oddiyan is in the Swat valley in Pakistan in the north west of India not much far away from Jalandhar. Oddiyan was centre of Vajrayan. Guru Padmasambhava of Uddiyan was called to Tibet on the advice of Shantrakshita who then was successful in founding of the Samye monastery there. The scholarship of Shantarakshita had failed to do so. In Tibetan Buddhism Tantrism is an essential element.

Tucci writes that in the Tibetan system of Tantrik practice Vajrakāyā, the body of the Vajra deity, is divided into twenty four parts, and each of these are identified with twenty-four Pīṭhas, places or regions, of India. At each of these 24 places there resides a guardian deity called Vīr. The vajrabody is first divided into three main spheres: I. Sphere of the Spirit: II. Verbal Sphere, and III. Sphere of the Body. Then in each sphere eight places are allotted in the following manner:

I. Sphere of the Spirit: 1. Pullīra Malaya (head), 2. Jalandhara (top of the head), 3. Oṭṭiyāna (right ear), 4. Arbuda (nape of the neck), 5. Godavari (left ear), 6. Rāmeṣvara (space between the eyebrows), 7. Devīkoṭa (two eyes), 8. Malavar (two shoulders).

II. Verbal Sphere. 1. Kāmarūpa (two armpits), 2. Oṭe or Oṭeviṣa (breasts), 3. Tiṣakune (navel), 4. Koṣala (tip of the nose), 5. Kaliṅga (mouth), 6. Lampaka (neck), 7. Kā–cī (alternately Campā) (heart), 8. Himalaya (pupils of the eyes).

III. Spheres of the Body. 1. Pretapurī (sexual organs), 2. Gṛhadevatā (anus), 3. Saurāṣtra (thighs), 4. Suvaraṇadvīpa (calves of legs), 5. Nāgara (sixteen fingers and toes) 6. Sindhu (upper part of the foot), 7. Maru (four thumbs and big toes). 8. Kulūṭa (Knees). Tucci gives name of each of the twenty-four presiding deity, Vīr, alongwith some other details. At Maru and Kulūṭa reside Vairocana and Vajrasattva, respectively.

Regarding the identification of the places Tucci remarks that, 'While in the school properly Indian, this "adamantine body" is identified with twenty four places mentioned above, corresponding, except for few exceptions, to countries easily identifiable in the Indian territory in a large sense, in a second time, and possibly when the fortune of Buddhism started declining, the zone of the geographical Vajrakāya has been limited to the Himalayan region. This transposition which has often done violence in the geographical traditions of India, is already an accomplished fact in the tantric schools of Tibet. For instance, Urgyanpa and sTag tshaṅ raspa do their pilgrimages from Tibet to the valley of the Swat taking care to visit the twenty four places of the Vajrakāya already presided, according to the theories of the Śaṁvaratantra, by the twenty four vīras. Now all these places are through Zanskar, Kashmir, Kullu, the district of Hazara and Swat', (Tucci 1935, III-2: 38-43).

Padmathangyig, a supposed biography of Guru Padmasambhava, gives the same list, with slight difference. It states that each of the twenty-four places is presided over by Lord 'Jigs-byed mi-bzang (Bhairav) and the places are held by the various categories of beings in the following manner:

I. The first four places are held by the gods.

II. Four places are held by the Gandharv.

III. Two are held by Yakshas.

IV. Two are held by the retinues of the Yakshas.

V. Two are held by Devils.

VI. Two are held by the retinues of Devils.

VII. Two are held by Nagas.

VIII. Two are held by the retinues of Nagas.

IX. Two are held by the Non-gods.

X. Two Pithas Ma-ru and Ku-lu-ta, the last two, are held by the retinues of non-god. (Padmathangyig, 15b.).

Lahul as a Tantrik Pith in Buddhism

Nawang Norbu provides a list of 24 Pithas from the book Cakrasamvaratantra in Bhoti from Lahul. On comparison of this list with the above we find some variation in it. The description appears to make a favour towards Lahul. Firstly the copyist in the first entry instead of Puliramaya writes 'Gar-zha'i Pu-li-ra-ma-ya' i.e Puliramaya of Lahul. Thus he adds the name of Lahul among the twenty four Pithas. At serial number three he writes 'Great Tīrtha Ma-ru' and in the end, at serial number 24 it gives Maru and Kuluta two separate places in one place, which reads as 'Maru and Kuluta'. He also seems to give prominence to Maru. Maru and Kuluta, according to the particular tradition, are situated in Lahul. The following description explains the grounds on which the above referred author might have been tempted to introduce the changes in the text.

At the confluence of the rivers Chandra and Bhaga near the village Tandi, the mountain range lying between these two rivers ends in a sheer cliff. The whole place, especially the peak, is holy from many angles. This was the sacred site of the most ancient temple in Lahul named Gandhala. The mountain peak is named Drilbu Ri, Ghantaparvata, named after one of the renowned scholar-siddha Ghantapad among the 84 great siddhas of India. He is said to have a lineage of pupils. This is also the place devoted to Cakrasamvara, the tantric god. Nawang Tshering (1657-1730), a great Lama from Zanskar, while visiting the holy place, prays in the words: 'Bowing to the Guru Cakrasamvara, at the holy place of Dril bu ri, like the palace of Shri Cakrasamvara, I seek the accomplishment of the union with the Vajaradhara.'

The holy guidebook (gnas-shad) about Dril-bu-ri and Gandhala states that this place is similar to the king of Mountains (Tise, Kailash). If one visits here all his desires are fulfilled. The religious arrangement in the valley of Chandrabhaga appears to be exactly like that at the Kailash mountain. In Lahul the two deities reside at the two ends of the valley and at Kailash they reside on the peaks of mountains which are situated near to each other. Swami Parnavananda writes, 'The presiding deity of Kailash is Demchhok (Dharampala) also called Pavo (Vir). He puts on tiger skin and garlands of human skulls and holds damru (vibrant drum) in one hand and khatan (= khtvang) (trident) in the other. Round Kailash are some more deities sitting in 990 rows with 500 in each. All these also put tiger skins etc. as Demchhok. The Shakti or the consort of Demchhok is Dorje Phagmo or Vajravarahi, who is shown in

Tibetan paintings and idols, clinging to him in inextricable embrace interlocked in sexual union. Adjacent to the Kailash Peak is situated on its western side a smaller snowy peak called Tijung which is said to be the abode of Dorje Phagmo,' (Parnavanand, 1949: 8).

Bhattacharyya, in his work 'Indian Buddhist Iconography', writes that the union of Vajravarahi with Heruka is the cult of the celebrated Cakarasamvara Tantra. She is also called a Dakini.

Drilbu Ri, Ghantaparvata, is dedicated to Dechhog (bde-mchhog), the lord Cakrasamvara. This is situated at the head (phug) of the Chandrabhaga valley. The guidebook (gnas-shad) of the holy places Drilburi and Gandhala writes that at Margul-Udaipur, 'At the end of the valley (mdo) is situated the thumb of Vajravarahi and thus signifies its being unparalleled among the twenty four countries, i.e. Piths.

Thus the two partners of the yugnadh (union) Cakrasamvara and Vajravarahi reside, even at distant places, but facing each other. This area between the two holy places of Dril-bu-ri and Margul covers the large part of the geographical area of Lahul.

There is no doubt that in all the above lists Kuluta stands for the present Kullu and in ancient tradition it must have been an important Pith. But on the decline of Buddhism there it lost the recognition as a Pith. In the medeaval period the Tibetan siddha travelers and the lamas in Lahul shifted the identification of Kuluta to Lahul. The village of Gushal on the confluence of Chandra and Bhaga, also known locally as Gus, Guī and Gudung, is also known as Kuluta. sTagtshang Raspa (1574-1651) while going through Lahul mentions the place as 'Gus Mandal Kuluta, corresponding to the knee'. Similarly Maru of the list of the Pithas is identified with Margul/Udaipur, near Triloknath in Lahul. Nawang Tsehering identifies Margul with the Thumb of Vajravarahi as mThe-bong-Maru, similarly others. Maru might have been a great place outside Lahul. Thus we find that the ancient Pithas of Kuluta and Maru, in the tradition of Tibetan Buddhism, came to be located in Lahul. It may be noted here that in the biographies of rGod-tshangpa and sTag-tshang repa there is no indication if they visited Kullu. Their descriptions of the Kuluta Pitha relate to the places which lay in the geographical area of Lahul. Nawang Tshering visited Kullu but not as a pilgrim to a Pitha. Thus we observe that Lahul has long tradition as Buddhist tantric centre.

Pithas in the Kashmir Saiva tradition and Lahul: It is a matter of great interest for us that Lahul figures in the list of Pithas according to the Kashmir Saivism. Abhinavgupt of Kashmir of the 11th-12th century, was a great scholar of Tantrism. He has a number of works on the subject. Hemendra Nath Chakravarty, in the chapter on Introduction to his translation of Tantrasār of Abhinavgupt gives list of 33 Piths from his works. According to him the principal Pīṭhas are three namely: i. Kāmarūpa, 2. Pūrnagiri and 3. Uḍḍiyāna. Here we observe that the name of Jalandhar is missing as a principal Pith. But it is found in the list in a different class.

The Piths have been classified in six divisions as follows, given with the number of Pithas in each division: Pīṭh -3; Upapīṭh-3; Sandohak -3; Kṣetr — 8; Upkṣetr-8; and Upsandohak -8.

Kṣetr: Lahul figures here as a Pith in the division of ksetra which are like the petals of the lotus of the heart. These are: 1. Prayāga. 2. Varaṇā, 3. Aṭṭahāsa. 4. Jayantikā. 5. Vārāṇasī. 6. Kalinga. 7. Kulūtā. 8 Lāhulā, (Chakravarty, 1986: liii).

The name Lāhulā at number eight here in this category can easily be identified with Lahul. This identification of the name Lāhulā with Lahul is corroborated from the presence of the name alongside Kulūtā. which certainly stands for Kullu. It may be added here that in the lists of Piths in the Sanskrit texts of Hevajratantra and Cakrasamvaratantra published from Varanasi the name appears as Kult whereas in other sources the name is Kulūta or Kulūtā. We find Kulūta listed among the Pithas in Buddhism and Saivism of Kashmir. The relevant sloka with a reference to Lahul from the famous work Tantaloka of Abhinavgupa is read as follows:

क्षेत्राष्टकम् क्षेत्रविदो हृदम्भोजलाष्टकम्।
प्रयागो वरणा पश्चादट्टासो जयन्तिका।
वराणासी च कालिङ्ग कुलूता लाहुला तथा।
उपक्षेत्राष्टकम् प्राहुर्हत्पद्मग्र दलाष्टकम्।

(Mukund Ram, Tantraloka:XV: 89-90).

Thus we learn that the name of Lahul too is found included among the Piths in the Kashmir Saiv tradition.

Natha Tradition in Lahul

Natha follows the Siddha. Nathas had been a great power in spreading the practices and traditions of Siddhas and Tantrics. The faith spread to Lahul as it gained great strength in the lower neighbouring areas. It introduced here great transformations. Then as the faith disappeared in other places here also some of the practices disappeared slowly and some others continued in their changed form. The practice of Natha faith in Lahul arrived from the lower direction. It came to Lahul from the sides of Kullu, Chamba and Pangi-Kishtwar. In Lahul it spread very deeply throughout the region. The period of most forceful entrance was in around between sixteenth and eighteenth centuries of the present era.

In Rwaling village there is a small temple devoted to the deity named Naunath or Virnath. It has a rath, a vehicle of a deity, and nine metal mohras, masks, all like those of the devatas in Kullu. Three of them are inscribed in Tankri script and one of them reads the name of Raja Tedhi Singh of Kullu, of the middle of eighteenth century. The tradition may be older.

Temples dedicated to the Natha deities were founded in the Pattan valley. Some of them though not known outside the place are still in practice but at least one known to us is missing. One dedicated to Naunath or Virnath at Rwaling still stands at a changed place. Although the structure is not impressive but, in Lahul, it carried a big tradition. There are temples dedicated to Tilo Devi, sister of Virnath, at several places. These had come from the side of Kullu. There was also a temple of Nahar Singh in Gushal. The periodical tradition of Dhadhi Jātrā i.e. Pilgrimage to Dhadhi, Manimahesh, in Chamba, during the annual great festival, is an evidence of its entry from the side of Chamba. Others are in the form of songs, stories and some social practices. The movement is perhaps connected with some great event occurring in the history of Lahul in around the middle of the second millennium. We identify the subject from two topics: Vir and Baliraja.

In this faith Vir (Hero), although a term of older use including Buddhism, is a very important character. The term appears to apply to a benevolent deity and also to a guardian deity. There is a carving of a deity on stone slab, there were more, planted on an open plain, at Srangbar, Khangsar, known locally as Vir. (Plate 19). It wears a crown and holds a sword or club in his right hand resting on right shoulder. One of the family deities of Khangsar Khar, says Thille Namgyal, is named as Phela Vir. Phela (phye-lha = god of flour, corn), a deity of folk tradition, here is modified to Phela Vir. Ajaypal, revered at many places in Kullu as a powerful devata having raths, is known to be a family deity of one of the families in Lahul who also possess a golden icon of the deity.

In Margul there is a Vir, not exhibited for public view, carved in wood similar to the two guardian deities standing on either side of the main entrance who are known as Bhairav, and also as Vir. The first sacrificial offerings in the temple were offered to this Vir.

Following is a part of a poetical work stated to be a mantra, a sacred formula, from a region of Himachal, outside Lahul, which makes mention of Lahula Vir.

संगलदीप का राजा जियापाल, जियापाल का लहूपाल,
लहूपाल का कुसलपाल, कुसलपाल का नमो नाहरसिंह वीर।
हाथ में डंडा, पवन का घोड़ा फिरे नग खेड़ा, कौण चले।
नाहरसिंह चले वीर, गद्दी वीर चले,
पहाड़िया वीर चले, वरोधिया वीर चले,
क्रोधिया वीर चले, वरोधिया वीर चले,
लाहुल वीर चले, सिंहडु वीर चले,
दोदिया वीर चले, क्रोधिया वीर चले।
जटाधरिया वीर चले, केलू वीर चले। (BR Sharma, 1986: 141)

The description may be summarized as, Jiyapal is the king of Sangladip, his son is Jiyapal, his son Lahupal, his son Kusalpal, his son is Nahar Singh, the Hero, I bow to him. He holds a stick in his hand and rides a horse, roams in the villages. Vir Nahar Singh is followed by many other Virs designated by the name of a tribe, area, type, etc. among whom is present the Lāhulā Vir, the Vir from

Lahul. The Vir from Lahul is designated by the name of the area therefore it is easy to identify him with Lahul. This tradition relates to Nathpanth.

The tradition of Bali Raja in Lahul: Bali is remembered for his generous act of bestowing gifts and wealth. He is famous in the traditions of some parts of Himachal Pradesh: in the districts of Shimla, Sirmaur, Solan, Pangi in Chamba and in Lahul, and may be in some other parts also. The deity has numerous followers in the country.

The tradition of Bali Raja in Himachal Pradesh: With the spread of the faith of the Saiva, Siddha and Natha, the legend of Bali gained great popularity in Himachal. Although Bali belongs to daitya, non-human, race, yet he is revered as a benevolent deity. He is deified although there is no temple known to have been dedicated to him and no iconographical representation given to him. But there are some rich cultural traditions associated with the deity and there also exist some valuable folk literature about him.

In Himachal the celebrations and the literature about Bali Raja are also known as Bralaj, Blaj, etc. This tradition is found in the districts of Shimla, Sirmaur and Solan. Bralaj is a drama of reciting the story of Baliraja in the form of song with music and dance. This song is considered as sacred and is recited as an auspicious prayer sung before beginning the recitation of the story of Ramayana and before the plays and festivals like Thoda, Karyala, Vishu, Diwali, etc.

During the Diwali, it is held a day before and on the day of the festival. A big bonfire is burnt and people sit around it. The recitation goes on through the whole night. There are four recitors. They wear woolen coat, tight woolen pyajama and white turban. Each one carries a stick having metal head. The story-tellers place this stick under their right armpit and they keep standing resting on it. They stand two on each side facing each other. Besides the Bralaj they recite the song telling the stories of valour of their khund, the area or village, stories from Ramayan, etc.

Thoda is played traditionally in the districts of Shimla, Sirmaur and Solan and in Uttrakhand in the areas near Sirmaur. It is a dramatic performance in which the characters display their skill in archery. This is played between two parties named Shaathii and Paashii. They represent the Kaurav and Pandava of Mahabharta, respectively. It is played in the day in an open ground. The players wear special dress: woolen pyjama and thick shoes. They carry in their hands arrow and bow. The fighters form pairs and compete with each other. One throws arrow on the opponent but the rule is to hit not above the knee and not below the ankles. The opponent keeps on dancing and also trying to escape the arrow. The role changes turn by turn. There are number of pairs playing on the ground at a time.

Nathapanth and Bali raja: Raja Bali was a good and virtuous King. But he was a daitya and harmed the devatas. He was humbled down and tamed by Vishnu. There is a story called Blaj, narrating his story, which was current in the Shimla Hills. The story begins as many stories of the Natha faith begin with the statement like, "In the beginning the Narayan, the almighty, created the earh. The whole earth was drowned in water. Mansa devi was kept guard." This expresses a relationship of Bali Raja with the Nathapanth.

Bali Raja, born in the avatar of a local Raja named Bali Chand in a small principality in the Shimla Hills which is identified with Koti State just close to the Shimla town, made his ambition to work with the festival of Diwali clear in the song. The followers of this faith appear to have worked simultaneously in the areas of Himachal with that of the Nathas. This belongs to the late medieval period. The ambition contained in the last paragraph of the song reads:

> Bali Chand exclaimed, "O Diwali, when will you come?" She said, "in Kartik"
> "With what greedy desire?"
> "With the desire of walnuts and greed of roasted grains,
> And with the desire of beautiful women and handsome youths,"
> (Tika Ram Joshi, 1911: 157).

Here it highlights the characteristics of the festival of Diwali that perhaps is intended to be given shape. In the middle hills this festival is named Phagli and is celebrated on different dates with some differences from place to place in the winter season. At places during the festival men of the village take round of the village with the band of music and singing some obscene songs. Women throw ash on the processioners. Then they are given walnuts, nuts of small apricot and may be at places parched grains of wheat. Transformations and additions may be attributed to the sect and the period as may be understood from the song.

Baliraja in Lahul

In Lahul there is no festival comparable to Diwali. But there is one common festival which is celebrated in all the three valleys as New Year festival with different names like Khogal, Losar, etc., celebrated at different dates at different places, in which fire torches are displayed and is partly like Diwali. One core ritualistic performance common in all the areas is that a mandala is drawn on the wall in which in the centre of the square a figure of the deity or an effigy is painted and around it in the square the drawings like that of sun, moon, etc. are drawn. This is the principal figure which is worshipped in the festival which runs for seven days. The second such ritual is the throwing of halda, torch of splintered wood. In Lahul Bali Raja penetrated the core of this chief traditional cultural entity.

The deity 'Raja Bali' is worshipped in the festival of New Year i.e. Khogal in the Pattan valley. Lahul is an area of many cultures and languages. The central figure may be that of the chief premordial deity of the particular culture or region. At places this central figure has been replaced and is presently occupied by Bali Raja. But in the lower regions of Pattan in Triloknath and Udaipur the whole mandala is covered by the single figure of Bali Raja eliminating all the other figures. He is shown standing and holding a bow with arrow ready to shoot (Plate 20). In Tinan totu (ṭoṭu) an effigy of dough, is offered to Baliraja. In Pattan there is a song in praise of the deity related to the same occasion as given below:

Song of Bali Raja

बलि राजा का गीत

बारा ना बरूशिए, बड़ी दानों तिहारा।

बड़ी दानों तिहारा, बलि राजा लिखी जै।
बलि राजा लिखीजै, शिरे भागुण कीती जै।
बड़ी दानों तिहारा, चूली मूके चौका जै।
चूली मूके चौका जै, फूल चढ़ी यौरा जै।
कोटा बेटी कोटा शीणी, थालू भरी सोना जै।
बड़ी दानों तिहारा तऊंएं मुके नावां जै। (Courtesy Shakun).

Translation

Song of Baliraja: It has been twelve years. O Baliraja, you have made great gifts. You are great gift granter. We have painted your figure (on the wall), O! Bali Raja, We have placed offerings on your head (in the figure painted on the wall). We have completed the work of preparing chauki (a small purified place in the room) by smearing cowdung and mud, over it. We offer flowers of Yoara, the fresh plants of barley, grown in the room. Your daughter Kotashin resides in the kot, dehra, temple. Now your spirit has entered in the priest and he is in play. The priest plays your spirit. The plate is filled with gold. You are a great gift granter. You have proved your name truly.

The Pantheon of Nathpanth: The sect reveres deities of several classes viz. Siva, Mahadeva the premordial god and Narayan i.e. Visnu the creator of the universe. Narayan is famous as village deity in many villages of Kullu and Kinnaur. Baliraja is great deity. Nrisingh is known as Naar Singh. The other deities are: Ajaypal, Naunath, Vir or Virnath, Bhairav, Gugga, Jogini, Virs, Tilo Devi, Katasan, etc. The human leaders are Gorakhnath, Bhartarihari, Gopichand, etc.

There was a temple dedicated to Nar Singh at Gushal in Lahul, and also of Tilo devi. There are temples dedicated to Tilo devi at some places in Pattan. Bali is famous as Bali Raja or Raja Bali, king Bali. He is a great donor of wealth. Katasani is the daughter of Baliraja. She is revered in Kullu as a village diety. Tilo devi is sister of Virnath. Sadavrat a term of Nath sect means a place of boarding and lodging for the pilgrims. There is Sadavrat kothi at Malana, a separate structure of two stories.

Some Stray Figures: We have found two stray figurines, one from Lahul and the other from Pangi, which cannot be associated with any of the three faiths described above. These two images tentatively may be identified with the Nathapanth.

i. A Non-Buddhist stone image resembling Buddha, from Margul, Udaipur. Not indentifieable. (Plate 21).

ii. A Non Buddhist unidentified image in-wood, Parmar Bhatori, Pangi. (Plate 22).

Baliraja in Pangi

Jukaru: The festival of Jukaru (Jakāru)is celebrated in whole of Pangi in the month of Phalgun. It is celebrated in three stages: Silh, Padod and Malang (Mālang). On the day of Silh the head of the household prepares an effigy of buckwheat and wheat flour, the images of cattle are prepared. At this time the members don't talk with each other. The articles of worship are kept in a separate room. After the dinner on the floor in a small space it is plastered with clay and cowdung. Over it are sprinkled the urine of cow and water from Ganga. A mandal is written with the flour of barley. Over the mandal an image of the Baldano (Baldāno) or Raja Bali is placed along with the images of wild goat and ram. Then Raja Bali is worshipped. Some members draw pictures of Raja Baldano on the wall in the other rooms and they do worship. In honour of Raja Baldano no body speaks loudly for three days. Splitting of wood is also prohibited. On the second day it is Padaddh. Early in the morning after taking bath members of the family bow before the image of Raja Bali. The younger members touch the feet of the elders and receive blessings. Water is brought for Raja Bali from the water-collecting-point of the village and the deity of water is also worshipped. On this day the head of the family also worships the Choor (= mdso, a cross breed of yak, a ploughing cattle). People visit each other's house and exchange greetings.

The third day is celebrated as Māngal or Panehi (Paṇehī). On this day the villagers gather at a fixed place in a field. They come with sattu, ghee, honey, eggs, effigies of goats, etc., made of wheat flour, and rākh (local beer), and they exchange them with each other. They enjoy dancing and then they worship the earth. This is called māngal. After singing ghure, songs, they depart to home. Then the image of Raja Bali, made of wheat flour, is thrown away and he is given send off. At home they find the door of the house closed. They knock at the door. From inside one asks, who are you? The person outside replies, I am Manglu (= auspiciousness). What do you have brought? He answers Prosperity and Pleasure. And then the door is opened. The festival of Jukaru is closed on the twelfth day after visitng the temple of devi Malāsani. The temple of Malāsani is situated at Purthi, four kilometers from Shaur, the first village of Pangi from Lahul. (Kedar Sharma, 1995: 82-84).

10

sTag-tshang Ras-pa's Visit to Urgyan and His Hindi Conversation

Urgyan is the birthplace of guru Padmasambhabva. Therefore Urgyan (Uddiyan, in Swat valley, Pakistan) and Jalandhar (Kangra) in north and north-west India, had been always a tempting pilgrimage places for the Tibetan siddha Teachers. rGodthangpa (1189-1259 C.E.) was perhaps the first such pilgrim who made move towards this direction and travelled upto Jalandhar. His disciple Urgyanpa Rinchhen dPal (1223-1303 C.E.) went further and was the first pilgrim who was able to fulfill his object of visiting Uddiyan, Urgyan. Therefore he became famous and was honourably addressed as Urgyanpa. He was the first Urgyanpa. The second such successful pilgrim was sTag-tshang Raspa. Urgyanpa travelled comparatively under easy social conditions. But by the time of Ngag-dbang rgya-mtsho alias sTag Tshang Raspa (1574-1651 C.E.) the conditions had become worse. Tucci writes, "The comparison of the two iteneraries, viz., that of Orgyan-pa and that of his later imitator proves very interesting: we realize the progress done by Islam during the three centuries which approximately intervene between the two travelers," (Tucci, 1940: 30). His first attempt failed due to the unwillingness of his companions who had accompanied him from his homeland. They were unaccustomed to the hot climate of the plains of north-west India and some of them also died. However, no impediment could deter sTag-tshang Ras-pa's resolve to accomplish the pilgrimage to Urgyan. He spent some time in Zanskar and Lahul and after more than a year the Teacher resumed his journey afresh. This time he was accompanied by a companion named Zhi-ba rNam-rgyal from Lahul. The Teacher, taking lesson from the first attempt, had contracted a strict agreement with his companion of no responsibility for each other's sake and no promise of help by one to the other during the course of their journey. The Teacher had made a determination to the extent of do or die. The companion returned from midway seeing too much danger to life on the way. But sTag tshang Ras-pa, continued his journey alone till his completion of the journey. The circumstances which the Guru describes and in which he completed his journey are horrible. He was the second Urgyanpa.

During the course of his stay in India, the Teacher had learned Hindi conversation fairly well for his practical use. He has recorded some sentences in Hindi transcribed in Bhoti. These sentences were all used within a short period while he was on pilgrimage in socalled Urgyan and was undergoing through greatly torturous conditions and was under deep stress all the time. He maintained his spirit by keeping the companionship of his teacher continuously in thought. rGodtshangpa also noted some sentences similarly. His conversations were also recorded under similar condition of extreme distress.

sTagtshang Raspa had used most of these sentences himself. Some are those he heard from others during the course of his conversation and encounters. The instances of the language give us a picture of the kind of language that was used in common intercourse in those days in the area. The language is very close to modern Hindi. Panjabi may be observed in the vocabulary in the use of such word as changā, good. These sentences under the shadow of Tibetan accent would have been difficult to decode. But the learned Teacher at many places has given, alongwith the Hindi sentences, their meanings in Tibetan and this has made our task easy. At places the meanings as given by the Teacher differ from what appears from the text. At places the Teacher is being made confused by using pun, for his poor knowledge of the language, for example: Kapoor (place name) and kapdā (cloth), adami (person) and Atumi (real or assumed name of a person), etc.

The journey was conducted in 1615 CE and the manuscript was ready by 1620 which indicates that the work was conducted under the supervision of the Teacher himself.

The Teacher confronted difficulty due to another reason. He was going to Uddiyan or Urgyan, the name by which he knew the place. But the local people were unaware of the term. So he was directed to: Hillo, Rukala, Kapoor, etc.

The class of the Teachers visiting Urgyan or having some kind of relationship with the place appear to have created an iconographic distinctiveness. sTagtshang Raspa wears a round woolen hill cap. Its top is flat and circular. A strip of about four inches broad cloth folded up to half falls down round the seam of the top going round the head. It may be a legacy inherited from the Guru himself, Guru Padmasambhava. At Chhukutsi gonpa there is a small and simple stucco image wearing simiple round cap and a thin upper garment. The left hand is open, empty and rests facing upwards on the lap and the right hand is raised touching the chest in abhaya mudra. The image carries no identification mark. It is shown as Urgyan Padma by the priests here. The term Urgyan is retained here and may be identified easily with Urgyanpa.

We observe another distictinve mark in sTag tshang Raspa, a further development. He was ordained into Nathapantha as we learn from his travelogue. He wears a large earring. This feature is not noticeable in the narrations of Urgyanpa and his image. He wears small earrings, a symbol of Natha Yogis. Below we give the text, which occur in the lam-yig, travelogue, of sTag-tshang Raspa (pp. 7b. to 15b), first in devanagari script, its transcription in Roman, its edited rendering in Hindi and thereafter English translation.

sTag-tshang Ras-pa — Hindi Conversations

Text in Nagari

(p.7b) क्य तुम ह–रमज़–ति। (L-4)
स–सि लिम स–पर्छ़ धरति।
तु–मि हरमज़–ति क्य हु–व। छु–टी मु–ह। **(L-5)**
भ–भ फ–ल। ह–मि मो–सूर–म हु–व।
सा–प कं–हं च़–ले। तिल–क मर्तु मि–मु–त। (L-6)
(p.8a) तु–मि अ–बो। ए–हं भे–ठ। रो–टि वे–ल।
खा–हि क्यि न–हि। खा **(L-2)**–हि। खा–हि।

ह–मि डम–ज़े हु–व। तु–मि थोर–र भ्य–ठ।
संगि र्दो–नो हो–ज़। (L-3)
(p.8b) भो–टन्ति जो–कि क–पुर्तित च़–ले।
ह–मर आ–चि़ क–पुर धु–यि।
सब च़–लो। संगि (L-1) धो–नो हो–ज़।
अ–चि़ भ्ये–ठ। स–पा आ–धु–मि। संगि धो–नो हो–ज़। (L-2)
आसुम भा–तिल ह (L-3) –ये। क–पुर धु–ङ न–हि। (L-4)
देम् झ़ंख न–हि। क–पुर घु–ङ न–हि।
तु–म–र भु–र। ह–मि च़–ले।
तु–मि स–प च़–ले। संगि धो–नो।
अ–चि़ भे–ठ। (L-5)
ह–म–र अ–चि़ अ–यि। अ–यु–स्म भ–ति न–हि।
क–पुर धुङ न–हि।
तु–म–र भु–र ह–रम ज़–ति क्य क–त। (L-6)
(p.9a) भो–टन्ति ह–रमज़–ति चो़–रे ह–यि (L-7)
(p.10b) तु–मि अ–यंघि (L-3) क–हं ते अ–यि।
ह–मि भो–टन्ति जो–कि हु–व।
क–शि–मि–रि भो–टन्ति अय।
ह–मि क–शि–मि–रि न–हि।
ह–म–र म–हा चि़न्द हुव।
क–शि–मि (L-4) – रिथि–बन्द प–रि।
दश म–यि–नि–घ–य–ह–यि।
भो–टन्ति जो–कि झ़ंख हयि। (L-5)
झ़ंख जो–कि। (L-7)
(p.11a) फ–ल हो। (L-1)
(p.13a) क–पुर–र ति–र क–रि। हमि संगि धो–नो हो–ज़।
ह–मि पद्म–न पु–रु सि च़रखा।
स्य–लोम पे–लोम तिर हु–व।
पठन्न ला–र–इ। हमि स्मरि।
तु–मि (L-4) –स च़रख। संगि हो–ज़। झ़ंख ह–यि।
दिम् दरश म–यि ई हम् भ्यठ।
ह–मि ह–सो न–गर च–ले।

दरश म–यि (L-5) घ–य। ईं ह अय।
संगि धो–नो हो–ज़।
ह–मि तु–मि मेल़ ल। (L-6)
(p.15b) अन्तर अप्से। चुप्ते क–रे। (L-6)
अन्तर न–हि। ह–मि ज़ो–कि हु–व।
जु–रु न–हि। अ–लि–कध्य। (L-7)

Transcription

(p.7b) ky tum h-ra mdsa-ti. (L-4).
s-si-lim s-partsh dharti.
tu-mi hrmds-ti ky hu-v. tshu-ṭi mu-h.(L-5).
bh-bh ph-l. h-mi mo-sur m hu-v.
sā-p km-hm ts-le. til-k martu mi-mu-t.(L-6).
(p.8a) tu-mi a-vo. ai-ham bhe-ṭh. ro-ṭi ve-l.
khā-hi kyi-n-hi.
khā (L-2)-hi khā-hi.
ha-mi ḍ(br)am-ze (Tib. bram-ze = Brahmin) hu-va.
tu-mi thor-r bhy-ṭh.
saṅgi rdo-no ho-dsa. (L-3).
(p 8b)bho-ṭanti dso-ki k-purtirt ts-le.
h-mr ā-tsi k-pur dhu-yi. sb ts-lo.
saṅgi(L-1)dho-no ho-dsa.
a-tsi bhye-ṭh.
s-pā-ādhu-mi. saṅgi dho-no ho-ds. (L-2).
āsum bha-tīl ha(L-3)-ye.
k-pur dhu-ṅ n-hi.(L-4).
dem dshṅkh n-hi. ka-pur dhuṅ n-hi.
tu-m-r bhu-r. ha-mi tsa-le.
tu-mi s-p ts-le. saṅgi dho-no.
a-tsi bhe-ṭh.(L-5).
h-m-r a-tsi a-yi. a-su-sm bh-til n-hi.
ka-pur dhu-ṅ n-hi.
tu-m-r bhu-r h-rm z-ti ky k-t.(L-6).
(p.9a) bho-ṭanti h-ramds-ti tso-re h-yi. (L-7).

(p.10b)tu-mi a-yṅghi(L-3) k-haṅ-te a-yi.
ha-mi bho-ṭanti dso-ki hu-v.
k-shi-mi-ri bho-ṭanti a-y.
h-mi k-shi-mi-ri n-hi.
h-m-r m-hā tsind hu-v.
k-shi-mi(L-4)-ri thi-band p-ri.
dash m-yi-ni-gh-y-h-yi.(L-5.)
bho-ṭanti dso-ki dshṅkh h-yi.(L-5).
dshṅkh dso-ki(L-7)
(p.11a)ph-l ho.(L-1).
(p.13a)k-pur-r ti-r k-ri. h-mi saṅgi dho-no ho-ds.
ha-mi padm—n pu-ru-si tsarkhā. sy-lom pe-lom tir hu-v.
pṭhnn lā-r-yi. ha-mi smari.
tu-mi(L-4) sa tsrkh. saṅgi ho-ds. dshaṅkh ha-yi.
dim drsh m-yi ī ham bhyaṭh.
h-mi h-so n-gar ts-le. drsh m-yi(L-5).
gh-y. īṅ-h a-y.
saṅgi dho-no ho-dsa.
h-mi tu-mi mel-l.(L-6).
(p.15b) antar apse. tsupte k-re. (L-6).
antar n-hi. h-mi dso-ki hu-v.
dsu-ru n-hi. a-li-k-dhy.(L-7).

Edited Hindi rendering

(p.7b) क्या (तुम) हरामज़ादा। (L-4)
सच-सच बोलो(?)। धरती स्पर्श (छू) करके।
हरामज़ादा तुम हो। तुम क्या करते हों। छोटी मुंह (बड़ी बात करता है) (L-5)
"बा बा, भला हो। हम मुसलमान हैं।"
सुबह कहां चले (जाओगे)? तीर मार कर मौत (के घाट उतार दूंगा) (L-6)
(p.8a) तुम आओ। यहां बैठो। रोटी का वेला है।
खाओगे कि नहीं।
खाऊंगा। (L-2) खऊंगा।
हम ब्राह्मण हैं। तुम थोड़ा बैठो।

हम दोनों साथ हो जाएंगे (चलेंगे)।
(p.8b) भोटन्ति जोगी कपूर को तीर्थ के लिए जा रहा है।
हमको आज कपड़ा धोना है।
सुबह चलेंगे। (L-1) दोनों साथ चलेंगे।
आज बैठो। सुबह तुम इस आदमी के साथ होकर
(L-2) दोनों साथ जाना।
आस्मान में बादल हैं (था)। (L-3) कपड़ा नहीं धो सका। (L-4)
दिन चंगा (अच्छा) नहीं है। कपड़ा नहीं धो सकते।
तुम्हारा बुरा हो। मैं जाता हूं।
तुम सुबह चलो। दोनों संग चलेंगे।
आज बैठो।
मैं आज आया। (आज जब मैं आ रहा था तब)
आस्मान में बादल नहीं थे। (फिर भी तुमने) कपड़ा नहीं धोया।
तुम्हारा बुरा हो। हरामज़ादा क्या करता है? (L-6)
(p.9a) भोटन्ति हरामज़ादा चोर है। (L-7)
(p.10b) तुम यहां को आए। कहां से आए? (L-3)
हम भोटन्ति जोगी हैं।
क्या कशमीरी भोटन्ति हो (है)?
हम कशमीरी नहीं हैं। हमारा (देश) तिब्बत (महाचीन) है।
कशमीर से तिब्बत परे, बहुत दूर, है। (L-4)
दस महीने हो गये हैं, वहां से आकर।
(p.7b) भोटन्ति जोगी चंगा है।
भला हो जोगी।
(p.13a) कपूर तीर्थ की य़ात्रा करेंगे। हम दोनो साथ जाएंगे।
मैं पद्मपुर (तीर्थ) को गया (च़रख=चला)। स्य–लोम पे–लोम की तीर्थ यात्रा की।
पठान लडाई करता(मारता) है। हमको मारा। (L-4) तुम साथ चलो।
साथ जाएंगे। चंगा है। दस दिन (महीना) यहां बैठो। हम हसोनगर च़ले।
दस दिन में वापिस आऊंगा। (L-5) यहीं आऊंगा। दोनों संग चलेंगे।
अब हम और तुम मिल गए हैं। (L-6)
(p.15b) अन्दर आओ। चूत करेंगे। (L-6)
अन्दर नहीं। हम जो़गी हैं।
जोरु नहीं (रखते)। हम अलख (ध्यायी, धारी हैं)। (L-7)

English translation

(p.7b) Are you Bastrad? (L-4).

I tell the truth, touching the earth. You Are bastard. What are you doing? You worthless man, you talk so high. (L-5).

Oh, Oh. Well, we are Muslman.

Where will you go in the morning? I will kill you with arrows. (L-6)

(p.8a). You come. Sit down here. This is time for meal. Will you have or not?

Yes, yes. I will. (L-2)

I am Brahmin. You wait a while. We will go together. (L-3)

(p.8b). Tibetan monk is going on pilgrimage to Kapoor.

Today I have to wash clothes. We will go in the morning. (L-1). We will go together.

Stay here today. Go in the morning with this man. You go together. (L-2).

It is cloudy. (L-3). I could not wash clothes. (L-4).

The day is not clear. I could not wash clothes.

Worse may come upon you. I am going.

You go in the morning. We will go together. Stay here today. (L-5). You wait today. (L-5). When I was coming today, it was not cloudy. You did not wash clothes. Worse may come upon you. You are bad. What do you do, you bastard. (L-6)

(p.9a) Bastard Bhotanti is thief. (L-7).

(p.10b) You have come, from where did you come?

I am a Tibetan monk.

Are you Kashmiri Bhotanti?

I am not from Kashmir. I am from Mahachin (Tibet). Tibet is far away from Kashmir. (L-4). It has been ten months (since I left Tibet).

Bhotanti monk is good). (L-5)

Well yogi, good luck. (L-7)

(p.11a) Well.

(p.13a) We will go on pilgrimage to the holy place of Kapoor. We will go together.

I journeyed to Padampur. I visited the holy place of Sya-lom Pe-lom. Pathans are quarrelsome. They beat me. I will go with you, (L-4).

We will go together. It will be good.

You wait here for ten days (months). I am going to Hasonagar, (L-5). After ten days (months) I will come here. Then we will go together. I and you, we have met together, (L-6).

(p.15b) Come in. We will play, (L-6).

Not in. I am a yogi. Not wife, (we don't marry). I am Alakhdhayayi or Alakhdhari (one who meditates on God, a yogi of Natha sect), (L-7).

Notes: The phrase "bha-bha pha-la pha-la" has origin from Acharya Shantarakshita in the middle of eighth century CE who on the completion of the Samye monastery pronounced "pha-la pha-la siddhi siddhi". It then was transcribed in the sba bzhed (Dharamsala) as such, and is seen followed generally in the same manner, which should have been "bha-la bha-la siddhi siddhi", well, well, accomplished!

tsarakh = Charakh (?), Pali.

smari (maari) = Tibetan system of spelling adding 's' as prefix to a word like in smad, skar, etc.

rGod-tshang-pa

Below are given a few sentences from the Namthar of rGod-tshang-pa which he says are in 'phral-skad, vernacular. It is difficult to decipher the sentences meaningfully. Not even the equivalents of the key words like sprang-po (Tib.) (= pauper), Bhot, sonā (gold), etc. given in the translation by the Teacher himself can be identified in the text.

i. Text

(p.50a)

अ–री ध–भान ध–त–री। (L-2) ध–न की–चे़ न–हे।)

तु–म–रे म–हा बौ–ते। पो–ने बुत अ–चे़।

अ–म–र बोन–धे। ज–ग–र–धे। (L-3)

अ–म–र भीद म–री ल ज़ा–जा। ग–अेन धे। ध–र्म क्र क–र। (L-5)

(rGod-tshang-pa, p. 50).

ii. Edited version

P. 50 (a)

अरी धभान धतरी। (L-2) धन किछ़ नहीं।

तुमरे महा भोट। सोना बहुत है।

हमारा सोना दे। झगड़ा दे। (L-3)

हमारा भीत मरी ल ज़ा–जा। गोए (=कपड़ा) दे। धर्म का कर्म कर। (L-5)

Translation

P. 50 (a)

(मैं गरीब हूं।)। (L-2) मेरे पास कुछ धन नहीं है।

तुम बड़े तिब्बती हो। तुम्हारे पास बहुत सोना है।

हमको सोना दे दो। नहीं तो झगड़ा, लड़ाई, करेंगे। (L-3)

मैं ठंड से मर रहा हूं। मुझे मेरा कपड़ा दे दो। धर्म का कर्म होगा। (L-5)

iii. Transcription and translation

P. 50

(a). a-ri dh-śan dh-t-ri.(L-2). dh-n ki-tse n-he.

tu-m-re mhā bau-te. po-n bud a-tse.

a-m-r bon-dhe. dsa-gar dhe. (L-3).

a-mar śid-mari l-dsā-dsā g-aen dhe. dh-rm kr kar. (L-5)

iv. Translation

p.50a.

[I am pauper]. L-2.I have no money.

You are great man from Tibet.

You have much gold.

Give us this gold. Otherwise we will quarrel, will beat you. L-3 I am dying of freezing cold. Please return my clothes. It will be a virtuous task. L-5

11

Genealogical Lists of the Thakurs of Lahul and the Style of Writing Their Titles

The ruling chiefs of Lahul, known by the title of Thakur, were: the Thakurs of Tinan (Gundhla), Barbog, Khangsar (Kolong) and Gumrang. They are in possession of genealogical lists of their families written at different times in the past. We have the oldest specimen from Gundhla i.e. Tinan. It reads: gser-gyi me-long zhes-pa'i rgyal-rabs, (Francke, 1926- II: 211). It may be translated as 'The Chronical called Golden Mirror.' This is the earliest available such document which belongs to the period of Raja Bahadur Singh (1532-1559) of Kullu. The title is in Bhoti language and written in Bhoti script. Its objective is single and the meaning of the text is easily understandable. It is evident that till this period the makers of such documents had no contact with any other language. But the later titles are difficult to understand. Here we have some later similar documents from three Thakur families as under. These titles are long descriptive sentences.

1. **Tinan:** nag-se chi-k-ba'i ba-mu-zu-ba-na-mu-ne lam-bar-2. ba-ba-ta ji-min gar-pa-na ko-khri gun-da-la, yul gun-da-la. (Pl. XXIII).
2. **Barbog:** nag-se-tsi-ka-b'a-be-mu-dzab-na-mu-na-lam-bar-2. ('number two') bā-paṭa ji-min-gar-pa-nra-ko-khri-bar-bog ('province of Barbog'), (Francke, 1926-II: 220).
3. **Khangsar:** nag-śa—cig-kyi ba-yi mu-jub-bad na-mu-na lam-ba'r-2. ba-bad ji-min gar-spran-na ko-khri ko-long, (Francke, 1926- II: 208).

Of these three the text of Barbog was found written in Tankri, writes Francke, and the other two are in Bhoti. Their language is complex, mainly Urdu but that is not clear. The object here is dual: 1. As a title of the genealogical list, and 2. Title of the land record. 3. Both, as in the case of Tinan. Here both the documents are given under one title, firstly the genealogical list and then the revenue record. The texts of the three statements are broadly identical therefore indicating to one single source. The language of all the three documents is broadly Urdu, which apparently may be related to Mughal tradition.

On the history of the Mughal contact of the Punjab Hill States, Hutchison and Vogel write that, the whole of the Hill States became subject and tributary to the Mughal empire in the time of Akbar. Soon afterwards Todar Mal, the great finance minister of Akbar, was deputed by his master to create an Imperial demesne in Kangra by confiscating territory from the various States of the Kangra group. In accordance with his instructions, Todar Mal annexed a large portion of the Kangra Valley, and made a similar demand on each of the other States proportionate to their means, (Hutchison and Vogel, Vol. I, 1933: 298).

Barnes, Settlement Officer of the first settlement of district Kangra, writes that the hills, however, do not appear to have been thoroughly subjected in the Imperial rule, until the time of the great Akbar, in 1556 A.D. Farishta narrates that in that year the young Emperor himself headed an expedition against Kangra, subduing the country and receiving the Katoch chief, Dhurmchund, with favour and liberality, (Barnes, 1855: Para 47).

According to Ahluwalia, Raja Todar Mal came to Kangra in 1573 CE and carried out the settlement. "We still see the revenue records of the state government in old format with Persian terminology. The British perhaps only strengthened the tradition", (Ahluwalia, 1988: 94).

From the above we observe that the Mughal system of maintaining the revenue record could have been introduced in Himachal Pradesh earliest in the last quarter of sixteenth century CE. In Lahul such impacts could be felt much after their settling down firmly in Kullu, because this is the most possible channel.

On this subject Lyall remarks, "Every Kulu man ascribes the jeolabandi or distribution of the fields into jeolas, etc, to Raja Jaggat Singh' (1637-1672), (Lyall, 1876: para-92). Further the Vansavali of the Rajas of Kullu records that Man Singh (1688-1719) introduced some new provisions in the system of revenue assessment, like measuring the land by the measure of kind of seed required, etc., (Tobdan, 2000: 87-88).

Hutchison and Vogel write that under Man Singh the Kulu State reached the zenith of its power. He fought against the states all around Kullu. He fixed the boundary with Ladak at Lingti and came plundering through Spiti, which was being ruled by Ladak.

Harcourt brings out a record of the visit of Man Singh to Lahul. Writing about the Thakur's house at Gundhla, he notes, "In one apartment is shown a cooking place that was used by the Kooloo Rajah, Man Sing when proceeding on pilgrimage to Triloknath, and on a beam in the roof is to be seen an order of the chief in the Nagari character, but it is so defaced by age and smoke that it is now quite illegible," (Harcourt, 1871: 100). Thus if any new system in maintaining the revenue record in Lahul was introduced by the Rajas of Kullu these could have been the dates earliest.

Francke concludes, although based on an erroneous fact, that these documents i.e. the genealogical lists with titles as discussed, were drawn after 1680, or say in 1700 A.D. (Francke, 1926-II:207). This is the period of Man Singh.

The above document at serial number 1 relating to Tinan was drawn at Sultanpur, Kullu, by Bilchung of Barbog, as is stated in the original document itself. The document of Barbog ends with the name of Bilchung from which it may be concluded that this document also was drawn during the same period and most probably by the same person Bilchung.

Francke on the strength of the statement of the 'old ex-chief' of the family of Barbog Thakurs of his time, c. 1906, records that 'Bil-cung and his four cousins were contemporaries of the Kulu king Man Singh', (1688-1719), (Francke, 1926-II: 220-Note). But this oral information is not found to be reliable.

The genealogical list of the Thakurs of Gundhla drawn with the help of Bilchung ends with the name of Thakur Hira (Hir) Chand who was contemporary with Harcourt, Assistant Commissioner, Kullu (1869-1871). Incidentally the date of birth of Thakur Hira Chand is given separately on the same document in Urdu as June 5, 1852. Hira Chand was the chief of Gundhla but he was still a boy, during the time of Lyall, as he writes. Therefore Bilchung's time cannot be much earlier than this date. There is no other Bilchung in the genealogy of the Thakurs of Barbog or any other in Lahul.

Francke while copying the genealogical list of Barbog gives at the end the name of the Chief as Tan-dzin chos-rgyal and his son as Bilchung, (Francke, 1926-II: 220). Lyall knew the two persons directly. Lyall (c.1870) writes about the Thakurs of Birbogi i.e. Barbog that, 'The present head is named Tangan Choigyal, an old man of eighty, his son is the lambardar of the kothi,' (Lyall, 1874: para 139). The two persons referred to here, father and son, are the same as described by Francke. The fact that Bilchung was a young boy during the time of Lyall is also corroborated from the Tinan document wherein Bilchung writes for himself as No-no i.e. a young boy or man. All these facts point that there was only one Bilchung, the author of the genealogical lists of Tinan and Barbog, and his life time is evidently the second half of the nineteenth century CE.

The genealogical list of Khangsar ends with the name of Tara Chand (Francke op. cit.), who too was contemporary with Harcourt. As such all the revised genealogical lists of the three Thakurs, as given above, were drawn simultaneously most likely during the time of Settlement of district Kangra by Lyall 1865-1872. Evidently these belong to the period of Lyall's work of Settlement of Kangra district.

Apparently all the three titles appear to be copies of one original source. The language of the text is broadly Urdu/Persian. In the present form they are not easily understandable.

F.W. Thomas, examining the title as above the document of Khangsar reads in the manner: "naqsh-i-chaki ba mūjib namūnā lambar 2 bābat zamin parganā koṭhī koloṅ," and translates it as: "Statement of property according to form number 2: account of the lands of the Parganā (district) of koṭhī koloṅ," (in Francke, 1926-II: 209-note). Thomas has made it clear without doubt as far as the first part of the statement, containing the Persian words, is concerned. The scribes had changed the Persian technical words unintelligible to them with the words of their own choice.

We, for example, now take the title of Barbog in its transformed form and translate it as we understand, which reads: nag-se-tsi-ka-b'a-be-mu-dzab-na-mu-na-lam-bar-2. ('number two') bā-paṭa ji-min-gar-pa-nra-ko-khri-Bar-bog. We may rewrite it as: nak-sha gchig-gi bahi ba munh-zuban na-mu-na lambar 2. We translate it as: Register in form one as per oral information according to sample number 2. Here the translation is defective because the scribe has changed the Persian word 'chaki' (= property, in Thomas) to Bhoti chig (=one)' and further ba mujib to muh zuban (oral).

All the three Thakurs mention the name of the Kothi of which he is the chief or in which his residence is situated. The Thakurs of Khangsar and Barbog were chiefs of one kothi each, Kothi Kolong and Borbaog, respectively. The Thakur of Gundhla was although chief of three kothis yet he writes 'garpana kothi gun-da-la' i.e. 'garpana of Kothi Gundhla' and adds 'yul gun-dala', i.e. area of Gundhla, the valley of Tinan.

Kothi, a circle of certain villages, more or less equal to modern Panchyat, was a subdivision of a Waziri, in the administrative system followed in Kullu.

Thomas while explaining the sentence introduced a slight change replacing the word garpan found in all the three titles in the original sentence with the term pargana. He writes 'Parganā (district) of koṭhī koloṅ'. Perhaps he presumes garpan a mistake for pargana, Further he takes paragana a synonym for Kothi. 'Garpan' is a typically unintelligible word but is important because it exists in all the three titles. Here we are not following Thomas. We at first attempt to explain the term Pargana.

Pargana: Pargana is a term in administration which came to the Hill States perhaps from the Mughals. In Himachal this terminology is used in Kangra and Chamba and is not in use in Kullu. In Kullu a Waziri was divided into Kothis which is equivalent to Pargana elsewhere. The part of Lahul under the reign of Kullu followed the system of Kullu and there were fourteen kothis. In Chamba a Waziri was divided into Pargana, which was equivalent to Mandala of the classical system, and of kothi of Kullu. Each Pargana had a Kothi which was the headdquarters and place of residence of Paragana officials. Pangi was one of the five Waziris of Chamba in which there were four Parganas. A part of Lahul, which was also known as Chamba Lahul comprised one Pargana of Waziri Pangi, (Gazetteer Chamba: 1910: 262-263). Here as there already exists the term Kothi in the statement, addition of similar term 'pargana' is not wanting.

The term garpan is a term quite strange for us. However, application of the term garpan had been acknowledged in relation to Lahul and explained several years before by J.B. Lyall. He writes about the nature of the holdings of arable lands in the jagir kothis in Lahul as follows: "The whole produce of certain fields is taken by the Thakur; this land is cultivated by farm servants, assisted on certain occasions by gatherings of the regular landholders; it is known as the Thakur's "garhpān" or home farm, and, as a general rule, the greater part of it is situated in villages near which he lives. Other fields are held rent-free as maintenance by his 'dotoen', i.e. by the dunnewassals, or junior branches of his family, or rent free in lieu of continuous service by his 'chāksīs', or family retainers, or by his kāng chumpa, or farm servant," (Lyall,1874: para-136). Here the word 'garpan' is rendered as 'land owned by the Thakur'. Lyall has improved the form of the word with explanation. But even this form of the word is literally not meaningful for us. Lyall has used the word slightly changed from the form occurring in the titles of the Thakurs as "garhpān". The term garpan was perhaps adopted for the first time during this period and was used by all the three Thakurs.

This term garpan is found used in two other documents of Khangsar which were constructed during the time of Lyall. They are examples of local practical application and good illustrations for understanding its true sense.

At the time of settlement work being done by Lyall the three Thakurs appear to have prepared the revised list of the geneology of their families and at the same time they also prepared their own revenue records. Lyall had prepared record for the Khalsa kothis and not for Jagir kothis as he writes, "The administration papers for khalsa kothis in Lahaul prepared at Regular Settlement were on the same model as those for Kulu." "No records were prepared for jagir kothis. In them therefore, in my opinion, the old customary terms of land remains in force." (Lyall, 1874: para 135). The kothis falling under the administration of the Thakurs viz. the valleys of Chandra and Bhaga constituted jagir kothis. The kothis falling in the areas administered directly by the Raja of Kullu were known as khalsa kothis. The Thakurs of Khangsar and Tinan conducted the task of settlement under the guidance of Lyall as is known from the Khangsar document, for Khangsar. We find the evidences in regard to these two families from the documents they own. About Gumrang Lyall has reproduced some examples in his Report.

Following are the titles of the registers of land record and revenue assessment of Khangsar, of the settlement conducted by Thakur Tara Chand and maintained in two languages, in Urdu and Bhoti :

i. Title in **Urdu:** "fard kist-bandi kothi kolong vaziri Lahul jagirdar Thakar Hari Chand Sahib hon. Magistrate va-ruye nakal khevat mustaba mister G.B.(sic.) Lyall sahib bhadur mohtmim bandobast zila Kangra," This title is made very nearly on modern official lines. It may be translated as, 'Register of installment, Kothi Kolong, Vaziri Lahul, Jagirdar Thakur Hari Chand, Hon. Magistrate, according to the sample of rent-roll prepared by Mr. J.B. Lyall, Settlement Oficer, district Kangra.'

ii. Title in **Bhoti**: "fa-d-kist-ban-di ko-thi ko-long va-zi-ri la-ho-la ba-mu-jub na-kal khy-'di bando-bast san 1868 la is-bi-la song. Si-ri sam-ba-t 1925 lo-la bris." This title appears to copy partly from the Urdu title, partly from an unknown source and the rest is the scribe's own addition. Translation: 'Register of installment, Kothi Kolong, Vaziri Lahul, according to the copy of the sample of rent roll of settlement which was done in 1868. It was written in Sri sambat (vikram sambat) 1925, i.e. 1868 CE.

The document in both the languages mention the settlement to have been conducted in 1868 corrsponding to Vikrami sambat 1925. The document in Urdu was prepared by a trained modern revenue official hailing from Hoshiarpur, Punjab. The second one in Bhoti was prepared presumably by a local lama. Both the documents are prepared in the same proforma, in seven major columns. The two documents are complementary to each other for proper understanding of the full record.

The typical term garpan has been used in both the above two documents under the column named in Urdu as 'kind of land as known in kothi Kolong' and 'kind of land-and-house' in Bhoti. In the column below this heading appear, in both the documents, downwards, the names of various classes of households paying tax or not. At the top comes the family of Thakur or jagirdar who is described as garpan, Below this are others: dotoen, chāksī, khral-pa (tax-payer, the middle class of farmers), khang-chung-pa (small landholder), etc. Thus the term garpan here distinguishes the family of the Thakur as a 'higher class of landholder', or say the highest among all categories of landholders in the Kothi. Here we follow the local recorder who explains the term garpan as 'kind of land-and-house' because he is better informed of the application although he may be ignorant about the literal meaning of the term.

Now we attempt to consider the etymology of the term. The term garpan independently is unintelligible. The term garpan is unrecognizable to the languages known to us. Thomas authoritatively removes it from the Persian vocabulary as we have seen above. It definitely does not belong to Bhoti also. We also do not see the word in use in any of the various languages of Himachal Pradesh either in spoken or written form like in Hindi, Pahari/Himachali, etc. But we also cannot go beyond these in search of its origin. It is not an ancient term but is most probably a modern current word. Its first part is clear. In this manner the word can be identified with the nearest current common Hindi phrase 'ghar parivar' which literally means 'house and family'. It matches somewhat in form and meaning with that of 'garpan'. There is another similar term in colloquial 'gharvaar' which means 'house and those related' like the family and the paroperty. In fact the term appears to be a thoughtful invention. Here although the words are imitable but don't include the connotation of land which is an essential part. The objective appears to use a term like the term zhing-khang (land and house) used in Khangsar, in sTod. Here a household may be defined like 'zhing-khang chhed-mo' = 'a big landlord' where the. family and land both are included.

Thus just as the records of Khangsar were prepared in the format for which the samples were provided by Lyall, as is stated in the titles of the two documents from Khangsar expressly, the samples of proforma for preparation of the documents including the titles of the genealogical lists of all the Thakurs were also evidently provided by Lyall. There might have been forms or samples number one and two. This also solves the presence of the English word 'lumber or number 2' in the statements. Thus the four Thakurs of Lahul viz. Khangsar, Gundhla, Gumrang and Barbog prepared their revenue records and the genealogical lists according to the samples of forms provided by J.B. Lyall, the Settlement Officer, district Kangra. In Kullu there were no suzerains or subordinate chiefs like the Thakurs in Lahul from where the sample could have come to Lahul. The subject has been made complicated by the copyists due to their unfamiliarity with the difficult language and various technical words. The statements have become so complex that they comprise words from four different languages: Persian, Bhoti, English and Hindi.

12

rKyang-chhu Thang : The Meeting Point of the Territories of Lahul and Ladakh

The border between Lahul and Ladakh: Lahul and Ladakh are neighbours and are located adjacent to each other, but the inhabited territories of the two areas are situated at a great distance. It takes full seven days for making a journey with a pack of ponies through the barren uninhabited land to cover the distance between Dartse (Darcha) the last inhabited village in Lahul to reach the first village of Gya in Ladakh. In history, however, this deserted part of the land did not remain wholly neglected. A busy trade route passed through it joining with the famous International Silk Route. This road joined the rich, fertile and productive plains and hilly regions of northern India on the one side with the rich wool producing region of Jangthang, the extensive pasture land extending across the border of India and Chinese Tibet and the markets of Central Asia, like Yarkand, Kashgar, etc. on the other. The high hilly regions of Himachal produced grains like wheat, maize, rice, etc. Many articles of necessity were imported from the lower areas and the plains such as gur, cotton cloths, spices, utensils, etc. for trade. Lahul produced the best kind of Ne, huskless barley. Jangthang including Ladak produced salt, borax, jang-bal (the long stapled wool of Janglug, sheep from Jangthang), pasham, and sheep and goats. These were traded and exchanged at seasonal markets at various places, between Lahul and Ladakh. Goods of trade from both the directions passed through Lahul and some Lahulas traded, some brought for their own use and some others worked as carriers. These goods from the two opposite directions went further like from Kullu down to Mandi, Kangra, Hoshiarpur, Amritsar, Lahore, and further. From Ladak the goods went to Central Asia. Ashokan Buddhism also travelled through this most hazardous route.

Given the geographical conditions no state would have liked to make any claim over this vast unproductive land in those days. In such a situation the border point could have been fixed either at Dartse in Lahul or Gya in Ladakh, or anywhere in between. Yet the history is different from this. The position depended somewhat on the fact as to which Raja is more powerful at the moment. Again these border points in the ancient times were not permanent. They were changing from time to time as the strength of a state changed or due to some other powerful factor.

In the ancient times in the hills two states lying close to each other shared borders marked by some existing prominent unchangeable natural object like a nallah, river, hill range, ridge, etc. The boundary between Kullu and Rampur Bashahar was formed by the river Satluj. The boundary between Lahul and Pangi is demarcated by a small hill range named Ghod-dhar emanating from the Shinkon-Paddar range and ending at the bank of Chandrabhaga. Between Kullu and Lahul it is the top of the Rohtang Pass. At many places between Mandi and Kullu the border is formed by small nallahs and hill ranges.

The boundary between Lahul and Ladakh is fixed somewhere in the middle of this vast stretch at some distance from both the sides at a place called rKyang-chhu Thang, the Plain of rKyang-chhu (plain where rkyang, wild ass, come to drink water) (others call it Lingti = Water of Ling), a large level plain lying on the other side of Baralacha pass, towards Ladakh. In the middle of this plain there is a big Phalong, boulder. This has been chosen as the border marker between Lahul and Ladakh and named as Phalong Danda, dividing rock [phalong = boulder. dran-'dra (colloquial) and 'dra-'dra (literal) = equal]. This has been done uniquely despite the fact that there is no dearth of any natural mark like streams and ridges. There are three high passes: Bara Lacha, Lachalung La and Tanglang La between Lahul and Ladakh.

From the side of Lahul this act of fixing the border is attributed to the Rajas of Kullu having been done during their rule over Lahul.

Moorcroft and Trebeck when crossed the area in 1820 were the first to observe the mark. They describe in the words, "A high, square, and insulated rock in the middle of one of these plains divided into two portions by the river constituted the boundary mark between the states of Kulu and Ladakh. It is called Ling-ti by the people of Kulu, and by those of Ladakh Fa-lung-danda. Other landmarks of a similar kind were observable across the river", (Moorcroft and Trebeck, 1841-I: 220).

In 1839, A. Cunningham, of the first boundary comminssion, surveyed the Lahul district. He fixed the boundary between the states of Lahul and Chamba two tributaries of the Chandrabhbhaga, Nalda on its left and Tsokhang (Chukum) on its right bank. From the head of the Tsokhang Nullah the Commissioners determined that all the country to the eastward which is drained by the Bhaga, the Chandrabhaga and their tributaries belonged to the British district of Lahul and that the boundary between Lahul and the Zanskar district was the snowy range (called Paralassa by Dr. Gerard) dividing the drainage of the Bhaga and Chandrabhaga from that of the Zanskar river, (Cunningham, JASB, 1848b: 296).

Beyond the Baralacha Pass to the eastward, the Commissioners found that there was an old well known boundary stone, named Phalong danda which marked the limit between Lahul and Ladak. It stands in the midst of an open plain on the right bank of the Yunam River. As there was no known or recognized boundary mark on the other side of the stream, the Commissioners selected a remarkable cream-coloured peak, called Turam, as the northern limit of the British territory on the left bank of the river. As this peak is situated at the end of one of the spur of the great snowy chain, already determined as the northern limit of the Lahul district, it forms a natural continuation of the boundary line from the westward.

Neil Howard narrates, giving the geographical details of the plain and the history of formation of the place as border, that the Lingti Plain i.e. rKyang-chhu Thang, lies to the north-east of the Baralacha Pass, on either side of the Gar zha'i chu, i.e. the Yunam River of many maps. The plain begins upstream at the Ra bo mchod rten, which stands above the river's left bank, and ends, downstream, at the junction of that river with the Tsarap River. It is crossed by the old frontier between Ladakh (including Zanskar) and Lahul (part of the Kingdom of Kulu since at least the late 17th century) which is now the boundary between the modern Indian states of Jammu & Kashmir and Himachal Pradesh. For as far back in history as we can surmise, and long anterior to any period for which we have documentary sources, Lahul (as we name it today) or Gar zha (as at least the northern part was named in Ladakhi Tibetan) was a borderland which seems to have belonged to whichever of its neighbouring states was the strongest. During the Ladakh-Tibet-Mongol war of 1679-1684 Raja Bidhi Singh of Kulu saw his chance and occupied Lahul in 1682. His successor Man Singh (1688-1719) established his border with Ladakh on the Lingti Plain, where it too has remained. In 1835 Ladakh was conquered by the Dogras of Jammu, whose ruler, Gulab Singh, was subordinate to Maharaja Ranjit Singh of the Sikhs. The Dogras did not rule Lahul. In 1840-1841 the Sikhs conquered Kulu, and Lahul became a part of the Sikh empire which it remained until 1846. Following the 1st Sikh War, the state of Jammu & Kashmir, now independent of the Sikhs, was established by the Treaty of Amritsar in 1846. It included Ladakh, and therefore Spiti, while Lahul became part of British India.

Neil Howard further writes that the Second Boundary Commission was constituted in 1871-1872 because trade from Ladakh to Turkestan had been suffering due to several reasons, particularly the extortionate duties imposed by the Maharaja Gulab Singh and the corruption of his officials. It was decided that the relatively direct route through Kulu and Lahul to Leh would be the most physically desirable route to Central Asia. In 1871 the commission representing the British government and the Maharaja were deputed for demarcating the boundary firmly. The Phalong Danda in the middle of Lingti Thang was retained, the members agreeing on the mark fixed by Cunningham. They however raised an additional structure to highlight the line of demarcation, (Neil Howard, 2005: 224).

Construction of Road: Construction and maintenance of road on this important route was essential and was of benefit to many.

However, to construct and maintain a usable road covering such a long distance, that also through a constantly physically active surface of land, during the early times of rules of the Rajas of small states, was extremely difficult, if not impossible.

During the British period the work of construction of the road and bridges was taken up expeditiously. The traditional local kind of old bridges of the ropes of branches of birch-wood were replaced by wooden suspension bridges. Rest houses and Sarais were built at many places for the benefit of the travellers. In Kullu during the time of the native rulers there were Dharamshalas at certain important places under the religious institutions. A. Cunningham had stayed in 1839 in the Dharamsala, attached to the temple, at Dwara near Katrain which later on was occupied by a Gosain to the exclusion of the needy travelers.

Till 1870, during the time of Harcourt, Assistant Commissioner of Kullu, there were at Khoksar and Tandi the traditional birchwood rope bridges called Jhoola or Rope bridges. At Dartse on the Zanskar river there was bridge which was swept away in 1870 and was rebuilt immediately.

There was also a sarai at Dartse. Rest houses were located at Rahla and Khoksar. At Marhi there was a small structure in ruins known after Lehna Singh, the Sikh Governor of the Hills, who had built the structure, (Harcourt, 1871:15-18).

Gazetteer of 1917 reports further progress of the work stating that by that time canti-lever bridges had been laid at Khoksar and Tandi. At Dartse there was already a similar bridge laid earlier. The footways were taken away each year before the winter. There were rest houses at Kyelang and Jispa. There was sarai and a shop at Zingzingbar and at a place on the other side of the Baralacha Pass. There were shelter huts at Rohtang and Baralacha Pass. There were six rest houses and seven sarais on this route of the length of 100 miles, (Gazetteer, 1918: 230).

After the independence of the country, although the highway lost its economic significance of great value, it became important from the angle of defence of the country. This became important after the Ladakh war of 1948 with Pakistan and gained further importance after the 1963 war with China.

Construction of road on Baralacha Pass

Dealing with the subject of construction of road on the Baralacha Pass we have an old document from the archives of the Thakurs of Gundhla (Annx. II). It states to have accomplished the work of construction of road over the Baralacha Pass. Two kinds of roads were constructed one for the sheep and goats, and the other for mules, during the period of Raja Pritam Singh (1767-1806), the Raja of Kullu, making reference to Sing-ge Namgyal (1634-1642), the king of Ladakh. From this we may also presume that the tradition goes further back. During this period Lahul was under the rule of Kullu.

The Document: This document, a separate sheet of two pages, termed as tho-yig, register, is placed after the title page of the main book entitled 'brom-ston pa rgyal-ba'i 'byung-gnas kyi skyes-rabs bka'-bsdams bu chhos le-'u nyi-shu-pa. (Biography of Dom-ton gyal-bayi jung-ne, the twentieth volume of the smaller collection of Kadam Literature.). Dom-ton (1005-1064) was chief pupil of Atisha and founder of the Kadampa sect. A copy of the work was made on the occasion of celebration of the death ceremony of Tashi Paljor, the Thakur of Gundhla, and was hosted by Paari, his son, the then existing Thakur. The document has now been digitised by the Shantarakshita Library, CUTS, Sarnath-Varanasi and forms book 5 of the volume 1/12 of Gondhla Kangyur- Misc. collection'. Below we give translation of the document.

Some initial sentences, the part forming prayer, have been excluded from the text here.

Tho-yig: In the west of the holy places of the white snowy Ti-rtse (Kailash), where the Arhats reside; and the turquoise-lake of the wish-fulfilling water, lake Ma-pang (Mansarovar) are situated and are connected by a continuous mountain chain, the Dril-bu Ri, Ghantaparvat, the great pilgrimage place; and the Gandhala mountain, prophecied by the Jina, the Buddha, which is the wonderful assembling place of the spiritual Heroes, male and female.

Hello! The religious king Pritam Singh resides at the great castle at the capital Makarsa (Ma-khar-sa) and his crown is held high. Sing-ge Namgyal resides in the castle in the great capital of Leh and his crown is held high and his kingdom is flourishing. Although we could not visit the country and the place of refuge, Leh in Ladak, but the work and objectives being related to each other, depended on his name as famed. The sun and the moon are adorned in the firmament between the earth and the sky like in an amulet box. Pray, this is in the practice of exchange of love and friendship between the two of us.

The red path for the mules like the great red lightning has been constructed on the pass of Baralacha (Ba-ra-la-sa) the border. The hard and rough white path like ribs of the spine has been constructed for the sheep. The people, like own sons and servants, gathering in legion like the planets and stars, are travelling happily.

No-No Paari and Sinsau Kum-jed (sKum-mjed), the two, father and son, belonging to the pure lineage and famed clan emanating from the god 'Od-gsal, (Abhasvara), possessed of miraculous powers, reside at the self-born palace at Tinan. While their reign is expanding and dominion is flourishing in Lahul, the country of Dakinis, the two for repaying the kindness of their kind (deceased) father, for removing the causes of difficulty in his life and for attaining the pure status in the next life, raised the good Ka-bam and literature of the class of father and son. The great merit amassed due to this is here praised by all. Hello!

Moreover, the Lady Donor, Grandmother, sister (address by the scribe), Nangka Palmo, for raising the holy books did great assistance. The excellent mothers Sonam Palmo and bLo-gro, the two mixed the god's nectar in the meal of men, served nice meal. Everybody appreciated and the scribes were all pleased. Hello!

The other important kinsmen who offered zong (offerings in a ceremony) gathered like birds in the garden or bees collected over honey. They are enumerated here:

The excellent daughter in law, sister Dri-med and sister Samdub Palmo, and the bride, the three, did good service while preparing the holy books. (The notable guests attending the ceremony were as follows):

From the house of Labrang of Khyinang (Khyim-nang), Pad-dkar, the religious Lord of the siddha lineage, and Padma Senge, father and son; Thakur Padma and sister Nom-tsel, husband and wife from Thorang Ling; Thakur Nom-chhog husband and wife; Thakur Ngang-tse and Tashi bu-khrid; Thakur Bhag-tu and sister Bel-mo; Thakur Logro rgya-mtsho and Buthid; Thakur dBang po and Tshe ring skyid; Thakur Nangka rGya-mtsho and sister Tashi dolma; Thakur Paljor and sNum-tse from Sra-sren; Thakur Sonam dpal-lde and Mugulu father and son; Tashi rgya-mtsho and sister Dolma from Bar-bog Khar; Nono Sonam Rgyalpo and sister Tashi Palmo, from Magon.

gNyer pa, the manager, Jogi Chand and Logro from Gundhla (Gunla); Phagspa Tashi and Sonam Dsom pa; Zang skyab and Pa-Le from Shuling. Alam the Lambardar and sister Bhelmo, the two from Lod, Lote.

Explanations: This ceremony was performed on the occasion of the death of Tashi Paljor. Paari, his son, is the present Thakur. He hosted the ceremony. It mentions Sing-ge Namgyal of Ladak. The document mentions that these people framing the document had not met him. Sing-ge Namgyal's period is slightly earlier (r.1634-1642). The road was constructed on the Baralacha pass sometime after the period of Sing-ge Namgyal.

Here we read the former form of the name of the village of Gundhla or Gondhla as Gun-la. The local interpretation of the name is that it originates from the term dgu-lha, nine gods. We are now firm that the correct form of the name of the seat of the Thakurs of Tinan is Gundhla, and not Gondhla as we sometimes write.

Makarsa: The document mentions the capital of Kullu as Makarsa. This is done according to the old practice followed in the area. At the time of Pritam Singh the capital was situated at Sultanpur which was shifted here sometime after 1650 CE. In a document in Tankri from Kullu regarding Pritam Singh his capital is named as Sultanpur.

Lahul has typical geographical situation and the travelers were always much in number. Lyall gives the internal arrangement made by the people among themselves for providing the carriers to meet the requirement of the outside official travelers. 'The forced labour which falls upon the Lahula is peculiarly heavy, as their country is a highway used by many travelers and officials on tour, and is surrounded by high snowy mountains and large tracts of elevated waste. The demand all occurs within the six months of summer, the time within which all field work and all trading journeys have to be done. It is distributed equally on each jeola or holding, but at times it may be ruinous to certain families to have to give perhaps the only man, or there may be none at home, all being away engaged in the carrying trade between Tibet and Kulu, in which almost all Lahuli landholders are concerned. The arrangements which have grown up owing to these difficulties and which have now become fixed institutions, deserve I think, to be briefly described. For the periodical repairs of roads a man is demanded from every house. For the carriage of travellers' baggage a man is taken from every jeola, or full allotment of land only, and the demand for supplies of all kinds required for travelers is distributed in the same way. Each kothi or group of kothis repairs certain lengths of highway, and carries baggage, and furnishes supplies for the stage nearest to undertake the carriage from Lahaul over the Rohtang Pass into Kullu. There remains the most difficult task of all, that is the providing supplies and carriage to travelers wishing to leave Lahaul for Ladakh, Spiti, Zanskar or Chamba by the Baralacha, Shinkal or Kukti passes, which are all over 16,000 feet in height, and involve a camping out for several nights in the wastes. For the work of these passes the ten kothis of Gara and Pattan have put themselves on a common roll or roster. Each kothi keeps an account with the other kothis of its contributions, and within each kothi each holding keeps an account with the other holdings. If a holding cannot furnish its man in the turn, a substitute is sent, and there are fixed sums which the defaulting holding is obliged to pay to the substitute in addition to the pay which he gets from the travelers', (Lyall, 1874: para. 140). An example of the kind of payment a defaulting member has to make, as given by Lyall, for a traveler going to Rubsho over Baralacha pass is: three rupees, 70 lbs. barley meal, one pair boots, and butter 2 lbs. Similar are the rates for the other three routes going to Spiti, Chamba and Zanskar. For the Rohtang pass it was the sole responsibility of the residents of the kothis of Chandra valley.

13

Two Little Known Languages of Western Pahari Group from Kinnaur

A number of languages are spoken in Kinnaur. Kinnauri, a class of languages of the district, is well studied and highly acclaimed. Bhoti, another important language spoken in the area of Poo, has not been studied well. Another class of languages from the same area spoken by the class of craftmen is found only in a few references with some sentences as examples from some language. Here we give some samples from the two languages of this neglected class of languages.

Kinnaur - Nomenclature: The early European writers writing about Kinnaur transcribe the local name according to their own understanding, there not yet being any standard model to be followed. Therefore the name is found written in several forms. The Gazetteer, therefore, writes that, "The earlier names and spellings were: Kanawar, Kunavur, Koonawur, Kanaur, Kunawar, and Kanauring," (Gazetteer-Kinnaur, 1971:1). Many modern scholars display the same view. We, however, observe that, in all these names there is one common factor: they tend to sincerely follow and transcribe in the manner in which the native speakers pronounce the term Kanaur or Kanauring. In the transcription the scholars were following strictly the principles of Phonetics, of which we are unaware. They all transcribe the word Kanaur or Kanauring as is pronounced locally even today. Here the letters u and a indicate the unstressed vowels in the word. Therefore all these older forms of the name may be pronounced in single form as Kanaur or Kanauring.

The Kinnauri society: The whole Kinnauri society is traditionally divided into two classes of Khasia, constituting the original inhabitants, and Beru or Ores, the lesser class. Beru and Ores are local traditional terms. A common term used all over the state is Koli which is also applied here. Harijan is a term used in official works.

In the Census of 1961, according to the district Gazetteer, of the total population of 40,980 the indigenous population numbered 36,800. Of this 11,133 constituted Beru, the Scheduled castes and 25,667 Scheduled Tribes. Their spread in the three different administrative sub divisions of the district was as under:

Sub-division/Number	Caste	Non caste
Nichar	4,429	6,584
Kalpa	4,365	9,146
Poo	2,339	9.937
Total	11,133	25,667

Thus more than 30 percent of the whole population constituted Beru. The data also indicates the direction of immigration of the population. The ratio between the two classes is the narrowest in Nichar division in southern direction touching the Shimla district, indicating the influx of the immigrants. It is the widest in Poo sub division, in the northern end. This class consists of several sections comprising the families practicing different crafts and trades, and known by different traditional names.

The Gazetteer mentions the three groups of the class as: Chamang, Domang and Ores. It writes further, Chamangs make and mend shoes and also weave woolen cloths. The Domangs are practically blacksmiths. The Ores who are equal to Domang work on wood and are carpenters, (Gazetteer, 1971: 76). While this may be taken as general explanation, some of these names are used at different places to address different sections of the society.

The term Ores appears to be in use loosely and much widely, and also as substitute for Beru, and to be applied to any group of the class. Thus in certain villages the term is used, instead of the particular name, to designate the weaver, Badi (Bāṛī) the carpenter, mason, metal worker, leather worker, etc. Separately leather worker is called Chamang, worker on iron as Lohar, worker on silver and gold as Sunares, worker on wood, and mason, as Badi, and the rest like weaver are known as Ores. The names are mostly of Sanskrit/ Hindi origin transformed to local environment. At places they may also create some confusion. For example the term Domang which is applied to the section working on metals does not appear to be a proper designation for the section. The word domang applied to the section of skilled craftsman is derived perhaps from the Sanskrit word 'dom' which indicates a class of unskilled labourer.

B.R. Sharma says that Ores, who work on wood, and Koli speak the same language. Chamang work on leather and are settled all over the district. They also do the work of weaving. (Sharma, B.R., 1976: 29-30).

The languages of Kinnaur may be divided into three classes: Kinnauri, Bhoti and Beru or Ores. The Beru or Ores belongs like the languages of the lower hills to the Western Pahari Group of languages of Indo-Aryan family. There is no definite information about the extent of prevalence of this class of language or languages in the district and their kinds.

The district Gazetteer mentions that there are spoken in Kinnaur about ten dialects and the one among them is given as 'Standard Harijan Kinnauri spoken in Kalpa and nearby villages'. In a note it further states that "No separate sub-dialects are spoken by Harijans". (Gazetteer, 1971: 70-72). Thus it provides that there is one Harijan language and it is spoken in and around Kalpa.

Thakur Sen Negi identifies two languages of the Harijans. He mentions three groups of speakers in the class as: Koli, Lohar and Badi (Bāṛī). Lohar and Badi speak the same dialect with a minor difference. Koli, who are larger in number, speak a different language. He reports presence of the languages of the class in many villages where they speak their own language and not the main Kinnauri, except at Ropa where both the classes speak the same main Kinnauri language, (Negi, 1975: 8-9). Negi and the Gazetteer quote some sentences with translation from a language as examples.

The population of the section called Beru or Ores, as seen above, forms a sizeable portion of the Kinnauri society. All of them do not speak their language. Here we give samples of two languages of the class spoken in Kalpa, the ancient capital of Kinnaur, and in Roghi situated at about five kilometers south of Kalpa. The speakers of both the kinds of languages name their language as Kinnauri. Here they are named as Roghi-Kinnauri and Kalpa-Kinnauri otherwise customarily called Chamang and Domang. The speakers of the latter language, who live in Kalpa, work on metal and are also known as Sunares and Ores. The former work on leather. We have no further first hand data on these languages, for example, the extent of use of these languages in other areas of the district.

As regards the role of different classes in the social functions it is told that the main drum of the devata of the village, which is made of silver and called shirang ḍhol (= leading drum), is played by a Domang and not by a Chamang. There is said to exist a social distinction between the sections in the class.

The two languages reveal sometimes quite unfamiliar vocabulary. Roghi-Kinnauri has no helping verb. Kalpa-Kinnauri has a helping verb but is found used rarely. There are words from the major Kinnauri languages. Some words seem to belong to quite distant places. For example there is a word 'Pishi' for cat in both the languages. This word is found in sTodpa of Lahul, a language of Tibeto-Himalayan group. But this word is not known in other languages in the state.

Both the languages possess the letters ts, tsh and z, non-aspirated and aspirated affricates and fricative.

The Domang don't have traditional songs. The Chamang have song describing the founding of the universe and some other religious songs revering Narayana.

On the question as to which section arrived first here we may argue that the work on the iron being an essential economic function specially in a agricultural society, the workers on iron can be said to have been the forerunners. Another point is that these families occupy the central place in the capital village of the area.

Roghi-Kinnauri and Kalpa-Kinnauri which are traditionally known as Chamang and Domang may be placed among the class of Western Pahari languages. But they are archaic. Some samples from the two languages are given as under.

A. Roghi-Kinnauri

Words : Noun

दिऊस *di-ūs*	=	Sun	ज़ोत *zot*	=	Moon
तारो *tāro*	=	Star	बादल *bādal*	=	Cloud
ढोखरो *ḍhokhro*	=	Earth	ब्याल *byāl*	=	Night
माटी *māṭī*	=	Soil	पाणी *pāṇī*	=	Water
बासल *bāśal*	=	Summer	छारमी *tshārmī*	=	Autumn
हिमद *himad*	=	Winter	ज़ाण *zāṇ*	=	Stone
ढोक *ḍhok*	=	Rock	लूड़ो ज़ाण *lūdo zāṇ*	=	Gravel
खौर *khaur*	=	Grass	बूट *būṭ*	=	Tree
पातरंग *pātraṅ*	=	Leaf	बारच्चो *bārtso*	=	Branch
हियूं *hiyūṅ*	=	Snow	स्राणे ठांग *Ṣāṇe ṭhāṅ*	=	Ice
गोयेन *goyen*	=	Rain	स्रे *Ṣe*	=	Foam
राठ *rāṭh*	=	Evening	दोती *dotī*	=	Morning
पौशी *pauṣī*	=	Day after tomorrow	आज़ *āz*	=	Today
कले *kale*	=	Tomorrow	घौरे *ghaure*	=	House
घौरे *ghaur*	=	Room	द्वार *dvār*	=	Door
खिड़की *khiṛkī*	=	Window	मेलिंग *meliṅ*	=	Hearth
घोड़ो *ghoṛo*	=	Horse	घोड़ी *ghoṛī*	=	Mare
पुस्रो *puṣo*	=	Man	देहन *dehan*	=	Woman
छेलड़ु *chelṛu*	=	Son, Boy	छेलड़ी *chelṛī*	=	Daughter, Girl
तेते *tete*	=	Grandfather	आपी *āpī*	=	Grand-mother
अमा *amā*	=	Mother	भाई *bhā-ī*	=	Brother
दाय *dāya*	=	Sister	बुआ *bū-ā*	=	Father
बापू *bāpū*	=	Uncle	नने *nane*	=	Aunt (father's sister)
कनाल्डू *knāldū*	=	Grandson	कनाल्डी *kanāldī*	=	Grand-aughter

सोसउ *sosa-u*	=	Mother in law	सेओरो *se-oro*	=	Father in law
मुटकन *muṭkan*	=	Head	आखी *ākhī*	=	Eye
कान *kān*	=	Ear	हाथ *hāth*	=	Hand
खुंडी *khunḍi*	=	Leg	आऊंठी *ā-ūnṭhi*	=	Finger
पेट *peṭ*	=	Stomach	नाक *nāk*	=	Nose
थुकांग *thukāṅ*	=	Sputum	चावल *cāval*	=	Rice
घीऊ *ghī-ū*	=	Butter	शाग *śāg*	=	Vegetable
दाल *dāl*	=	Pulse	दोयंग *doyaṅ*	=	Curd
दूध *dūdh*	=	Milk	दोतिर खाऊ *dotir khā-ū*	=	Morning meal
दिउसे रो खाऊ *diuse ro khā-ū*	=	Lunch	ब्याल रो खाऊ *byāl ro khā-ū*	=	Dinner
टौफी *ṭauphī*	=	Cap	सूतन *sūtan*	=	Pyajama
चोरकू *corkū*	=	Bangle	शोपोटक *śopoṭak*	=	Neck ornament
कोनताई *kontā-ī*	=	Ear ornament	शांगली *śāṅglī*	=	Chain
लोहा *lohā*	=	Iron	रूपा *rūpā*	=	Silver
बैर *bair*	=	Sheep	धागो *dhāgo*	=	Thread
ऊन *un*	=	Wool	मासोंग *māsoṅ*	=	Flesh
सोतू *śothu*	=	Stick	दुराहि *durāh*	=	Wood
दाम *dām*	=	Bullock			

Adjective

शूईक *śu-īk*	=	Red	पीक *pīk*	=	Yellow
राक *rāk*	=	Green	गोरया *goryā*	=	Grey
ठोह *ṭhoh*	=	White	रोक *rok*	=	Black
कोड़वो *koṛvo*	=	Bitter	खाटो *khāṭo*	=	Sour
मीठो *mīṭho*	=	Sweet	मारी *mārī*	=	Bad
बोड़ो, बड़ो *boṛo, baṛo*	=	Big, Elder	बोड़ी बड़ी *boṛī, baṛī*	=	Big, Elder
कालो, काली *kālo, kālī*	=	Black	आछा *āchā*	=	Good

इन्छे *inche*	=	Here	बालो *bālo*	=	More
लम्बो *lambo*	=	Long	हसल–हसल *hasal-hasal*	=	Quickly
लूड़ो *lūṛo*	=	Small	होदिन्छे *hodinche*	=	There
तुल *tul*	=	Below	पिछें *picheṅ*	=	Behind
आंगमये *āṅgmye*	=	Before	आउखा *ā-ukhā*	=	In front
बादो *bādo*	=	Many	घाटो *ghāṭo*	=	Some
केथरे *kethre*	=	When	किन *kin*	=	Where
केओसे *ke-ose*	=	How	मोटो *moṭo*	=	Thick
सारी *śārī*	=	Beautiful	कोचरो *kocro*	=	Bad
बोलो *bolo*	=	Good	पटले *paṭle*	=	parti-coloured
रादो *rādo*	=	Red	कालो *kālo*	=	Black
पीलो *pīlo*	=	Yellow	सुकलो *śuklo*	=	White
हारो *hāro*	=	Green			

एक, द्वी, त्रोण, च़ार, पांच, छ़ो, सात, आठ, नौ, दौश, ग्यारह, बीश, बीशो–एक, बीशो–दौश, त्रोण–बीश

ek, dvī, troṇ, tsār, pāṅts, tsho, sāt, aṭh, nau, dauś, gyārah, bīś, bīśo-ek, bīśo-dauś, troṇ-bīś.

One, Two, Three, Four, Five, Six, Seven, Eight, Nine, Ten, Eleven, Twenty, Twenty one, Thirty, Sixty.

Pronoun

हांऊं *Hāṅ-ūṅ*	=	I	अमोरे *amore*	=	We
होसो *hoso*	=	He	तमोर सेबे *tamor sebe*	=	They
तू *tū*	=	Thou	तुमोरी *tumorī*	=	You
मेरो *mero*	=	My	अमोरो *amoro*	=	Our
तेरो *tero*	=	Thine	तुमोरी *tumori*	=	Your
होतिन रो *hotin ro*	=	His	होतनो रो *hotno ro*	=	Their
की *kī*	=	You (hon.)			

Imperative

स्रावो *Ṣāvo*	=	See	अन *an*	=	Bring

Verb

नाशिन *naśin*	=	To go, going
लोसिन *losin*	=	Beats
शाईन, *śa-īn*	=	Is seeing
लिखिन, *likhin*	=	Writes
नाशिन *naśin*	=	Sits down
जुटिन *juṭin*	=	Is drinking
सौ नाशिन *sau naśin*	=	He goes.
सेबे नाशिन *sebe naśin*	=	They go.
साननू साचि्मो *sānanū sātsimo*	=	To kill to death
टोमू *ṭomū*	=	To beat, thrash
ठुरेस *ṭhures*	=	Run
बहन *bahan*	=	Laugh
क्रमिग *kramig*	=	To cry
क्रवो *kravo*	=	Is crying
यमहो *yamho*	=	To fly
वसरचिमो *vasarcimo*	=	Get up
तोशिमो *tośimo*	=	Sit down
स्रीमी साचि्मो *Sīmī sātsimo*	=	Live, To kill
गोभू *gobhū*	=	To bend
रोएन *royen*	=	Crying
स्रांदवी *Ṣāndvī*	=	To get tired
खोटिन *khoṭin*	=	To work

Case Signs

कुकुर ला *kukur lā*	=	To, for dog
आप ला *āp lā*	=	For self.
घौरे *ghaure*	=	To, at home
कलमे *kalme*	=	With pen

छेलडुए *chelṛu-e* = By child

सूरते *sūrte* = By Surat

घोरे का *ghaure kā* = From home

बाजार का *bājār kā* = From bazar

होतिन रो *hotin ro* = His

होतिनोरो *hotno ro* = Their

नदी के *nadi ke* = In river

Sentences

Present Tense

छेलडू रोएन स्रावो। *chelṛū royen Ṣābo.* = Child cries.

दो बियो *do biyo.* = He is going.

होसो किताब बाकलोस। *hoso kitāb bāklos.* = That book is thick.

रादो घोड़ा वाल्ल नासिनस *rādo ghoṛā bāll naśins.* = Red horse runs fast.

होसो किताब कछवी स्कूल के नासिंस *hoso kitāb kachvī skūl ke naśins.* = He went to school carrying book.

दो किम छज़ा बियो। *do kim chazā biyo.* = He went leaving house.

होई नाचिन सोई। *ho-ī nācin so-ī.* = I am watching dance.

होई मानुश मारी। *ho-ī mānuś mārī.* = He is a bad man.

हाऊं पानी पी मे। *hā-ūṅ pānī pīme.* = I drink water.

गावो खोर खाएम स्रावो। *gāvo khor khā-em Ṣābo.* = See, Cow eats grass.

सूरते कुकुर ला लोसिन। *sūrate kukur lā losin.* = Surat beats dog.

सूरत घौरे का बाजार के नसिन। *sūrat ghaure kā bājār ke naśin.* = Surat goes to bazar from home.

होई घौर सूरत रो। *ho-ī ghaur sūrat ro.* = That is house of Surat.

नदी के मछली। *nadī ke machlī.* = There is fish in the river.

राजा राणी ला शाईन। *rājā rāṇī lā śa-īn.* = King looks at queen.

होसो कलमे लिखिन। *hoso kalme likhin.* = He writes with pen.

होसो घौरे नशिन। *hoso ghaure naśin.* = He stays at home.

सौ घौरे नशिन। *sau ghaure naśin.* = He goes to home.

कालो पिशि दूध जुटिन। *kālo piśī dūdh juṭin.* = Black cat is drinking milk.

Past

जुरेई *jure-ī* = Made, constructed

ठूरी *ṭhūrī* = Went

शिखी *śikhī* = Read

गीत लाई *gīt lāī* = Sang song

सूरते घौर जुरेई। *sūrate ghaur jure-ī.* = Surat constructed house.

सूरते आप ला चा जुरेई। *sūrate āp lā cā jure-ī.* = Surat prepared tea for himself.

होसो घौरे ठूरी। *hoso ghaure ṭhūrī.* = She went to home.

छेलड़ुए चिठी शिखी *chelṛu-e ciṭhī śikhī.* = Boy read the letter.

सूरते गीत लाई। *surate gīt lā-ī.* = Surat sang song.

Future

खोटसू *khoṭsū* = Will do.

नसू *nasū* = Will go (sing.)

नसूंगे *nasūṅge* = Will go (plu.)

हांऊं काम खोटसू। *hā-ūṅ kām khoṭsū.* = I will do work

हांऊं घौरे नासू। *hā-ūṅ ghaure nāsu.* = I will go home.

अमोरे स्कूल के नंसूगे। *amore skūl ke nasūṅge.* = We will go to school.

हांऊं पाणी पीमेसू। *hāṅ-ūṅ pāṇī pīmesū.* = I will drink water.

Imperative

बाजार का कुन नशिन। *bājār kā kun naśins.*= Who is coming from bazar?

ओई कासरो दुकान। *o-ī kāsro dukān.* = Whose shop is this?

की बिम यातना। *kī bim yātnā.* = Do you want to go? (hon.)

क बिम यातना। *ka bim yātnā.* = Do you want to go?

तू पाणी पीमेस। *tū pāṇī pīmes.*= Will thou drink water?

तुमोरे सबे पाणी पीमोसे आ। *tumore sabe pāṇī pīmose ā.* = Will you all drink water?

तुमोरे पाणी पीमोसो। *tumore pāṇī pīmoso.* = You will drink water?

हांऊं पाणी पीमे। *hā-ūṅ pāṇī pīme.* = I want to drink water.

मैयी–या पाणी पी। *mai-yā pāṇī pī.* = I drank water.

अमोरी पाणी पीमोसी। *amorī pāṇī pīmosī.* = We want to drink water.

अमोरे पाणी पियो। *amore pāṇī pīyo.* = We drank water.

गावो खोर खाएम न खाएम स्रावो। *gāvo khor khā-em na khā-em Ṣābo.* = See whether cow is eating grass or not.

सतजुग का गीत Song of Satjug

सतेजुगे सोरो मोरो तला satejuge soro moro talā
तला मांजे स्रे पोजो रिंगो talā mānje Ṣe pojo riṅgo
तोदु जुगे मोनु नयीं मया todu juge monu na-yīṅ ma-yā
तोदु जुगे माटी नयीं सारेगा todu juge māṭī na-yīṅ sorgā
सतेजुगे सोरो मोरो तला satejuge soro moro talā.
तला मांजे स्रे पोजो रिंगो talā mānje Ṣe pojo riṅgo.
स्रे स्रो पुटिन्दे स्रे रास्रो ज़मा Ṣe Ṣo puṭinde Ṣe rāṢo zamā
स्रे स्रो मांजे कोनला फुला रोज़ो Ṣe Ṣo mānje konlā phulā rozo
स्रे स्रो पुटिन्दे कोनला फुला रोज़ो Ṣe Ṣo puṭinde konlā phulā rozo
कोनला फुला के आपू ब्रमा रोज़ा konlā phulā ke āpū bramā rozā
तू ई बोड़ो ब्रमा बिशनु tū-i boṛo bramā biśnu

The Song of the Age of Truth: Summary: In the beginning there was only lake. There was no soil, no trees, no man, there was nothing. Brahma-Vishnu for seating himself created a foam in the lake. It burst out. From it grew a big and beautiful flower. Brahma-Vishnu sat over it. He looked out and saw the whole universe from here. Then there grew soil. The soil was ploughed with a pair of bear. The soil was made terraced. Then there grew seed of mustard. Then man was born.

B. Kalpa-Kinnauri

Words: Noun

सोरगो *sorgo*	=	Sky	दौं *dauṅ*	=	Sun
ज़ोत *zot*	=	Moon	तारे *tāre*	=	Stars
माटो, *māṭo*	=	Earth, soil	पहाड़ *pahāṛ*	=	Mountain
बोड़ो ढांक	=	Rock	जन्टो *janṭo*	=	Stone

boṛo ḍhāṅk

गिंटो *giṅṭo*	=	Rain	हियूं *hiyūṅ*	=	Snow
स्रन्टो *Ṣaṅṭo*	=	Ice	बादो *bādo*	=	Cloud
बुट *buṭ*	=	Tree	बारचो *bārtso*	=	Branch
पतरंग *patraṅ*	=	Leaves	खौर *khaur*	=	Grass
बेई फिरन *beī phiran*	=	Evening	दोती बियान *doti biyān*	=	Morning
आज़ *āz*	=	Today	काले *kāle*	=	Tomorrow
पौशी *pauśī*	=	Day after tomorrow	फरेज़ *pharez*	=	Yesterday
देनी मिद *denī mid*	=	Woman	मोर्द लेया *mord leyā*	=	Man
याणो *yāṇo*	=	Boy, Son	लारी *lāri*	=	Daughter, Girl
बोड़ो *boṛo* (mas.)	=	Elder, bigger	बोड़ी *boṛī (fem.)*	=	Big, Elder
कुंडो *kunḍo*	=	Hearth	आग *āg*	=	Fire
मुटको *muṭko*	=	head	आखी *ākhī*	=	Eyes
कान *kān*	=	Ear	हाथ *hāth*	=	Hand
ओंगटी *a-oṅgṭi*	=	Finger	थूक *thūk*	=	Sputum
डमटो *ḍamṭo*	=	Bullock	गऊई *ga-ū-ī*	=	Cow
बेरी *berī*	=	Sheep	घोरो *ghoro*	=	Horse
घोरी *ghorī*	=	Mare	ऊन *ūn*	=	Wool
धागो *dhāgo*	=	Thread	मांस *māṅs*	=	Flesh
लोह *loha*	=	Iron	रूपो *rūpo*	=	Silver
पीतल *pītal*	=	Brass	बकरो *bakro*	=	Goat
तेते *tete*	=	Grandfather	आयी *āyī*	=	Grand-mother
अमा *amā*	=	Mother	बिदा *bidā*	=	Brother
बुआ *bū-ā*	=	Father	बबू *babū*	=	Uncle
मुमा *mumā*	=	Uncle	अमनी *amanī*	=	Aunt
वरी *varī*	=	Daughter in law	ससु *sasu*	=	Mother in law

स्रेओड़ा *Ṣe-oṛā*	=	Father in law	बोद दई *bod daī*	=	Elder sister
लोड़ी बाटी *loṛī bāṭī*	=	Younger sister	बोदी दा *bodi dā*	=	Elder brother
चा़व *cāv*	=	Rice	साग *sāg*	=	Vegetable
घीऊ *ghī-ū*	=	Butter	दाल *dāl*	=	Pulse cooked
दोयन *doyan*	=	Curd	छाछ *chāch*	=	Buttermilk
खीर *khīr*	=	Milk	खाऊ *khā-ū*	=	Morning meal
होलिओ *holio*	=	Lunch	देई खाऊ *deī khā-ū*	=	Dinner
सुतनटो *sutanṭo*	=	Pyjama	चि़न्दरो *tsindro*	=	Shoes
टोपी *ṭopī*	=	Cap	दगलटू *daglaṭū*	=	Bracelet
कंगनी *kaṅgnī*	=	Finger ring	स्रोक पटोंक *Ṣok paṭoṅk*	=	An neck ornament of three balls.

Adjective

काओ *kā-o*	=	Black	शुकलो *śuklo*	=	White
होरो *horo*	=	Green	पिआ *pi-ā*	=	Yellow
रतो *rato*	=	Red	नील *nīl*	=	Blue
मोटो *moṭo*	=	Thick, Fat	शारी *śārī*	=	Handsome
खोरा *khorā*	=	Lame	बोलो *bolo*	=	Good
मरे *mare*	=	Bad	ओन्चे *once*	=	There
बोधी *bodhī*	=	More	इन्च *inc*	=	Here
कम घटो *kam ghaṭo*	=	Small quantity	लोड़ो *loḍo*	=	Small
पाड़ *pāṛ*	=	Below	आकशे *ākśe*	=	In front
पाछ बला *pāch blā*	=	Back side	हसल हसल *hasal hasal*	=	Quickly
मुलुक *muluk*	=	Many			

एक, दी, त्रोण, चा़र, पांच, छो़, सात, अठ, नौ, दौश, बीस, बीसो एक, बीसो दौश

ek, dī, troṇ, tsār, pānc, tsho, sāt, aṭh, nau, dauś, bīs, bīso ek, biso dauś.

one, two, three, four, five, six, seven, eight, nine, ten, twenty, twenty one, thirty.

Verb

हसीनो *hasīno*	=	to laugh
उड़नो *uṛno*	=	to fly
बैठनो *baiṭhno*	=	to sit
लो सल्ले हौल्ले *lo salle haulle*	=	to beat
होल्ले ज़ान का मारवेनो *holle zān ka mārveno*	=	to kill
हसियन *hasiyan*	=	to laugh
ठूरन *ṭhurn*	=	to go
हन्डन *handan*	=	to walk

Case Signs

आमाए *āmāye*	=	For mother
रानी ले *rānī le*	=	To rani
मेले *mele*	=	For me
घौरे *ghaure*	=	To home
लारी ले *lārī le*	=	For girl
गोपाले *gopāle*	=	By Gopal
कोलोमे *kolome*	=	With pen
बाजार का *bājār kā*	=	From bazar
घौरे का *ghaure kā*	=	From home
कोसरो *kosro*	=	Whose
मेरो *mero*	=	My
गोपालो *gopālo*	=	Of Gopal
गाडे के *gāde ke*	=	In river
घौरे *ghaure*	=	At home

Pronoun

हूं *hūṅ* = I

हमरी *hamri* = We

होरो *horo* = He

एकले होरो *ekle horo* = He alone

होरी *hori* = They

होरेरी मुलुक ज़ोन। *horeri muluk zon* = They, many people.

तू tū = Thou

तुमरी *tumrī* = You (pl.)

मेरो *mero* = My

तेरो *tero* = Thine

अमरीयो *amrīyo* = Our

तुमरीयो सबियो tumrīyo sabiyo = Yours, of you all

एसरो *esro* = His

होरे रियो *hore riyo* = Their

कम मानुश *kam mānuś* =

Some, some people

Interrogative

केवी *kevi*	=	When
किन्दे *kinde*	=	Where
कीनो *kīno*	=	How

Present

रौ मानुस हंडन *rau mānuś haṅdan.* = That man is going.

गोपाल पाणी रूटना। *gopāl pāṇī rūṭnā.* = Gopal drinks water.

राजा रानी ले स्रान। *rājā rānī le Ṣān.* = King is looking at queen.

रौ कोलोमे लियन। *ro kolome liyan.* = He writes with pen.

होरो घोरे दी मायरा थाकते। *horo ghore dī māyrā thākte.* = There live two persons in this house.

रौ मानुश ठुरन। *ro mānuś ṭhuran.* =That man runs.

रवो घोरो वाल तेज हांडदोआ। *ravo ghoro vāl tez hāṅḍdoā.* = Red horse runs very fast.

काओ पिशि खीर रूटन। *kāo piśi khīr rūṭan.* = Black cat is drinking milk.

छ़ोकरू खेलन। *tshokrū khelan.* = Child is playing.

चो़रखी उड़न मयन। *tsorkhī uṛan mayan.* = Birds are flying.

तू बाल सच बतान्दो। *tū bāl sac btāndo.* = You tell very much truth.

गोपाले घौर जराओ। *gopāle ghaur jarā-o.* = Gopal constructed house.

घौर गोपाले असा। *ghaur gopālo asā.* = This is house of Gopal.

गाडे के मछी असा। *gāḍe ke machī asā.* = There is fish in the river.

रौ घौरे का वै नाहन। *ro ghore kā vai nāhan.* = He goes out of house.

बाजार का कुन आछ्ना। *bājār kā kun ātshnā.* = Who is coming from bazar?

अरो कोसरो दुकान असा *aro kosro dukān asā.* = Whose shop is this?

मेरो किताब बाको असा *mero kitāb bāko asā.* = My book is thick.

रोया नो रोणा। *royā no roṇā.* = Boy cries.

हूं ना नू। *hūṅ nā nū.* = I go.

तू किन नान्हे। *tū kin nānhe.* = Do you go.

रहरी किन नान्ह। *rahrī kin nānh.* = Do you go?

घौरे का मुलुक दूर ठूरो। *ghaure kā muluk dūr ṭhūro.* = He goes far away from home.

आमाए लारी ले हलुवा जराओ। *āmāye lārī le haluvā jarāo.* = Mother prepared pudding for daughter.

Past

गोपाले पाणी पियो। *gopāle pāṇī piyo.* = Gopal drank water.

होरो मानुश मेले फूल आनन। *horo mānuś mele phūl ānan.* = He brought flowers for me.

होरे देईनी घौरे ठूरी। *horo de-īnī ghore ṭhūrī.* = She went to home.

मैयें सेब खाओ। *maiyeṅ seb khāo.* = I ate apple.

होसे गीत लाओ। *hose gīt lāo.* = He sang a song.

होईं गीत लाई। *ho-īṅ gīt lāī* = She sang song. (fem.)

होईं गीत लाओ। *ho-iṅ gīt lā-o.* = You sang song. (mas.)

Future

काले हूं काम खोटूं। *kāle hūṅ kām khoṭūṅ.* = Tomorrow I will work.

काले हूं घौरे नाशुंग। *kāle hūṅ ghaure nāśuṅg.* = Tomorrow I will go to home.

हुं गीत लाऊ। *hūṅ gīt lā-ūṅ.* = I will sing song. (mas.)

हूं गीत लांदी। *hūṅ gīt lāndī.* = I will sing song. (fem.)

I am greatly thankful to Surat and Pyare Lal of Roghi, and Gopal Kirshan and Seva Buthid of Kalpa for helping me, and Ashwani Negi for the difficult task of arranging the meetings.

14

Traditional Methods of Distribution of Irrigation Water in Lahul

In Lahul there grows only one crop a year in the summer. Therefore it is essential that this crop should fail on no account. If one crop fails the gap between the two crops becomes of two years. Therefore every family must make stock of grains and essential commodities lasting for at least two years. It is the blessing of the nature that whereas it creates scarcity on the one hand it has blessings on the other hand that things don't rot and worms don't attack the grain stocks early. There is also no report of any instance of total draught in the area.

Due to lack of rain in the summer season all kinds of crops even the plantation trees like willow, poplar, etc. and grasslands are required to be irrigated. It receives a good precipitation in the winter in the form of solid snow a good part of which remains deposited on mountain tops. This mass of snow stock keeps on melting and releases water slowly and constantly. In the summer as the weather gets warmer the rate of melting accelerates and the volume of water in the dogpos, streams, increase. Some part of these flow underground and come out on the way in the form of spring water. At this time the need of water for the inhabitants becomes acute. Thus the bulk supply of water during this period is received in two ways through the flow and springs, besides the occasional rainfall.

Water is drawn from the dogpos flowing on the sides of villages, through yu-ra, water channels. Many of these dogpos become dry in the winter or the volume of water is reduced very much. But in the summer they become turbulent. Their usual behavior in the peak season is that while in the morning they are calm, in the afternoon they become muddy and forceful. Sometimes they bring rubbles by boring and cutting its banks. It often swells to bring flood. It then damages the heads of the yu-ra and carries away the small bridges which are put up in the Spring season every year with great labour. Communications break up abruptly stranding the flocks of sheep and cattle and the men working in the fields on the other side of the dogpo. They sometimes become so forceful that it dams the main river. But in Lahul few villages are gifted with such beneficial dogpos running nearby. Therefore proper control and management of the supply of water from the yura is required for the utilization of the scarce resources judiciously. In the tough topography it is difficult to construct yura. Here we attempt to examine the system of management of the scarce resources of water for irrigation in sTod.

Za-chhu: For za-chhu, water for the purpose of use in the homes, there is generally a spring in most of the villages. At places it may have to be drawn from some distance either from a spring or the village yura. In whole of the village there is one place called *murti* from where water is collected by all the villagers. It does not need any supervision or management and there is no such arrangement in any of the villages in whole of sTod.

Water for irrigation: As regards water required for irrigation the villagers have customary collective right and control over the sources of water close to their village. Here for our purpose we take for example the traditional system of harnessing and distribution of water among the various users from different sources in the villages of Kolong and Karing in the upper Bhaga valley, sTod. Water courses or yu-ra are drawn from the dogpos flowing nearby on the sides of the villages. Every year the yura has to be repaired after sowing the crops in the Spring season. The labour is shared by all the households proportionately according to the number of chhu-re, water-days, which is based on the full size of land holding of each household.

Kolong village: Kolong is a small village and is also name of a cluster of small and scattered villages: Kolong, Kelad, Rangrig and Sarang. For certain purposes it also includes Khangsar. Kolong has three sources varying in period and kind of source. These are: two from yura and one from the spring. The first yura is drawn from the left or the southern side from Shiti lumpa from where another village, village Karing also shares. The Shiti lumpa has inadequate flow of water. Therefore the village has to draw yura from its right or northern side from Chatsi lumpa. Supply of water from here is unlimited but it is difficult to draw water from here due to sheer cliff of rock on the way and the long distance. But this is the most dependable source and has to rely on it much specially in the years when there is very less precipitation in the winter. Moderately it is tapped every year. The third source is a big natural spring which is metaphorically termed as Uthi (Uṭhī), big metallic pitcher, situated just above the village.

Shiti Lumpa: The village is divided into two parts according to its topography: Tog-gong (upper zone) and yog-gong (lower zone). Water from the yura from Shiti Lumpa comes at a level which covers about half of the village situated at lower level, the yog-gong. This water is divided among the 10 families of this zone in nine days. During this period the families in the upper zone have some small temporary source. At a point named Tatsi sPang there appears a small spring which is put in a channel called rgya-ti bar. This also receives water from the receding winter snow stock lying above the yura. This water is divided among the eleven households of the upper zone till the time of bursting of Uthi.

Fixing of individual turn: Chhu-re (chhu= water; re=re-mo = line, turn) means the turn of the day on which one receives water for full day of 24 hours. Fixing of the turn is termed as chhu-re rgyab-che. The traditional method is known as har-shing, or Ha-ra, rgyab-che, making demarcation, or making distribution i.e. fixing the turn of the day of chhu-re. A turn of full day is called chhu-re and fractions are phyed-ti and dbang-ti i.e. half day and a share i.e. quarter day. Earlier the days were marked by the method of har-shing. In this system twelve pieces of twigs of equal size were taken and each household marked it with his typical symbol called tshal-ma, sign. They were then collected in a cap or bowl and taken out one by one which fixed the turn of each household turnwise. Now a days lot is drawn and the turn is fixed by lottery.

Uthi: Kolong has a unique source of water for irrigation. Every year a big spring water, known as Uthi, situated just above the village, oozes out in the summer. Uthi means pitcher made of copper or brass of the capacity of about fifty litres for storing chhang which is used in most of the houses. This is located on the face of rock just above the village and conveniently covers the whole village and its cultivations. Half of the water from it goes to Khangsar Khar, the Thakurs of Khangsar, of Kolong, and the half is kept as share of Kolong Yul-pha, the villagers of Kolong. It is a seasonal source of spring water received at the peak period of requirement in the mid summer. It opens in the beginning of the summer, just when the requirement for water for the fields also begins and stops flowing in the Autumn. The beginning of the flow of water from the mouth is known as uthi-rdol-che, bursting out of pitcher. The Uthi has three mouths, it bursts at three places, at a distance of about 10 to 12 meters between each other. The central one is the largest in volume.

This spring of water opens every year systematically in the middle of summer in the 5th month of Tibetan calendar or July. The days are not fixed but the people say that it opens on an auspicious day of 5th, 15th or 25th day or Namgang (new moon) of the month. In the year 2015 the Uthi burst out on 11th July, corresponding to 25th day of the 5th month of the Tibetan calendar. When the Uthi bursts the volume of water in the Shiti Lumpa gets reduced. This observation is known since long past.

After this auspicious event of uthi-rdol-che a fresh chhure-rgyab-che, marking-the-turn-of-water, is done. This is known as ma-chhu-re, the mother-water-turn, i.e. the principal or the main distribution of water. For this the previous arrangement is stopped. If some families were left out uncovered due to inconvenient location of some fields or any other reason all have to be adjusted now carefully. Attempt is made to remove all the anomalies. The water is divided in full, half and quarter day. This arrangement is called Korti-Bangti: Circle water and share water. Now the dates are fixed by clubbing the two sources Shiti Lumpa and Uthi together as one source. For this one family is taken from the upper zone and one from the lower zone for one day. Now Har-shing is put again. This time two sticks are taken out at a time of which one should be from the upper zone and the other should be from the lower zone. If both the sticks come from the same zone, another one has to be taken. After this supply of water is doubled. One getting for quarter day gets for half day.

The total number of days of a circle and the number of households who share the water is fixed and are unchangeable. Here in a cycle the number of days are 12 and the number of households are 26. The first figure is fixed, it is traditional. The second is variable. Number of families may increase, but extremely rarely.

Chatsi Lumpa: To this resource are included the beneficiaries of two more villages of Sarang and Khangsar.The number of consumers of this course are 46. In this case four families are covered per day, two families from Khangsar and Sarang, and two families from Kolong. It is completed in the cycle of 12 days. On the first day it is given to two families then to four families each in order to complete the figure of 46 among the circle of 12. On the occasion of division of a traditional family, they get no relief from the village community. They have to divide the source of the family among themselves according to their own system. On the event of some new field is broken such as nautaur, he too gets no share in the water of the village source.

Lepha: There are two Lepha (las-pha), workers, who are changed every year. One is from the upper zone and the other is from the lower zone. His function is to keep account of the system and to see that the yura remains in working order. He calls the beneficiaries whenever the yura is breached or damaged and is required to be repaired. There comes one worker from each family. The actual number of days of work for each family are charged according to the number of chhu-re.

Further division has to be done at the level of a family for adjustment between the two or more shareholding families or any other fimily when they come in the same zone but have fields in different zones or at some distance from the sub-channel. This is fixed by arrangement with each other.

Karing village: In village Karing there is only one source of water. It is drawn from Shiti lumpa, from the right side or the northern side of the village. There are two yu-ra: gyen-yur or gong-yur and yog-yur, the upper and the lower channels, drawn from the same source. Karing has preferential right over the water of Shiti Lumpa. Therefore the head of its yura is above that of Kolong. The yog-yur is a later construction. Its head is below that of Kolong. All the three heads are in one line but one above or below the other. The feature of Shiti gorge is such that below the point where the three yura are drawn, the water flowing in the gorge is covered by the mass of flat chunks of rocks slipping from both side ridges of the gorge. So some portion of the water flows much below underground whose sound can be heard but the water is not visible. The water becomes visible below near where it meets the river. There the volume of water is so large that two water mills can run side by side. There run three or four watermills there but in one line. The villagers have to go to repair the yura every year after ploughing the fields and the crops have been sown. Thereafter as and when required. The water of Shiti Lumpa is always clean and white therefore it received this name: Shi(= white) + ti (= water), White Water. Both the words belong to a culture prior to that of the speakers of the existing language.

Chhure is divided as chhure, one full day; phyed-ti, half water that is half day; and bangti one share i.e. quarter day. The days are named as goti, nyi-ti, gsumti, i.e. the first water, second water, etc., upto twelve. One can say nyiti, the second turn, is my turn.

sKorti (Water Cycle): Firstly, in the beginning of the season, all the villagers get water one after the other equal in quantity for three cycles. One cycle is of twelve days and in each round all the householders should be covered. Thus this part is covered in three cycles of twelve days, total thirty six days. This is called skor-ti: circle —water because the turn to each member is circulated. Every household gets water for the same period irrespective of the size of holding.

Ma-chhure: Thereafter, after the completion of this period, the distribution is made again. This is called ma-chhure, mother or the principal chhure. Ma-chhure is divided according to the size of the landholding by the households. When ma-chhure starts the sixteen households get water in the cycle of eight days. As the korti finishes ma-chhure starts the next day. This marking of days is applicable only for the upper yura which is traditional. These periods of rounds of twelve days, or eight days or any other have been fixed from the early times. People go for the repair of yura according to the number of chhur-re a household has.

From the yog-yur, which is a new construction, all the 16 households of the village get equal share of water of one full day and the system is followed for the full season.

The days are assigned and the sequence is fixed presently according to a draw of lot. The turns are so fixed that two households should not come in one yu-ra in one day.

The day of watering starts in the evening. Karing is situated on the right side of the river Bhaga. A rock is identified on the face of the cliff on the other side of the river where the evening line of sun and shadow reaches. The day lasts till the same time on the next day. Similarly there are marks for half and quarter day. In case of cloudy day it is done according to estimate. These days time is fixed instead of the marks on the land. It starts around 6.00 p.m. In sTod all the households and all their fields have names. Below we give the type of chhure the household of Hayar has in one circle and how it utilizes among the fields named here located at different places from two yura.

go-zhing — one, gnyis-ti, second water; Hayar — one and half, bdun-ti, 7th; Gonpa - quarter, bdun-ti, seventh; Khor tsam — one; mKhar - half, gchug-shig-ti, 11th. Total 3.75 days out of the 24 days. We may read thus: For the field named go-zhing water is received for one full day, named gnyis-ti, the second water.

Lepha: Lepha (las-pha) is chosen every year.

Kullu valley: There is a concept of gāhar and balh which means the upper area and lower area. In the balh in the areas near the riverbed where there are flat lands and water for irrigation is available rice is cultivated under irrigated conditions. In the gahar areas, at higher reaches, where water for irrigation is not available rice is cultivated under dry conditions. In Kullu water is used only for cultivation of rice. Therefore the requirement of water is quite limited.

For other crops there is plenty of monsoon rain which also benefits rice plantation. As such the farmers get sufficient water for their use. There is no need of strict supervision and regulation of the water. Yet the supplies are not unlimited and some kind of management is essential.

Naggar village: In Naggar there are three Kuhls. These are Ki-ooshi kuhl, Balogi kuhl and Ladagi kuhl. These were all drawn from Tshaki nala. They lie one above the other. The first one, Ki-ooshi kuhl was at the highest level and it went further upto Jana village. The users were all recorded in the revenue record as beneficieries of the water. For the distribution of the water there was a mutual understanding as to who was to use and when. About three or four families could use at a time. For any kind of work required to be done on the kuhl there was a person called Jethāli who would give call to all the persons to come for the work. His post was hereditary and was paid in kind at the time of harvesting of the crop.

All the users were required to come to work at the head of the kuhl. But as the work progressed the workers left one by one as the boundary of one's last field came to end. The farmer would work on the kuhl only upto the point where the boundary of his last field ended. Those who had their field in the last end of the kuhl had to work starting from the head till the finishing point of the kuhl.

Kais village: There were two kuhls: one drawn from the south-west direction from the Raugi Nala and the other from the north-east direction from Kais Nala. The second one was more important.

From the Kais Nala which was the major source of water, was divided between the villages of Kais and Karadsu. The first was known as Kais seri (seri = patch of fields) and the other as Kookri seri. Each side used the water for fifteen days for the first time in the year. For the first fifteen days from 16th of Jeth to 30th of Jeth it was used by the Kukri Seri and from 1st Ashadh to 15 Ashadh by the Kais Seri. There could be no relaxation in the condition. But if some family had problem that his nursery of rice plants is drying up he could make request. After this then the water could be used by the others who were left and who was in need of water.

The kuhl was divided in distances. A farmer could use water for the time taken for walking from one point to the other. Sometimes as soon as he reached from the first point to the other point the water was cut from behind by the other user. In this manner it was used by the different farmers.

In the kuhls in multilayer, when there were thefts, sometimes the kuhls at lower level had a momentary gush of flooded water. It was called Jhalkā.

In order to prevent thefts guards were appointed who were called Mandānu. These were voluntary from among the users themselves. Actually they were the persons who were in need of water more urgently. They could be more than one at a time. They were compensated for the work according to the following principle. Those who watched during the day they were given water from the kuhl for irrigation in their field for the period of evening from the time of sun set to the time it became dark. Those who remained in guard during the night got water from early dawn to the sunrise. In case they were more than one on guard the water was divided among themselves.

In the year when there is extreme scarcity of water, sheep and goat were offered to the local deity and it was named dūt.

In Kangra there were professionals who managed the kuhls and they were called Kuhloo (Kūhlū), those related to Kuhls. There were Kuhloos at some places in Kullu also, as in Parvati valley. Perhaps they were immigrants from the lower areas.

15

Ancient Trade Routes and Wool Markets in Himachal Pradesh

Himalaya, the great, has been source of numerous valuable products since the time unknown. These goods were in great demand and the inhabitants of these regions exchanged them with those from the distant countries.

The western section of the Himalaya is broader as compared to the central and the eastern ones, and whole of Himachal Pradesh lies in this portion. Three major ancient trade routes passed through Himachal connecting with the big markets outside the state. Some markets lay on these roads within the state also.

The roads passing through Himachal Pradesh were longer and tougher as compared to those passing through Kashmir, Kumaon-Garhwal and further in the east.

1. Routes: We identify the three traditional trade routes as: eastern, middle and western, as they passed through these sections of the present state of Himachal Pradesh. These routes branched off or were joined by other smaller routes on the way. The routes crossed through several high mountain passes some of them going above 6182m. Some stretches of roads lay across vast barren lands being without human habitations, without cultivation and scanty vegetation where the necessary provisions could not be obtained.

a. **Eastern Route:** The route which ran along the Sutluj valley through Rampur, Kinnaur across Shipki pass to Gartok, Rudok, etc. in Chinese Tibet is the eastern route. The Bashaharies i.e. the Kinnauries mostly used this route. The people of Spiti crossed to Tibet from their own area. From there the merchandise reached Rampur, the capital of Bashahar state.

There it was exchanged in the fair held in November for the local produce and the goods of the plains from Ambala, Ludhiana, Amritsar, etc. brought by the merchants from there. The route also passed through Spiti to join the middle route in Rubsho.

b. **Middle Route:** This route started from the boundaries of the states from Bilaspur and Kangra and passed through the middle of Himachal passing through Mandi, Kullu and Lahul to Ladak and reaching Yarkand in the north. The route also branched off to Spiti and Guge from Kullu one through Manikaran valley and the other from Prini, through Hamta pass. The branch from Khoksar across Kunzom, although known, was not used much by the travelers and traders. The usual route to Spiti adopted from Lahul was through Baralacha pass to Chandra valley and then to cross Kunzom pass. The whole of northwest India including Afghanistan was connected through this route. Moorcroft and Trebeck went with a large contingent of ponies through this route to Ladak and further in 1820. Here the roads are easy, worthy for laden ponies, and necessary provisions were available at many places in the way.

c. **Western Route:** This route was a branch originating from the middle one at Nurpur, in Kangra near the plains. From Nurpur it led to Chamba and across the Pangi range to Chandrabhaga valley. From Paddar (Pāddar) or Pangi it crossed over to Zanskar and further to Leh. From Paddar or Pangi it could also go along the valley of Chandrabhaga and meet the middle route at Tandi in Lahul. There were shorter routes through higher but much difficult passes linking Chamba with Pangi and also Lahul.

We learn about the importance of Western route from several travelers. James B. Fraser gathered in about 1816 that, 'at present the bulk of this traffic goes entirely through the dominions of Ranjit Sing, the Sikh chief of Lahore, and the best roads are first through Chamba, Jwalamukhi, and Nurpur to Amritsar, by which horses, mules, and asses pass easily, next that through Kullu', (Fraser 1820: 276).

Vigne who journeyed in about 1835, writes, 'another way to Ladak from Chamba is by 'Burmorawur, Lawur, or Lahoul, to Chuchut, as that part of the valley of the Indus, a little above the town of Leh, in Ladak, is called. But there are fewer human habitations, and less cultivation. The Burmawur way is used by those who fear the passage over the deep and dangerous clefts in the glacier of the mountain of Zanskar, or Burdar (= Paddar), and is also more used than any other by the mountaineers of Chamba, who naturally prefer to travel as far as they can in their own country; whereas the merchants from Yarkund, or the native of Hindustan, being strangers, prefer the Chatur Ghur road'.

Vigne, writes further that, 'originally, the great road for merchants from Hindustan lay by Nurpur, Chamba, Chatar Ghar, Zanskar and Ladak. The Nurpur Rajah provided them with Kulis to carry their goods as far as Chumba, taking an ad valorum duty from the owners. The Chumba Rajah did the same to the end of his territories which then extended to the pass of Zanskar, at the mountain of Zaruk (?), at the extremity of the valley of Padar, or Paldar', (Vigne, 1844-I: 163-164). Alexander Gerard, a few years after Vigne, writes that, 'the merchants from the Punjab take to the capital of Ladak chiefly by the Chamba road', (Gerard, 1841:182).

In fact none of the above named authors who applause the importance of the route through Chamba had actually travelled through the route. Therefore they lacked complete knowledge about the length and nature of the route.

Thomas Thomson traversed this route in 1848. He passed through Chhattargarh in Paddar and then through Bhutna Nala and Umasi La 5295m (17370 ft) went to Zanskar and Leh. Thomson was not accompanied by ponies. Actually this route was not worthy for ponies. (Thomson, 1852: 346-359).

Pitts-Tucker, a mountaineer, went in 1979 from Kilar in Pangi, through Suraal Nala, crossed Sarsank Pass 5375m and reached Dharlang valley. From here instead of crossing the low Umsi La through which Thomson went, chose the higher one and went to Zanskar through Phota La. 5717m (18756 ft.) and then to Leh, (Pitts-Tucker, 1981:3-6).

Frederick Drew, an early geographer of Jammu, Kashmir and Ladak, also passed through Bhutna Nala in Paddar and crossed Umasi La to Zanskar and Ladak. He remarks that the road from Kishtwar via Zanskar to Leh is not fit for laden animals, and it would be difficult to lead a horse along it, but this has been done, (Drew, 1875: 535). He successfully took an unladen horse from Paddar to Zanskar and Leh. This pass remains open for four to five months in a year. Thus if anybody wanted to go straight from Chamba to Zanskar, without diverting to Lahul or else, perhaps this was the easiest route.

From the above descriptions it becomes clear that this route was not worthy for laden horses. Therefore it cannot be said that the traders from the plains who are accustomed to travel with only mules and horses, and not with sheep and goat at least in trading, passed through this route. None of the above travelers met any party even a small one with loaded sheep. There is no mention in the old Gazetteer of Chamba and that of Kashmir and Ladak stating that this route ever remained a trade route. But this route was used commonly by the lamas and pilgrims from Zanksar and the tough local traders of Zanskar, Pangi and Kishtwar, carrying loads on their back.

One route starting from Chamba crossed Tissa and Sach pass 4420m and reached in Kilar or Chhattargarh, and through Budhwar pass/Umsi La, reached Zanskar and Leh. The town and the fort of Chhattargarh was named after Chhattar Singh (1664-1690), the Raja of Chamba, in 1666. Historically Paddar had since then been effectively under Chamba. It was annexed to Jammu by Zorawar Singh in 1836 and then the town was renamed as Gulabgarh. From Gulabgarh the road after crossing the Chandrabhaga river ascends through the Bhutna Nala and crosses a low pass of 4420m and enters Dharlang valley. Another route starts from Killar in Pangi through Suraal Nala and crossing the Sersank Pass, enters the same Dharlang valley. From Pangi there is another pass which enters this valley. This valley of Dharlang is stated to be forty miles long and may be about ten miles or more wide. There is glacier and remains covered with snow for most of the time in the year. From here there are at least two passes which enter Zanskar:

Phota La 5717m (18756 ft) and Bardhar/Bardar Pass or Umasi La 5295m (17,370ft.). A traveler from Dharlang valley could take either of the two passes. The pass with lower height has two names both in Zanskari and Pangwali/Paddari from which it can be assumed that this route was used by the travelers and the inhabitants of both sides. There is evidence to indicate the movement of traffic from the side of Zanskar. The Zanskaris brought salt to Paddar on their back and the people from Paddar etc. also used to visit Zanskar for similar purpose. On the way one has to spend one night on the snowy plain whether one is going to Zanskar or is coming to Paddar.

The Gazetteer of Kashmir and Ladak notes that Rupshu people bring salt to Zanskar and take barley in exchange. Some of this salt is taken to Paddar and Pangi by a difficult route and there exchanged for rice, butter, skins, etc., (Gazetteer J&K, 1890: 865). This merchandise could have been brought by the inhabitants of Zanskar loaded on sheep and goats. There are some settlements at the top of Bhutna valley in Paddar who are said to belong to Zanskar.

The Bharmour path going through Kugati Pass was traditionally used by the Gaddi shepherds of Bharmour who take their flocks every year to Lahul for grazing. This road was not worthy of laden horses and also at Yobrang in Lahul there was no bridge on the Chandrabhaga.

Lyall informs that, between Jobrang Kothi, in Lahoul, and Kukti, in Bharmour of Chamba, there is the Kukti pass, about 16,000 feet in elevetation, rather steep. Near the summit the glaciers on both sides cut up with crevasses but otherwise not difficult. The Kukti pass is used by the greater number of the Gaddi shepherds from Kangra and Chamba who graze in Lahoul. A few Gaddis who trade towards Leh and Yarkand also use this pass, (Lyall, 874: Appendix No. III-vii).

From the above descriptions we gather that there was no great trade route which passed through Chamba to Kishtwar or Pangi and from there to Zanskar. Pangi itself was an inaccessible and remote region in the state of Chamba according to its history.

Moorcroft writes that the inhabitants of Lahul are much employed as carriers between Chamba, Kullu and Ladak. From this it may be presumed that Lahulies worked to some extent as intermediaries. Chamba may be taken for the Pangi. Kilar, Paddar and Chhattargarh from where the traders from the lower regions and plains picked up the merchandise. Alternatively these traders from the lower regions possibly after crossing Sach or some other pass travelled through the valley of Chandrabhaga and joined the main route at Tandi. Here it may be remarked that the track between Pangi and Lahul of 27kms which passed along the Chandrabhaga river was not worthy for horses, laden or unladen. The laden horses were taken upwards from Udaipur along the Miyar Nala. Then it crossed the Ghordhar and descended to meet the main road in Pangi through Saicu Nala. Any way the early people were using habitually all these routes. The Gazetteer of Chamba 1904 writes that ponies were brought to Chamba from Lahul through Ghordhar (between Miyara Nala and Pangi) and Sach pass. From Lahul the traders came mostly from the Bhaga and the upper region of Pattan valley. During the period of Independence they were mostly concerntrated on the routes to Kullu. But a small number of them were necessarily involved for transmission of goods through Pangi also carrying loads on the sheep and human back. People in sTod tell that they off-loaded merchandise from Jangthang of their ponies at Madgran, at the lower end of Lahul near Pangi, during the period of the Independence. There are also Bhutori settlements in the heights of Pangi who are connected with Zanskar. Loaded sheep and goats could pass from Lahul to Pangi along Chandrabhaga river.

This route, as stated above by some authors like Fraser, Vigne, etc. through Chamba, became activated during the first half of the nineteenth century due to some strong historical reasons.

During this period the area comprising the lower regions of the present Himachal Pradesh had become politically much disturbed for some time. The Raja of Kangra had started an aggressive movement against the other Hill Rajas. The Gorkhas had invaded the region. There was a Sikh intervention. The traders might have been oppressed heavily. They were compelled to abandon the traditional routes, the middle route, and take the alternative and more difficult route via Chamba. Vigne writes, 'a duty on merchandise is demanded at five different places: Bilaspur, Sukyt (Suket), Mundi, Kulu, Chamba and finally by the Sikhs at Ladak: and this was the principal reason for the disuse of this way', (Vigne: I, 1844: 99) i.e. the middle way. Thus it appears that this route had been adopted out of compulsion.

In the past this route was popular among the Tibetan lama pilgrims among others. Three famous Tibetan Lamas viz. rGod-tshang-pa (1189-1258), Urgyanpa (Dharmsinge Namgyal) (1223-1303) and sTag-tshang Repa (1574-1651), while going on pilgrimage to Jalandhar (Kangra) and Uddyan, the birthplace of Padmasambhava, journeyed through this route. They all came through Lahul to Pangi and from there, most likely through Sach pass, came to Chamba, and from there they went to Kangra and further. This route was advantageous to them for the reason that the traveler covered much longer distance in shorter time at the same time remaining in congenial colder climate.

By all means the middle route was the longest, the most important, and remained always busy. Even if the traders and carriers from the distant lands were obstructed temporarily due to some reason the inhabitants of the nearer regions kept on employing the road beneficially. According to Vigne, continuing the above description, writes, "The path from Mundi to Ladak is frequented chiefly by those who live in the former province, or near it', (Vigne,1844-I: 99). This route was useable by the laden ponies. This we confirm from Drew who writes, 'this road is fit for camels during the months it remains open, it remains closed by snow for about seven months in the year', (Drew, 1875: 537). Moorcroft passed through this route with a large pack of ponies carrying provisions and merchandise. He also met parties from Lahul with horses having carriages. This is unexplored Silk Route. The British government initiated improvements on the route.

According to Drew the length of the road from Palampur to Leh is 570 kms and has 28 stages. Five passes have to be crossed in the way: Bubu 3048m, Rohtang 3978m, Baralacha 4938m, Lachalung 4877m and Tanglang 5334m.

Nurpur: Nurpur lay on the highway connecting Lahore, Amritsar, Kangra, Chamba, Mandi, Kullu, etc. During the British period it had acquired more advantageous position. Hutchison and Vogel write, 'Of late years, since the opening of the branch railway from Amritsar, it has become the principal point of arrival and departure for all the trade of the Western Hills, between Kashmir and Kulu', (Hutchison & Vogel, 1918: 102). Nurpur was an importation station suited to the traders going to any direction.

Historically speaking, Nurpur, in the former times, was capital of Nurpur state. The family of its rulers was named Pathania. According to Alberuni, a great scholar from Central Asia, in the early eleventh century, the place was called Dahmal and was the capital of Jalandhar. Its antiquity is proved from the fact that Cunningham found coins relating to the periods of Greek, Indo-Scythian and Muhammedans.

Hutchison and Vogel quoting Cunningham, write that, possibly Audumbara was the ancient name of the state. This suggestion receives some support from the fact that the old Hindu name of Nurpur was Darmeri or Dharmeri, which is a not impossible abbreviation of Audumbara. The name was changed to Nurpur by Jahangir in honour of his wife Nur Jahan, (Hutchison and Vogel, 1918: 103). According to the Kangra district gazetteer, 1924, the city was renamed Nurpur in honour of the Emperor Nur-ud-din, whose title was Jahangir.

It is noticed that the bulk of long chain of this trade was carried out in parts. This division in work was essential because all the traders could not travel the whole length of the long distance, extending for example from Amritsar to Yarkand. The Jangpas, the originators of the great mass of the goods of trade, from northern direction came with the merchandise from the northern cold regions upto a point where they, particularly their animals, were able to bear the discomforts of the heat. Roughly these chosen stages were: Rampur in Bashahar, Parang La in Spiti, and Dozam in Lahul, where temporary trade markets were organized annually. The Bashaharies and Lahulis were generally the intermediary transporters. They took the goods from the Jangpas and handed over to the merchants of the lower hills and the plains in Kullu and

Rampur. But this was not always a very strict rule. The Hoshiarpuris reached Leh and Yarkand and the traders from Kullu and Nagarkot visited Leh, Rudok and Gartok. But a few Lahulis and Bashaharies also travelled long distances between Yarkand and Lahore.

We notionally divide the whole length of the middle route within Himachal Pradesh into three parts. The first part comprises the lower hills which are comparatively level and plain and the climate is hot. Then comes the middle region which is tough and hilly but the climate is moderate. Then comes the toughest part where climate is harsh and availability of the essential provisions is difficult. In the three odd kinds of geo-climatic conditions, there were need of men experienced and acclimatized to the particular harsh conditions.

2. Commodities of trade: Bulk of the trade was conducted by barter. The articles which were in universal demand and traded in large quantities were Jangbal (wool from Jangthang), ba-tsha (borax) of industrial use, le-na (pashm) and salt. Jang-bal (byang-bal), wool of Jang-lug, (Biyangi in Kullu) is obtained from a superior breed of sheep which is reared by the Jangpas of Janghthang. The sheep is large in size. Jang-bal has long staples and in Lahul it is used for warp with gzhi-bal, local wool, which is short and soft, for waft. No cloth of pure jang-bal is prepared for it is rough and less warm as compared to that of mixed wools. Pashm is used both as warp and waft or only as waft. From the southern direction came grains, sugar, utensils, cotton cloths, etc.

James B. Fraser, an early traveler, writes that Yarkund sends to Leh in Ludhak, silver, Russian leather, called Bhul-R,hal, felt carpets, called Numbdas, coarse and fine China silks, taffetas, velvets, and earthen ware, sable fur, small coral beads, and seed pearls; and in return receives all manner of produce from Hindostan, keen kabs, embroidered cloth, baftas, and other white cloths, moultan chintz, quantities of red tanned skins of sheep, goat, and kid nerbisee or zedoary, silk manufactures of Benares, soongrees, and all sorts of spices, (Fraser 1820: 275-276).

Gerard writes that the merchants from the Punjab take to the capital of Ludak and exchange red goats' and sheep's leather, which is brought by the mooghuls of Yarkund for boots, match locks, sabres, shields, all kinds of cloth and chintzes, spices and sugar, (Gerard, 1841: 182).

Shuttleworth reporting the volume of trade that passed through Kullu and Lahul in 1918-1919 writes that the main imports were: wool 3878 maunds, worth Rs. 1,49,907; salt 5820 maunds; worth Rs. 11,640; and borax 240 maunds, worth Rs. 1200 — all brought in on pack sheep and goats: 9050 of these animals were imported in 1917-18. Shuttleworth remarks this to be fairly considerable.

The exports from the Punjab via Lahul are only cotton piece goods, which have considerable value i.e. Rs. 24,898. In 1918-19 silver to the value of Rs. 99,893 in coin left Lahul. In all Rs. 3,06,689 worth of silver went into Central Asia and Tibet from the Punjab. It is remarkable that a larger quantity of inferior brick tea from China reaches Spiti and Lahul overland, though these countries are situated politically in a Punjab tea-growing district. In 1918-19 only 312 maunds of Kangra and Kullu tea passed the Lahul Trade Post. A constant stream of grain goes up from Lahul and Kulu to Rupshu and beyond, (Shuttleworth, 1922: 260-261).

Gerard writes that the Koonawurees take to Ladak, Kharwa or strong cotton cloths, white cotton cloth, and chintzes of various sorts both course and fine, a little broad cloth, a few silks, gongs or large circular metallic instruments struck with a hammer, and used by the Lamas in their devotions, from iron both wrought and unwrought from Nawur, and Kootlaha of Busehur, lead from Sirmour, and Jounsar, copper and brass pots, matchlocks, straight swords, sabres, shields, bows and arrows, knives, scissors, spectacles looking glasses, sunkhs or sacred shells used by the Hindus and Lamas in their religious ceremonies, crystals, precious stones, sandal wood, Purwa or vessels of juniper wood, otter skins, indigo, oil, ghee, or boiled butter, opium, tobacco, rice, wheat, barley, walnuts, apples, raisins, almonds, shungtee or Newza, gurh, masala, shaker, ghanti made in Koonawru, etc.

They bring back: Kesur, or saffron, coarse shawls of Ladak, Numdas, or felts, dochuks or ingots of silver, soom, a kind of blanket dyed red and blue, thermas, goodmas, punkhees, and pushmeenas, skins of red Russian leather, borax, agate, tea, (Gerard, 1841: 185).

Cunningham has given an exhaustive list of articles carried from India to Yarkand and the Chinese articles brought to India, (Cunningham, 1854a: 241-244).

3. Difficulties: The greatest difficulty experienced by the commuters was that there were a few bridges on the rivers and large Nalas. For this they had adopted a course that they began their journey in the early morning about four-five o'clock and stopped before noon at the time of morning meal. Thus they had enough time in the day for the animals also to graze. During this period the Nalas are at low ebb. After the mid day they swell up abruptly due to the melting of snow with the increase of heat of the sun.

The season for the business was very limited. It had to be covered within three four months. The inhabitants were adapted to a particular climatic condition. The Lahulis could not bear the summer heat of Kullu. Therefore during the summer they remained in the northern lands. The Jangpas did not come down below certain height, below Lahul and Spiti.

Secondly the necessary provisions, fuel and fodder could not be obtained at many places. The journey between Lahul and Ladak takes more than a week through barren and uninhabited land. There no provision can be procured and there is scarcity of fodder and fuel.

The road from Leh to Yarkand is more difficult than that between Lahul and Leh. There one has to travel through sandy land for several days where not even water can be procured. Sometimes on the way it is told, even the body of dead animals like camel or horse were not allowed to go waste. The first party uses as much as it can. The remainder was kept for utilization by the caravans following them. But this has to be saved from the predators. Perhaps there were few wild carnivorous quadruped animals in the desert. But there are vultures flying high in the sky with penetrating eyes from whom it is difficult to protect the valuable remains. For this the travelers laid the dead animal on its back and its four limbs raised up towards the sky. In this way the diligent earth-watchers were deceived.

Weather is a great threat on this journey. On this route snow can fall any time in the year. Sometimes the travelers are stuck up for a whole month. Sometimes they have to leave all the goods and run to save their own life. Then on the way there was fear of theft, pilferage, unlawful exactions, etc.

4. Major participants in the operation: The network of this commerce was spread over a very large area. In Himachal the inhabitants of the higher regions of Lahul, Spiti, Bashahar, and to some extent Kullu, were involved in large scale. Kangra, Chamba, Mandi were the other areas known to have been involved in the trade.

Lahulis: Sherring writes that from Lahul traders visit Rudok by means of a pass between Hanle and Demchok, in Ladak. (Sherring, 1916:340). Some of them also visited Gartok, Leh and Yarkand.

Bashaharies: The Bashaharis had close relations with the Tibetan government and they were a privileged class of trader in Guge. Sherring writes, the Shimla route follows the Sutluj river and goes over the Shipki and Sirang passes; this is the principal road for the traders of the native State of Bashahar, (Sherring, 1916: 340).

Fraser has much wider picture of the trading activities of the Kinnauries. He writes, the Kannaur merchants carry on a trade not only with the plains and the neighbouring Chinese provinces, but they are also the chief carriers between Gartok, Ladak and Kashmere, and they even push their commercial enterprises as far as Lahasa on the south east, exchanging commodities between that place and Nepal and between the latter and the Chinese towns in Little Thibet, and to the northward, trading between Kashmir, Yarkand, Kashgar, Gartok and the various cities and people of these quarters, (Fraser, 1820:274).

Kulu: Sherring writes that Kullu traders pass through Spiti and use the Shangrang Pass by means of a bad cooli track, (Sherring, 1916:340). Shuttleworth and Whistler write that Kullu traders come to Patseo, but they don't partake in the trade there.

During the British period Hoshiarpuris of the Kumhar class were involved in large number in the business. They went upto Leh and perhaps Yarkand. Later on some of them settled down permanently in Leh and Kullu.

Lyall writes that between Rupi in Kullu, in ilaqa Pandara Bis, and Kanawar, on this side and Pin Kothi in Spiti, there is a pass of about 17000 feet elevation. It is very steep and road is bad on Bishahar side below the highest halting place. The men of Pin barter salt, borax, etc. for iron with the Basaharis at the upper place, which is a small plain. He also writes that, the Hamta Pass is important, as the shortest road from Kulu to Spiti. A certain number of Kulu zamindars also go by this route to Spiti in the autumn, and there meet the traders and barter. The Spiti people come to Kulu when they have government business, (Lyall,1873: Appendix xiii).

In 1630 in the conflict between Ladak and Guge some merchants from Nagarkot (Kangra) were held up at Tsaparang in Guge. Petech writes "They asked sTag-tshang-ras-pa for protection. This was granted and they were escorted to sPurang without damage to persons or good". This indicates that the traders from Kangra were visitng Guge since quite early time.

5. Markets: The markets visited by the traders from Himachal outside the state were Leh in Ladak; and Rudock and Gartok in Guge; and Yarkand. Within Himachal annual trade markets were arranged at Rampur in Bashahar; at Phalong Baldag over the Parang La; and Dozam also known as Patseo in Lahul. The markets in Spiti and Lahul were held at places which were uninhabited. Presently only Rampur fair, although much changed, is held regularly. Dozam was closed sometime after the Independence.

a. **Rampur:** Gerard writes that Rampur, the capital of Bushahar, contains about one hundred houses and is situated on the left bank of the Sataduru or Satluj. It contains seven or eight shops. A fair is held in January and another in October.

   In Rampur a fair was held every year in the month of November which is famous as Lavi. The term Lavi originates from the local word loi which means blanket. In Rampur, in fact, three fairs were held by this name. But in due course of time the two fairs became obsolete and only one which was held in November remained in practice. Traders came for participation in the fair, besides all kinds of the local farmers and producers, from Punjab, Tibet, Ladakh, Spiti, Kulu, etc. A great setback was received to the fair during the Gorkha invasion in around 1807-8. This fair continues to be held, maintaining the tradition, at present also. It lasts for about two weeks,

b. **Phalong Baldak:** Trebeck visited Spiti in mid June in 1822. He writes, on the northern side of Parang La there is a small platform which is called Phalong Bal dak, i.e. the rocks where wool is clipped. The people of Piti and Rubsho annually meet here, to barter the former grain and the provisions for wool of the latter, and they find shelter in the lee of huge blocks of chert which are lying about, (Moorcroft, 1841-II: 52). We notice here that Trebeck makes no mention of the important market held annually at the same time at La Darcha these days said to be continuation of an old custom.

c. **Dozam:** Dozam (rdo-zam = stone bridge), also known as Patseo (poṭ-seo = stone-slab bridge) in Kullu, both of which mean stone-bridge, is situated below Baralacha pass, in a barren place, in the Bhaga valley, about fifteen kilometers up from Darcha, the last village in Lahul on the Manali-Leh road. A fair was held here every year in July-August which lasted for about two months.

Moorcroft and Trebeck passed through the region in the first week of September in 1820. But the travelers make no mention of Dozam or its market in their description. They were accompanied by a well informed person named Nama, Kanungo, an official of the Raja of Kullu stationed at Tandi, in Lahul, who was giving all kinds of information on the way. They give detailed information on the subject from the area. They write, "The inhabitants of this part of the country are much employed as carriers between Chamba, Kulu, and Ladakh, transporting merchandise from the latter country, chiefly wool, on ponies about thirteen hands high, well made, strong, and well trained in the peculiarities of mountain carriage. Sheep are also used to carry grain and goods. The hire of a pony from Tandi to Leh was ordinarily eleven rupees, each carrying two paka maunds: we were made to pay thirteen rupees. Although the charge was high, yet, as supplies were not likely to be abundant on the road, and grain is ordinarily dear in Ladakh, I laid in a considerable quantity of wheat flour in Tandi and engaged carriers and ponies for its transport, (Moorcroft-1841-I:198-199).

After Moorcroft there was another traveler who passed through the site by the time of which the marked had been established. Isabella passed through the route sometime thereafter in the month of August. She saw the fair going on and informing about the fair writes, "Lower down where flowers abounded and at the camping ground of Patseo 12000 feet where the Tibetan sheep caravans exchange their wool, salt, and borax for grain, the ground was covered with soft greensward and real rain fell," (Isabella,1894: 147).

Shigri glacier and the Beginning of the Fair at Dozam: It is not long past when the fair started at Dozam. The fair was shifted to the present site in the Bhaga valley from Bathal in the Chandra valley where it was held earlier. We have no ground to guess when the fair started at Bathal. But we know when and why the fair was stopped here. The cause was a great unusual natural phenomenon. The Gazetteer records that, "In 1836 the Shirgri glacier burst its bounds and dammed the Chandra, river so high that (as the story goes) guards were posted on the Kunzom pass to watch lest the water should flow over into Spiti. There are at any rate traces of a large lake formed at the time, and the glacier has ever since laid athwart the old trade route, and is the most formidable and convincing obstacle to trade between Spiti and Kulu," (Gazetteer, 1918:188). About Shigri it informs,'At the west ward turn the Shigri glacier crosses the road on the left bank: this is the principal obstacle on the route between Kulu and Spiti. It is a large glacier, over a mile wide, the spout is right on the river, and laden animals cannot cross it. The left bank of the Chandra is steep and bare, but there is good grazing on the right bank down to Khoksar, where the first village is met'.

The big incident of Shigri might have occurred in the summer, in August-September, perhaps due to heavy rain which might have caused a big chunk of the glacier to break away. This dammed up the flooded Chandra. The Gazetteer tells that the marks of the dam could be seen several years after. Winter avlanche only hit the standing structures and generally do not leave any trace of the disturbances occurring every year over the surface. This was a phenomenon occurring all over Lahul and Spiti and could have been much wider. Thakur Duchi Chand relates the incident of the same period occurring in Tinan valley on the Chandra in Sissu, as he learnt.

He tells that the fair of Dozam was earlier held at Bathal in the Chandra valley. People used to come here from Rubsho, Lahul, Spiti, Khunu (Bashahar) and Kullu. The market place was destroyed in a great flood and snow flood. Then the vanue was shifted to Dozam. There the people from Spiti did not come. In Lahul it is remembered that on the left bank of Chandra opposite to Sissu there were two small villages named Shi-chi and Du-chi and they were connected with Sissu by a ropebridge. These two villages and the bridge were destroyed in this catastrophe. The name of their god was Shurjum (shur = juniper; jum?). The route through the left bank of Chandra from Damphug (Khoksar) to Sissu avoided the frequent devastations of the three big Nalas of Damphug of heavy glacier, and the floods in the Teling Nala and Pagal Nala. There is a song in the language of Sissu i.e. Tinan about this event and the villages:

Shi-chi Du-chi (name of two villages),
Ko–ko Na-na (names of two persons),
Yangling Thalang (behind i.e. above the village of Yangling),
Dren Dren Buṭa (a big tree),
Dombu'u tumbok (in front of the household named Dombu),
Rus-po'o thor (there is a heap of bones).

Dunichand's narration may be linked perfectly with the incident recorded in the Gazetteers famous as the devastating glacier of Shigri (shig = louse; ri = mountain) which occurred in 1836. His statement is corroborated from the accounts of Moorcroft about Lahul and that of Trebeck about Spiti. Moorcroft in 1820 makes no mention of Dozam fair and Trebeck does not mention La Darcha. Spiti started a market in Spiti itself at La Darcha and Lahul at Dozam, both after 1836. La Darcha was started after independence.

A similar, partially agreeing, information has been gathered by Shuttleworth. He writes, 'The Changpas and their flocks are not supposed to thrive at low elevations. However, it is said that in old times they travelled further 25 miles south west direction to where the Bhaga joins Chandra at a little below at the 10,000 foot level from this instance and another in Spiti in which within the memory of man the mart has been shifted 40 miles eastwards', (Shuttleworth, 1923:556). In other words earlier the market was situated at Tandi where the traders both from Lahul and Spiti participated. Later on the vanue was shifted, cause not stated, and markets were founded separately in Lahul and Spiti. The information recorded by Shuttleworth partly affirms the event of Shigri. However, as we know, at Tandi there is not enough space to accommodate so large number of sheep and tents, such a large required for spreading market. This may also be understood from the description of Shuttleworth himself below, let alone space required for grazing the animals. Moreover we may argue that there was no reason that the people of Spiti should take trouble to travel so far in opposite direction to Tandi. Furthermore, Moorcroft makes no mention of such a big and important event occurring at Tandi.

So the fact is that the two markets were shifted from Bathal. This great devastation might have prompted to shift the site permanently and the fair might have started functioning at the new sites immediately at the next year.

Dozan being situated on the main line and important trade route attracted many visitors who were mountaineers, hunters, and high officials and some of them have left record of their visit. Here we give extracts from the accounts of some of the important visitors.

Bruce: Bruce was a mountaineer who visited Lahul in 1912 and stayed at Patseo for about ten days during which time he witnessed the Patseo fair very closely. He writes, 'There was a wide plane on which were spread out many traders' camps — a scene of busy bartering of tea and wool, etc. The sheep, both Tibetan and Indian were fascinating — the former with their beautiful fleeces which they had brought to markets — the latter little creatures, making marches pack-laden with tea and salt. To me there was an additional pleasure in knowing that none of them would be killed for food. Every morning the different flocks would stream over the narrow bridge which spanned the turbulent river in search of grazing and every evening saw them stream back to their respective camps', (Bruce, 1914: 259-260).

Shuttleworth: Shuttleworth has the description of the fair as follows. Each set of people keeps to its own tent-pitch and uses the same piled stone enclosure to keep the wind off. Besides regular traders the Lahulas buy or rather pay an advance on the wool the year before, and also own several of the Tibetan flocks-casual buyers from Lahul and Kulu attend, and the smiling Khampa wanderers, who once lived on the confines of China and still keep up the dress of the East, foregather and engage in peddling all sorts of worthless trinkets from the plains. In winter they descend as far as Hoshiarpur and Pathankot, whence some take train to Delhi and even Calcutta. At Patseo, too, we find a few tall picturesque Gaddis with their flocks, which in summer graze on the south westerly slopes of the Baralacha, and in winter are taken to the lower Kangra hills between the Dhaula Dhar and Outer Sivaliks. In August the trade fair is attended by a diversity of hill peoples, but in September Patseo is populated only by the large hords of ibex, which come to lick the stones where the Tibetan salt has been piled, (Shuttleworth, 1922: 260-261).

In the subsequent report Shuttleworth describes the market and the activities he saw there in more detail. Dozam is situated, 'Ten miles west of Baralacha pass on the Great Himalaya Range and eight miles to the northeast of the last Lahul village of Darcha'.

'Many Lahulas own flocks of the Changthang sheep or are shareholders in them with the Tibetan Changpas. Other Lahulas pay advance for the wool they will want in the coming year. The result is that practically all the wool that enters Lahul is in the hands of small number of dealers. Some animals are shorn at home and their wool is brought in small bales on the backs of sheep or goats the common carriers of roadless Tibet. There shearing is done only once in the year in late July or August. At this time great flocks of long fleeced sheep, each flock consisting perhaps of a thousand or so in charge of two or three men and a few fierce Tibetan mastiffs, arrive here'.

Trade at the Mart: For a whole month at the time every available piece of ground at Patseo among the rocks as well as on the little plains, is occupied by tents, men, animals, piles of fleeces, bags of salt and borax from the East and bales of cotton cloth, packages of tea, and bags of grain from the West. The merchandise from Punjab plains and Kulu or Lahul is carried up on ponies or pack sheep and goats of breeds different from those they meet at Patseo. The same animals with more bought from the Tibetans, take down the wool. A pony load is from 160 to 200 lbs or more according to the condition of the road. Men from Kulu and a few Lahula women also take away loads of 60 or 70 lbs on their backs in kiltas.

Accounts of the market are settled up and the balance due is paid in silver Indian rupees, together with an advance for next year's wool. In this way a large amount of rupees goes out of Lahul into Western Tibet every year. In 1918-1919 Rs. 99,893 were recorded as leaving Lahul. In the same year three times that amount of silver went to Tibet and Central Asia from the Punjab by the various routes to make up the adverse trade balance. It is interesting to recall that, while a constant stream of Indian silver enters Western Tibet annually, another stream one of gold some of it from Thok Jalung in the Chang Tang, flows out of Eastern Tibet into China. But none of this gold enters Lahul. It is strange also that though Lahul is situated in Kangra as Indian tea prodcucing district, some brick tea reaches Patseo and Lahul from far off China after traversing the whole length of Tibet from east to west.

'The wool that leaves Patseo does not go straight down to the railway. The bulk of it is carried by the Lahula pony men go through Lahul and over the 13,000 foot Rohtang Pass down into Kulu. There at the town of Sultanpur, 90 miles from Patseo, it is sold either to down country purchasers from Amritsar, Dhariwal, and Hoshiarpur, or to local dealers who will distribute small quantities to common consumers in the hills. Most of this buying and selling takes place during the Kulu Dusshra fair', (Shuttleworth, 1923: 556-558). The present author remembers only a glimpse of the fair—the crowd of the people, herds of sheep and goats, a Punjab Police in uniform with half nicker—when he walked with his grandfather with the herd of sheep, starting journey in the morning and reaching at Dozam in the evening. In the evening the feet had swelled and had to come back on horse after two or three days.

Fodder: In Lahul there is abundant grazing pasture of rich nutritious grass called jam-sa and in Kullui ni-ru. The gaddis bring their sheep to fatten them in the period of about three months journey and stay. Gaddis go upto Sarchu on the other side of Baralacha. It is observed that here most of the carriages of the merchandise had to be done through sheep, even the Bashaharis who had to come from the farthest. Those with the ponies went farther to Guge.

Hugh Whistler: Whistler writes that on the right of the rest house there is a comparatively large stretch of level ground. This was the site of the main camp of the traders from Rubshu. 'The tiny tents were all pitched in a row and by each were stacked the sheep packs, forming a low wall in the centre of which the sheep were tied at night. Long ropes were pegged down to the ground, and to these the sheep were tethered by the cord and peg which are always to be seen round their necks. These little camps are set out in this fashion wherever one meets them on the road from Ladakh. Some of the packs were also stacked about the tents to keep off the wind, while bales of wool awaiting sale made a luxurious couch for the owners.

On the first camp the owners of the tents had come from Rubsho, the Tibetan province of Kashmir, and they were dressed in the long robe and greasy wool-lined cap common to Spiti, Ladakh and Western Tibet. Amongst them were a few lamas with cropped heads and dirty frocks. At one side of the Rupshu camp were a party of Kampas, the curious nomads of Tibetan origin, who wander far afield, even to the edge of the Punjab plains, earning a living in various devious ways, of which the most prominent is begging. These Kampas must have intended to stay at Patseo longer than most of the traders, for their very exiguous tents were built up with walls of stones and piles of brush-wood gathered far afield on the hills — till quite a miniature village had been formed.

On the other side of the bridge there were tents of khampas, partly wool traders. Then there was Bashahri camp, who greatly resembled Lahulas, and like them were clothed in good brown homespun, neat to look upon and serviceable to wear. They wore silver made buttons. Traders and men of substance are these Bashiris, and they had marched many long stages to barter wool and grain. There a few Ladakis. There are gaddi shepherds from Chamba.

Wool shorn are twisted into long ropes, which were then coiled and tied into bundles, to be loaded on to the sheep that had brought up grain for sale at the fair. The trade there is mainly by barter, but the Tibetans like the British silver rupee, and the Lahulas pay for a certain amount of their purchases in cash. The trade there is mainly by barter. Tibetans did not bring money. They have no need of money on the road, for they bring their own provisions for the journey, which lies almost entirely through uninhabited country.

The Lahulas bring up their grain in similar saddle bags on their own flocks, and there is usually an understanding that the Lahula shall purchase his wool and salt from the Tibetan who has bought his grain, the two accounts being set against each other and the balance paid in cash. The extensive purchases of wool almost invariably throw the balance of cash payment to be made on the Lahula, who often has to make more than one journey down from Patseo to carry away all the wool that he has brought. Some of the wool is used in Lahul in manufacture of clothes and the remainder is exported to Kulu, and much of this finds its way to the factories of Dhariwal and Agra. In addition to the wool purchased at the fair, great quantities of it are brought direct from Tibet by hundreds of Lahulas, who take their flocks up for the winter grazing and return in summer with bales of wool. When the last bale has changed hands the traders and Kampas depart, and Patseo is deserted, (Whistler, 1924: 90-91).

6. The British Arrangement — Palampur

The British government attempted to introduce Tea as a trade commodity from Indian side. They developed tea plantation in Kangra and also introduced it in Kullu. They perhaps wanted to make it a substitute for the tea which came from China. They tried to make every effort to popularize it. It is noteworthy that Egerton, the Deputy Commissioner of Kangra, when on tour to Spiti had carried samples of tea from Kangra and distributed it in Spiti and was seeking reactions of the people on the product. They intended to include it among the silk, wool, salt, etc.

The British government made incessant efforts to promote this trade. They constructed roads, bridges, rest houses and sarais on the way. They founded market-town of Palampur. As stated by Alfred Drew the town of Palampur, in the centre of Kangra tea-district, was founded by the Britishers with a special purpose of promoting the Central Asian trade and also popularising the Kangra tea towards the north. Drew further writes that a fair is held each autumn which was established to attract Yarkandi merchants from Leh by this route. In some years it has been attended by them, but partly from irregularity in the arrival of the Yarkandi caravans at Leh and partly that this road is not open late in the year the fair has not answered this purpose well as was expected by its founders, still it remains a local fair of some importance, (Drew, 1875: 536).

Track to Rudok — Tradition in Lahul

Charles A. Sherring: Sherring visited the region of Gartok in around 1905, coming from the side of Garhwal-Kumaon. Thakur Jai Chand, from Lahul, who later on was ranked as Rai Bahadur, was appointed British Agent at Gartok, to protect the interests of the traders from India. Sherring writes about the Lahulis, 'Curiously enough, all the Lahaul residents are traders. Men from Lahaul are to be found at Rudok (they utilise a route between Demchok and Hanle) and at many other places in western Nari, and their principal trade lies in wool and pashim, i.e. fine goat's hair, and they annually import about pound 35000 worth of these articles. In return, strange to say, they have practically nothing to give in the shape of goods, but pay for these imports in solid cash, and this fact accounts for the popularity and the wide circulation of Indian coinage. At present Ladakh and Lahaul take the greater part of the trade of western Nari, for there is very little trade with Simla direct. Further the only other competitors, the Bashahris, come a long way behind these two (Sherring, 1916: 310-11).

Account of Chhimed Dawa: Lahulis used to go to Ngari-Guge every year in large number. Here we give the personal account of Chhimed Dawa, of village Goram, Pattan, of about 80 years age in 2007, who was a regular visitor to Jangthang. Name of his household is Larje i.e. doctor. His father was a gelong, monk, who was educated in Tashi Lhunpo. His grandfather Tanzin was an Amchi, doctor, famous in whole valley. He had learned the profession at Zangla in Zanskar.

Chhimed Dawa, used to go to Rudok, annually, on trade trip. He narrates his story. Rudok could be reached in about fifteen days from Goram. Actually it takes more than fifteen days. They have to give rest to the animals, called chag-mal, on the way. It is more necessary when the animals are fully loaded and there are sometimes places where there is scarcity of grass and at places there are good grazing grounds. The stages from Goram were: 1. Beeling, 2. Jispa or Brog, 3. Zing Zing bar, 4. Sarchhu, 5. Demra on this side of Lacha-lung, 6. Pang, 7. Chhokak Hog-da, 8. after crossing a small hill reach Chhogating, 9. Pugaa. Here there is hot water spring. Here Sulphur and borax (ba-tsha) are extracted. Some Ladakis reside here. This is in Ladak. 10. Nyoma. 11. Dungthe. This is on the border. 12. Tshaga. 13. From here we don't go towards Chhushul. Crossing a hill reached Shinthong. 14. Then comes Rezung. There lives none. 15. Chhubling. Nobody lives here. 16. Then comes Rudok. Here there are Bazar and monasteries.

At Rudok there are four monasteries. Labrang is the largest. It is situated at a height. There were about 300, 500, and 700 lamas in each monastery. The children become lama after three-four years of age. The chief officer of the Zong, fort, was a Lama. When the Chinese came they sent all the lamas to work leaving only two-three lamas in the monastery. We used to give tax ten percent called tshu-khral (?). This trade was stopped after the Chinese aggression of 1962.

There were Kazaks, Chinese and Yarkandis who used to loot the Ladakis and Lahulis. They had their eyes more on our horses. Tsog is ten days journey from Rudok with the ponies.

Salt was extracted near Rudok. The Tibetans used to bring goods from there to Dozam. From there they took back wheat and barley. No trading was done in gold.

From Rudok they went to Ruldor. It is of two-three days journey. They used to go to the ngo-shes, a friend of acquaintance. 'We used to take with us rice, tsampa, cloth and gur (sugar). They gave us butter. We used to bring about three horse loads of butter, besides salt, wool, and pashmina'.

From here we used to go for four more days ahead to Tsog. At Tarzi tak-tak there is plenty of grass. Here we used to stay for two days. From here we went to Dorag half of which falls in Ladak. Then Trandeb, Koktse and the last stage is Yarsa. There falls snow in July also. We return by the same route. Those with the sheep used to walk day and night. They started their journey in the morning at four o'clock. Donkeys also walked with them. We used to carry some dry vegetrables. We had to eat meat continuously. At Rwang there came the traders from Nyiti (Garhwal) and Bashahar. The traders from Gahar (Lahul) used to go eight-nine days journey ahead towards Kailash.

While returning those accompanying ponies used to stay there for a month. Those with sheep used to come early. We were stuck up on the way at Sarchhu twice. Then people were called from Dartse with yak. Sometimes we were stuck up in the way for whole month. The last traders to go to Rudok from Lahul were Thabaku from Srang-me (Shansha), and Barongpa (from Kyelang).

They went in July and reached back by the end of September or by the 4-5th of October. The goods were sold at Kullu. There were many thieves there. Maddi was the chief merchant there. He sold them at Amritsar. He knew the languages as Bhoti, Gahari and Manchhad. Pashma of tso was costly. It sold at the price of four hundred rupees for a batti (two seers). Tso is not seen in the summer. They were seen in the winter. It is in colour like almond. The Tibetans killed it for meat. There were many other wild animals. Kyang (wild ass) used to come in the groups of 50s. The Chinese extinguished them. Others were dong (wild yak), nyan (like an Australian sheep), na-bo (dan) and tangrol (ibex). The skin of Dong (wild yak) is costly, it is very tough and strong.

The number of the families going from Pattan from different villages is given with the number of households going as under:

Goram -1, Yambe (Jahlma) — 3, Srangme (Shansha) — 2: (Thabaku and Dhoko), Haaling — 1, Loat -1, Wari — 2, Krozing — 1, Tholong — 6, Tandi — 4, Srumnam — 2: (Bogtapa), Gushal — 4: (Bhat, Rashpa, etc.). There was none from Mooling and Bargul, and none from Tinan valley. There were many from Gahar and sTod.

The traders in Lahul used to borrow from Kushok Nawang Dondub who possessed Da-yang (Chinese rupee coins) in a sack.

It may be summarized that of the three routes the eastern route was the shortest and the easiest. But it was used not more than by one kind of traders. The western route was not worthy for loaded ponies. It is not found to have been used as a regular route. The middle route was the most reliable since ancient times. We have some monuments on the grand route in the form of rock carvings of Bodhisattvas belonging to the Indian Buddhism which go back at least one thousand years back.

16

Revenue System of Lahul and the Socio-economic Classes in sTod

Before the takeover of Lahul in 1846 by the British, it was ruled by Kullu except for a brief period by the Sikhs. It was ruled in two manners. The whole of Pattan valley, excluding Chamba Lahul, was directly under the Raja of Kullu, who had appointed an officer with supporting staff, in Lahul. During the time of Moorcroft in 1820 their office was located at Tandi. The valleys of Bhaga and Chandra were ruled by the Thakurs and they paid nazarana to the Raja. Whole of Tinan valley was ruled by the Thakurs of Gundhla. The upper part of Bhaga, sTod valley, was ruled by the Thakurs of Khangsar known generally as the Thakurs of Kolong. The lower part of Bhaga valley known to the sTodpas as Punan, and to the others as Gahar, was ruled by the Thakurs of Gumrang. Whole of Lahul was divided into 14 divisions known as kothi. Those directly under the Raja of Kullu were known as khalsa kothis and those under the Thakurs as jagir kothis. The arrangement of the Raja with the Thakurs of Gundhla for procurement of rent was different from those with the other two Thakurs.

In 1865-72 regular settlement of revenue of the Khalsa kothis was done under James B. Lyall, Settlement Officer, district Kangra. The three Thakurs, perhaps under the guidance of the Settlement Officer, conducted settlements in their areas in their traditional manner. These documents give some good information about the older past. The document from Gundhla is sketchy and is not of much help for us in the present context. The settlement of Khangsar (Kolong) was done by a trained person in the profession. The document is written in two languages: Bhoti and Urdu. The entries are given for each individual whether tax payer or not in seven columns sub-divided into thirteen. The primary data is the same in both the documents but the two differ in the description of individual entries in the last column of 'remarks'. About Gumrang Lyall (1874: para 137) discusses the system as it prevailed there in detail. Below we reproduce a summary of the report by Lyall about Lahul and Gumrang kothi.

Lyall writes that under the Rajas the Thakurs who were allowed to exist were supreme in their own estates, but paid a heavy annual tribute or nazarana for them in the shape of a certain number of ponies, piece of cloth, etc.

Revenue in Khalsa Kothis: In royal kothis the Raja took the place of the extinct Thakurs, and managed them through an official with the rank of a wazir. The Thakurs, with a following of their tenants, and one man for each holding to the royal kothis, were, I believe, compelled to attend the Raja at his capital Sultanpur for the six winter months of the year, and do any service, menial or military, which might be committed to them. This was the origin of the present annual emigration of a very large part of the Lahaul population to their winter quarters in Akhara, a suburb of Sultanpur.

Lyall further writes, when the Sikhs ousted the Raja of Kulu, they collected the cash and grain from the khalsa kothis, and nazarnas from the Thakurs as before, but on the pretence that they did not demand any service of either Thakur or landholder, they imposed an additional cess, under the name of betangna, of rupees six per jeola on every holding, whether in the Khalsa or the jagir kothis.

The nature of the holdings in Gundhla (Tinan): About the territory of Gundhla it is said that half was described in former Settlement papers as resumed. One of the last Rajas of Kulu did in fact resume half, but practically the whole remained undividedly in possession of the Thakur who accounted to the Raja for half his collections of all kinds. After Regular Settlement he continued in the same way to exact the old dues and services from all the landholders, and to pay the Government the land revenue for half the kothi, plus nazarana on account of the other half. The whole of his payment may be considered to have been of the nature of nazarana, (Lyall, 1872: 109. 136).

Gungrang and Khangsar (Kolong) : The whole produce of certain fields is taken by the Thakur. This land is cultivated by farm servants, assisted on certain occasions by gatherings of the regular landholders, it is known as the Thakur's garhpan or home farm, and as a general rule, the greater part of it is situated in villages near which he lives. Other fields are held rent free as maintenance by his dotoes i.e. by the dunnewassals, or junior branches of his family, or rent free in lieu of continuous service by his chagshis, or family retainers, or by his kangchunpa or farm servants.

The great bulk of fields, however, form the jeolas or holdings of the yulfa or villagers, which are held subject to payments of thal i.e. rent or revenue, the performance when required of begaar or forced labour for the State, and of certain periodical services to the Thakur. An average jeola contains about 15 lakh, or 5 acres. A dotoen's holding is on an average equal in extent to from one to two jeolas, a chakasi's holding varies between a half and a whole jeola, a kangchumpa generally holds only about a quarter jeola, or less. There are some other small miscellaneous rent free holdings, the revenue of which must I think, be considered to have been remitted, not in lieu of service to the Thakur, but for the good of the whole community. For example garzhing, Lhazhing and gonzhing (land of smith, folk deity and monastery).

The garphan land, no doubt belongs solely to the Thakur, who is also, I consider landlord or superior of the whole kothi. The yulfa or villagers hold to be the subordinate proprietors of their holdings, so are the dotoens. At first I was inclined to think that the chaksis and kangchumpas were mere tenants in the garpan or private lands of the Thakurs, but on further enquiry their title did not seem to be essentially weaker than that of any other class. They are never evicted, and the custom with regard to inheritance and power of mortgage, with regard to their holdings and landholders appears to be precisely the same. I consider them therefore to be also subordinate proprietors of their holdings, differing only from the yulfas in as much as they pay no rent, and do private service only to the Thakur, whereas the latter pay rent, and do public service for the State, begaar, as well as occasional private service to the Thakur.

The best way to describe the nature of the rents and services rendered to the Thakurs by the subordinate landholders will be to give a detail of them as they exist in one jagir. We may note here that in the matter the whole description about Gumrang applies to sTod also. Lyall continues, for example Kothi Gumrang contains 58 jeolas or retainers, and eight of kangchumpas or farm servants.

The following is list of the periodical services rendered to the Thakur by the farming class according to the custom existing in Gumrang.

On certain days known as besti days, each jeola has to furnish one man to work on the Thakur's garhpan land. The Thakur supplies food and drink, but no pay. There are eleven besti days in the year, but two, the sowing and the mowing days, are distinguished as the big bestis, on them a man for each jeola attends, on the other nine only some 15 or 10 men who live handy actually attend, the others remain at home, and pay the Thakur annually in lieu of attendance, the sum of one rupee under the name of besti money.

Each jeola is bound to stable and feed for the six months of the winter one of the Thakur's horses, one horse to a jeola is allowed to be the old standard, but as the Thakur has not so many horses, it has been customary for two jeolas to divide between them the care and charge of one horse.

Each jeola is bound to convey once in the year eight or nine path, or about sixteen pounds of rice (a light goat or sheep load) from the Kulu valley to the Thakur's house in Lahul.

It is the custom in all kothis of Lahul for the regular landholders each year to provide in turn a certain number of men to undertake the duty of supplying the common quarters of the kothi at Akhara, in Kulu, with fuel. For the six winter months spent in Kulu, these men are steadily employed in bringing in fuel for general use and they are in some degree remunerated by being paid rupees six each, which sum is raised by a rate on all the jeolas of the kothi. In Ghumrang, each year four jeolas furnish four men for this duty, and they are also bound to carry loads for the Thakur in going to and from his house to Akhara, and to furnish him, as well as the subordinate landholders, with fuel while he remains there.

There are no dotoen or cadet families in the Ghumrang jagir. In other jagirs the dotoen are said after a time, when the sense of relationship to the Thakur has become faint, to be degraded into chaksis, and forced to do service for their holdings. A chaksi holding is held rent free in lieu of the following services: It is bound to furnish one man for continuous attendance on the Thakur, and for the performance of light work, such as cooking his food when on the march, leading his horse, etc. As however, there are many chaksi holdings in Ghumrang, the custom now is that three holdings at a time furnish one man each for ten days, and then recall their men till their turn comes again. But for the privilege of not supplying one man continuously, they pay the Thakurs eight annas per month per holding, or six rupees per annum.

A few of the chaksis are distinguished by the term of lalok or pass crossers. These instead of having to furnish a man for personal attendance, are only bound to furnish a man to cross a pass, either to Ladakh, Zanskar or Kulu on the Thakur's business. If they cross a pass once in the year, the rest of it is their own, and they have no payment to make, but if not called upon to cross a pass, they pay rupees seven per annum as relief or betangna. Some chaksis of all kinds now pay rupees seven regularly in lieu of all service by agreement with the Thakur.

All chaksi holdings send a man to work on the two big besti days, not on the other days.

Kangchumpa may be translated as cottager. The family in possession of a holding of this kind is bound to furnish one man for continuous work, at the Thakur's house or on his garhpan land. Some holdings of this kind will be found near wherever the Thakur has garhpan. When there is much work, the head of the family attends in person, otherwise he sends his wife, or son, or daughter. the person who is in attendance gets food five times a day, and does field work of every kind, or cuts and brings in wood or grass, sweeps the house, or combs wool, etc. Those who live at a distance from the Thakur's house cannot practically attend, they therefore, do only field, work on the garpan land near them, but as they in this way get off lighter than the others they are bound to feed and keep one sheep for the Thakur during the winter months. Some kang chumpas now pay five rupees per anuum to the Thakur in lieu of all service.

The Thakur takes the chatru or colts from landholders of every class. The custom is that when a mare foals, and her master sees that he is not the lucky owner of a filly, he at once takes both mare and colt to the Thakurs house. There he is presented with a new cap as a mark or favour, and leaves his mare to be kept for six months at the Thakurs expense. The nature of the holdings, and of the rents and services paid to the Thakurs, are the same in all the jagirs, there are differences in detail, but they do not require to be mentioned in this report.

The big monastery of Guru Ghantal, with its chapels of ease at Koksar and Sansa holds a good deal of land in different kothis rent free as endowment. More than half is held of the Gonpa by kang chumpa tenants, who by way of rent only present annually some shoulders of mutton, pots of whisky, and plaited sandals, but are bound to perform certain fixed services, such as the cultivation of the rest of the monastery land, the sweeping of snow off the roof of the monastery in winter, the bringing in to many fagots for winter fuel, etc.

The above descriptions by Lyall about Gumrang Kothi applies generally to sTod also. In sTod the society although very small was varied and much complex. Below we have a glimpse of the socio-economic classes in the sTodpa society existing at the time.

The Social and Taxpaying Classes: Here we attempt to present an analysis of the society of sTod as it existed in the nineteenth century CE. The information is based on an local document, the settlement report of 1868 conducted by the Thakurs of Khangsar. The Urdu document is dated May 5, 1864, although in the title it is given as 1868, from which it may be presumed that the work of compilation had been completed earlier than 1868. There also might have been some traditional system of preparation of the record of the revenue receipt as is known from Lyall.

The record of the settlement of Kothi Kolong has 75 entries which includes both the tax payers and those exempted. Out of the 75 entries 72 constitute those of the living households and the remaining three are institutions where there live no regular population. Now in the 72 households presuming on an average each household having residents of five members counts nearly to 360 persons. In the census of 1981 also the average population per household was five. This tiny society was highly classified and diversified. For the present we look from the view of payment of land revenue.

Here are given the name of each class, which have been explained in detail separately below, and the number of households contained in each: i. The Thakur who was called Garhpan -1; ii. Doethi — 3; iii. Chhagshikpa — 6; iv. Thalpa (Ṭhalpa) — 37; v. Nautaur or khru-chag — 9; vi. Khangchungpa — 15; vii. The monasteries Zong gonpa of Tinno, and Gemur gonpa — 2; viii. The lha-zhing, land of the folk deity, in Kyelad-1; ix. The garzhing, land of the gara, artisan - 1. Thus in all there are 75 entries.

The non-resident institutions are: Two monasteries and the lha-zhing, in Kyelad. The rest are all residential households.

We now classify into the two categories of: i. Those exempted, and ii. The tax payers.

The classes who are exempt from the rent are: (i) The Thakur who was called Garhpan -1. Chhagshikpa - 6. Khangchungpa - 15. (ii) Two monasteries Zong gonpa of Tinno, and Gemur gonpa - 2. (iii) The lha-zhing, land of the folk deity, in Kyelad -1. (iv) The garzhing, land of the gara, artisan - 1. Thus out of 75 entities 26 did not make payment in the form of regular rent. The old monastery of Chhukutsi is not found mentioned here.

The classes paying rent on the land are: (i) Doethi — 3. (ii) Thalpa — 37. (iii) Nautaur or khru-chag — 9. Thus 49 households are liable to pay the regular rent.

It is observed from the report that about fifty percent of the landholders were evicted partially or wholly. The estates were taken over by the jagirdar himself, or given to some close relative or to a third person certainly not without substantial compensation to the Gharpan. This may be due to inability of the cultivators to pay the exorbitant rent. The rate of levy constituted 50 percent of the produce and it went up to the higher authority in the same ratio.

There were the additional burden of begaar and besti. There must have been other occasional levies. Watermill was taxed additionally at the flat rate of rupees two per annum. The tax was levied in the form of cash, grain, ghee (butter) and blanket. Below we attempt to explain some of the important terms:

Gharpan: During the settlement in 1868 Thakur Tara Chand was the officiating Thakur. He is designated as Jagirdar and as Gharpan. Here for some of the terms we follow the spellings of the Urdu document. In Lahul the Thakur families, the ruling chiefs, of Tinan, Barbog, Gumrang and Khangsar call themselves as gharpan which we discussed in detail.

Garzhing: Garzhing (mgar-ra zhing = smith land) land of the gara, artisan. Of this class the family who owned the land was resident in Kyelang. He had a patch of land given to him ostensibly in lieu of his services of smith. In 1868 after the settlement he left the land and this was transferred to a family of the same class who was resident at Srangbar in Khangsar and it is stated he was providing the requisite services. The artisan was paid some fixed amount of grain by all the inhabitants at the end of the crop season. At the time of taking service from him coal was provided by the beneficiary, some people stayed for hammering, and some for blowing air. Some brought drink and eatables. They had to be compensated in some other ways also. They also played drums on all festive occasions and did work also on silver and gold.

Ṭīkā: The term means the designated and the heir apparent of the chief. This has been given in the description once in a document from Khangsar. Otherwise practically this term is not found in use in Lahul.

Dothi: This term is found written in several ways: dothi (doṭhī), dothai, doṭhaiṅ, and doethi. This term is found used in the narratives of the families of Thakurs of Lahul. Lyall writes that 'the dotoen are said after a time, when the sense of relationship to the Thakur has become faint, to be degraded into chaksis, and forced to do service for their holdings.' Lama Jangchub, who died in around 1990 at the age of around 90, informs similarly do-thi as a family having separated from Khangsar Khar, Thakurs of Khangsar. Further the families separated from do-thi are called chhak-shi. This term is found used in an old song from the area of Shimla as dothain. Tika Ram Joshi explains the term as the brothers of Tika, (Joshi Tika Ram, 1911: 150. 154).

In sTod, according to the document, there are three households of Dothi. They paid rent fully. All of them belong to Jo or Thakur class.

Dothi could relieve themselves of the services to the Thakur by making cash payment. One of the dothi paid rupees 28 which constituted rupees 21 and six annas in lieu of dothi service; rupees 6 and 8 annas as rent and rupee one as rent for watermill.

Chhagshigpa: Chhagshi, chhagshig or chhagshipa as explained above is known to be a degraded dothi. There are six households belonging to the category of Chhagshig. They are of mixed class. Three of them belong to the Thakur clan and three of them are termed as Kanait. They were not liable to pay tax. They did the service of Chhashik in the house of the Thakur. In a year one of the chhagshig paid in lieu of chhagshik service rupees nine cash.

This term is found in Ladak in two forms and Gergan explains as: byag-shi = chaprasi (p. 606) and phyag-shi = Tehsil jamadar (p. 611). These terms are not traditional of social applications.

In social terms the two classes of Dothi and Chhagshi appear to be a separate and slightly higher ranking class placed between the Gharpanh and the Thalpa. In Kullu the related terms are Mahant and Miyan.

Nautaur or khru-chag: Nautor (Nau-toṛ = new-break land), a newly broken land, is a word of Hindi/Pahari language and its equivalent is khru-chag, also khrub-chag, a local word. Here chag means breaking but the first part cannot be understood. There are nine households having wholly new land and they mostly lived around Dartse. But many others have small pieces of this kind of land. All kinds of holders, other than the Gharpan, of the land of the kind were liable to pay rent over the land to the Jagirdar. Khrub-chagpa, an economic class, was growth of a particular historical period. The class disappeared during the British period perhaps on the receipt of regular right over the land.

Khangchungpa: Khangchung or Khangchhung literally means small house and khangchungpa in social connotation means a small householder and also a class of such members. Lyall translates it as cottager. Here Khangchungpa has a different connotation. Here he has no land of his own or of his family. The land which he tills is owned by the Jagirdar. He did not pay rent for the land that he tilled but gave fixed services of khangchungpa on the lands of the Gharpan. He is tenant of the Jagirdar. The jagirdar can evict the landholder khangchungpa in case of nonfulfilment of certain conditions of contract. There were 15 households in this class. According to lama Jangchub one person from a house worked in the house of Khar from the day of Birshu (Kullui), i.e. around 13th April (Vaisakhi), till khu'i korche, the task of thrashing was over. This was the system in Kolong and Gumrang. We cannot explain how the class of khangchungpa under the economic system came to be in creation. It was a purely economic class different from social class of the same name.

Lalok (la-log = return from pass): It was a kind of service. Lyall writes that a few of the chaksis are distinguished by the term of lalok or pass crossers. These instead of having to furnish a man for personal attendance, are only bound to furnish a man to cross a pass, either to Ladakh, Jangthang, Zanskar or Kulu on the Thakur's business. They went with the flock of sheep or with the ponies owned by the Thakur. If they cross a pass once in the year, the rest of it is their own, and they have no payment to make.

Thalpa: Thalpa (khral = tax) means a tax payer. This formed the large middle class of landholders who constituted 37 households in number and have been termed as kanait. There were also two more categories of thalpa.

Besti: Besti, a term of unknown source, means a day of work in the fields of the Thakur. Perhaps this relates to the thalpas. This service was in addition to the usual rent. There were such ten bestis in a year in Gumrang. There were two big bestis, besti chhed-mo, the days of ploughing and harvesting on which attendance was essential. In others some households absented by paying the fixed amount.

Betangna: This was a levy charged in lieu of begaar.

Wazir and Hakim: During the time of Kullu Raj the charge to look after the affairs of Lahul was given to one of the Wazirs stationed at Sultanpur. There was no exclusive Wazir looking after the affairs of the areas of Khalsa kothis. An official was appointed to look after the affairs of whole Lahul who was stationed in Lahul. During Moorcroft's visit in 1820 the officer was designated as Hakim and his office was situated at Tandi. In a tradition Sadho from village Goram in Pattan, Lahul, was a Hakim.

Negi: During the British period administrative incharge of whole of Lahul was designated as Negi. This designation was assigned by Barnes, the Settlement Officer, district Kangra, in his first regular settlement of the district conducted in 1851. Baliram was the first Negi appointed on the takeover by the British. He belonged to the family named Hakim in village Goram. Harcourt writes that his office was at Tandi. Lyall writes that the first Negi was a Brahmin of Pattan.

Thakur Tara Chand of Khangsar was appointed Negi of Lahul on September 17, 1852. In around 1860 the British government directed the Negi of Lahul to discontinue a certain tribute which the Lahulis had been in the custom of paying through him to the representative of the Maharaja of Jammu in Ladak.

Lambardar: Barnes appointed Lambardars who headed a kothi.

17

Pungyin : A Brahminic Tradition of Ancestor Worship in Lahul

In Lahul there was a custom of celebrating the ceremony of worship of the ancestors called Pung-yin (puṅ-īṅ) among the class named Songla (soṅlā) which includes a sub-section called Bhatt (Bhaṭṭ). Pung-yin is a modified form of Sanskrit word punya (= virtue). Both the classes belong to Brahmin class. The former has a larger population and is a farming community. The latter functions as priests to the whole society in Pattan. Both the classes are included under the heading Songla. The term Songla remains obscure. They are settled in the Pattan valley, more thickly as we move down towards Pangi. They tell that they came from Kishtwar during the time of the oppressive periods of Aurangzeb. Some others tell to have come from Bharmour and some tell from Bhir Bhangal. While it may be that some of them came in groups many others came in trickles. They are a well settled class and own lands in prominent places of settlements and some villages are wholly inhabited by their class.

The Bhatt priests perform the rites according to the Brahminic custom but they don't read recitations from the scriptures. They have the requisite literature in translation in Pahari language.

Pungyin is not a regular festival. It was performed with one's own will or on the advice of the pandita, i.e. a priest, specially when there is some kind of trouble in a family. Some also say that it is a display of prosperity of the household. It involves a large amount of expenditure. Therefore the household has to make preparations for the ceremony several years in advance. This brings prestige to the family. In Sindhwari one household is named as Pungyin only because they performed this celebration in their house. At this time three physical structures were raised: Marh (Maṛh), Drawings of Pitra (mūrat) and Dhaj (dhāj).

Marh: A sacred house, called marh, is constructed. It is a structure of one room, of single storey, with three walls of stone and mud. The front side is left open without any wall like a shop. It is about 10'x10'x8'(height) having flat roof. In the middle of the inner wall there is a niche of about five inches deep and about more than a feet in height to accommodate the slabs on which the figures of Pitra (ancestors) are engraved. The length may be kept according to the individual requirement. In the centre of the room a pillar is raised which is carved. On the edges of the two walls inwards on each side there are placed a wooden plank carved with a large flower (Plate 24).

It is told that rarely there could be a marh of two storeys and there is reported no such marh existing or in knowledge of anybody. The upper storey, if constructed, is done on the occasion of new celebration. It is told that raising the second storey is much costly. These structures exist in the villages of Thabak, Yang Keerting, Shansha, Nalda, Triloknath, Tindi, Sumnam, Goram, Ruding, Baring, Sidhwadi, Yambe, Dhwansha, etc. There is no rule as to which direction the front of the marh should face. Generally it is observed that its front faces towards the opposite side of the valley as all the houses of the village face.

Marh is a Sanskrit term which means temple. In the lower areas of Himachal like Kangra, Bilaspur, etc. this term is applied for small shrines and are called Marhi, small temple, which are about 6x6x6' dedicated to a deity. In Kullu marh designates a structure near a temple where the retinue accompanying a guest deity rest in the night. In Lahul this term is used only for this particular purpose.

Pitra: Marh, a private temple, is constructed to enshrine the slab containg the drawings of the pitra, ancestors, of the household. On a flat stone slab of about one and half feet broad and of the desired length are carved the drawings of the ancestors. This is placed in the niche of the shrine. The number of figures represent the number of the members of ancestors for whom the ceremony is performed. In every celebration a new marh is constructed. Then on the day of Phagli, New year day and other auspicious days they are reverened. Ghee is pasted and ṭoṭu, a conical effigy made of sattu (barley flour), is offered. The marh is kept generally empty. But at some places they are now used as store for wood, hay etc. At some places such slabs were found where there was no marh, although they are kept in a safe place.

The artist first writes the names of all the pitras as dictated by the head of the household. He carves the figures for each member and covers it with a cloth. At home this slab is raised after offerings are made. A person raises the cloth taking name of the ancestors one by one. It does not include the name of his father. The writing might have been done for the fulfilment of the ceremonial requirement and was a temporary action. We find no inscription or record anywhere.

At all the places the figures carved on the stone slabs are similar, of the same size and shape, even in age. They generally appear like female figures wearing ghaghra, long frock, having number of folds. But all are aware that all these figures are only of males. The head appears bare, hairs are short and there appears nothing to cover the head. They wear a well tailored waist cloth like a woman's ghaghra hanging below the waist and reaching the ankles. The dress, however, appears undoubtedly hilly. Unlike these, the figures in carvings belonging to the family of the Thakurs of Triloknath give variety and better look. Here the figures are drawn both of male and female. Both wear different kinds of headgears and are clearly distinguishable. A male figure appears after three or four female figures. They all wear headgears. The headgears of women resemble with the samples from wider areas and the tradition appears slightly older than those found at other places here. The figures are more artistic. They perhaps exhibit royal tradition. But it is difficult to say if the carvings on the stone slabs, only two pieces from two different samples, really belong to this kind of celebration. There is total break up from the knowledge of the tradition and the past. Things are lying in total neglect.

Dhaj: Dhāj, Sanskrit dhvaja (banner, emblem), is a pillar of stone about five to nine feet long and about a foot or more in girth. One dhaj is raised in one ceremony. It is kept leaning against the wall outside the marh. Such pillars are seen generally one in one marh but at places there were around four-five placed in a cluster at one place. May be that they belong to some similar earlier performances. It is told that relatives bring them. It is told that at the time of ceremony the members of the household dance in circle around it. Although such pillars are found raised in sacred grounds or near the temples in Kullu, Kinnaur, Pangi and in Lahul, as above, its symbolic meaning could not be known from anywhere. These stone pillars are not revered afterwards. Such pillars have not been seen revered anywhere else.

Swahat: The whole ceremony is conducted by a person of traditionally experienced family. He is designated as Swahat (Swāhat). He is a Brahmin. There was a family whose members performed this ceremony. They resided in the village named Deldā, near Jundā, and were also known as deldadu (deldāṛu).

Invitation: The general statement of the informers is that whole of Lahul was invited in the ceremony. According to one informant persons from four-five panchayats were called. But actually the people from Mooling to Madgran comprising the Chandrabhaga valley were invited.

Feast: Almost all the informants tell in a rounded figure that about one hundred sheep and one hundred tin of ghee are spent in such a ceremony. This being a kind of item, the volume of the other materials like wheat flour, sattu, etc., can be estimated easily. In this ceremony no drink is served. In the meal roti, cakes, mārchu (cakes fried in oil) are served. Meat is also served. Tainta and the Rudingba were the last households who performed this ceremony. In the last all the people sing and dance. A drink of ghee was given to all symbolizing end of the ceremony.

The Household of Rudingba of village Ruding: The house of Rudingba (Rūṛīṅbā) in the village of Ruding celebrated Pung-yin last in 1940. The family tells that their ancestors came from Bhid Bhangal. They worked as cook at some Jagirdar. The name of the village was founded on the name of their house. It has three marhs standing and appears to have a long tradition. The house must have been prosperous for long period. Of the three marhs two face towards the other side of the river Chandrabhaga flowing here from east to west in the front of the village in the middle of the valley. The third faces opposite to the two.

Marh number one is situated nearest to the residential house. It faces, south, the other side of the valley. Its dimension is 13x12 feet and the height is about eight feet. The breadth of the wall is two feet. These structures are built by the laymen of the village and not by the professional carpenters and masons. Here these were built by three villagers of Mayling, Ruding and Telingba. They were given only food and drink. Repair, if any required, is also done like this. In every festival flowers, ghee and dhoop are offered to the pitras. They tell that when a marh is built more than one storey high the cost exceeds much. Its roof has to be kept sloping.

Stone Carvings: It is told that in the old tradition one slab was placed in a marh carved with one figure of the Pittra for whom the present ceremony is being celebrated. No marh containing a slab with only one figure could be found. But the existing slabs contain figures even of the persons for whom no separate celebrations were conducted. They say that about seven or eight Pungying have been held in their family. The carvers worked near the stone mine near the village. They worked in such a way that people could not see them. A man was kept to keep watch and keep the strangers away from coming near them.

Dhaj: One dhaj is raised in one pungying. The dhaj were brought by the bhaghiyad (bhagiyāṛ), the kinsmen, the collaterals of the family. If there was no bhaghiyad then one has to be made. This was called Sro-baghiyad (earthen god-brother). Then they brought the stone pillars. This family made two bhagiyads and each of them brought one dhaj each. The tradition in this regard as told in the household of Tainta, as shown below, is different. There are two long stone pillars measuring about eight feet above the ground leaning with the wall of the first marh outside. They are the longest I could see anywhere. There is a carved wooden pillar in the centre of the marh at equal distance from all the walls. Under it is kept a kumbh, pitcher, in which are kept eight kinds of precious materials. Two carved wooden planks are brought by the carpenter who has relation with the family. Lohars also brought something. Every body came with something.

The family presently is in possession of three Marhs. In the second marh, which is comparatively small, there is one slab with a carving of one figure. The niche is one square feet with the depth of about four inches. The height of the image inside is about nine inches. In this marh there is no dhaj, central pillar or the the carved planks on the walls in the sides. It is told that one of the living ancestors insisted that a celebration should be conducted for him also. This was not a regular but an odd celebration.

The third marh is located at about twenty meters away from the house which faces south like the first. There are in it two slabs with the number of carvings of three and eight on each.

In the three marhs there are eight slabs with total of thirty nine figures. From the eight slabs we can merely presume that eight celebrations were performed which agrees with their own statement.

Here it may be presumed that the marhs accommodate additional slabs belonging to the former marhs which were demolished. In the marh of the house of Tainta in Shansha there is one long slab with nearly twenty figures as the owners tell that in their celebration, performance was given for more than twenty of their ancestors.

The house owns two lists of ancestors. It is told that Chahnu, 13th in one of the lists, started first celebrating Pungyin. The last was performed by Chhape Ram and Nyima Ram (brothers), 21st in serial number in 1940. Seven or nine Puingying were celebrated in this family. Thakur Fatehchand of Gundhla was invited in the last ceremony. The people from the other valleys were not called because of the conflict existing between the spirits of the lamas and the goors.

It is told that a marh could be constructed of two storeys. But then the second storey should be having slanting roof. But this enhances the cost of construction substially. About the cost of construction of a marh of bouble storey the other informants also hold the same opinion. But nobody is able to explain why. This may be explained in the manner that in Lahul wood is used for laying the slanting roofs. But wood is an extremely scarce commodity here. Therefore it naturally increases the cost of construction. No marh of two storeys was seen and is not known to exist anywhere.

From the history of celebration of the ceremony in the household of Rudingba we may attempt to deduce some general rules that was followed in the tradition generally. It has already been stated as above that in a ceremony there was created only one slab on which were carved the figures of all the ancestors for whom the celebration was performed in one ceremony. The earliest tradition was that in a marh there was kept only one slab having one figure of the person for whom the ceremony was performed. We have not been able to find such an evidence. Later on the tradition became liberal and changed to include the figures of other ancestors of the family. Only one dhaj is raised in one pungyin but there can be more than one.

Another tradition is followed by the Chinals. They after the death of a person raise a small resting place called chog on the road side for resting for the travelers. On the back towards the slope they raise a stone slab in the memory of the dead person.

Triloknath: The Thakur or Rana family of Triloknath used to perform this kind of ceremony. It is told that after the death of each Rana a Punyin was held. Each time a figure was added in the line of the carvings of the ancestors on a slab which is kept in the marh (Plate 25). They invited the whole Lahul and also Gepang. The celebration was performed for the expansion of the lineage. Singh Ram, father of Surinder, one of the present generation, made the last pungyin. These informations call for verification. There were about twenty dhajs all lying uncared. Even the last marh, over the roof on which the Thakur used to sit with his retinue to watch the annual fair of Pori in the large ground before it, which the people still remember, is in shambles.

The family also used to follow the custom of Sati. There are carved sati stones placed at the cremation ground with figures in pairs of a male and a female (Plate 26). The figures are similar in all the samples. The declining workmanship in the figures displays comparative age of each work with the advancement of time. These models are much different from those seen in Kullu and Mandi.

The household of Tainta - the Last Pungyin

The last such ceremony of Pungyin in Lahul was performed in 1944 in the household named Tainta (Ṭainṭā) in village Shansha. Dola Ram is member of the family who had witnessed the performance fully. He was 91 and half years of age in the middle of 2017. Before this, similar rite was performed in 1940 in the house of Rudingba of the village Ruding. Master Budh Ram is member of this household witnessing this ceremony. But he tells that he was too young at the time to understand. Therefore he does not remember anything of the event. Below is given the account as narrated by Dola Ram as was performed in his household. They belong to the Songla community.

Pungyin is performed for the pitras, ancestors. Ancestors are worshipped in it. Pandits tell that the cause of any big trouble in the household is due to a curse of the ancestors. Then preparations are made for Pungyin. The family has to be economically very sound because in this performance the expenditure is very heavy.

On the auspicious day of Shektsum, in the month of July, the villagers were called. A list of the ancestors is prepared. Ghyāt, the owner of the household, tells the names of the ancestors. The carver writes all the names. The list includes the names of the brothers in the same generation. In Lote there was a person named Gopi. He wrote the names. In their family the number of the ancestors was more than twenty. Then they go near the mine of stone. Then the mason carves figures in the name of each ancestor named here. On the completion of the task an effigy of sattu is prepared and offered. Then the murat (mūrat= statue, the carved stone slab) is brought home wrapped in a white cloth and is kept at home.

The villagers start constructing marh from the beginning of the summer, in the Spring. A new marh is prepared in every pungyin. The old marh, if there is any, is dismantled. If there is space then the old one is not touched. One marh is constructed with the wood from one tree of pine. Carvings are done on the pillars of wood but it has no religious significance. This marh is about 10 to 12 feet long and breadth of the same size. Its dimension and the direction of the face is not fixed. It is constructed according to the space available. It is only of one storey and not above it.

In the Autumn, Dhaj is prepared. This is also prepared by the villagers. One sheep is given for it. One dhaj is prepared for one Pungyin.

Then a Sehṇu, chief, is appointed who is called Swāhat. He was hereditary and belonged to village Deldā ahead of Jahlma. There was a family in the village who only did the job. He was also called Deldadu. He explained all the works to be done and he also gave the estimate of the expenditure likely to be incurred in the performance.

This ceremony is performed in the month of Kyurlha, the month of October-November, as soon as the work of thrashing was finished. The people from Mooling to Madgran were invited, i. e. the whole of Pattan valley. All the musicians, who constitute the drummers and flute players, are invited. All the goors, priests, who numbered about 13-15 were also called. All the Pandits, bhatts, have to be called. They come about a week before. They sit inside and keep worshipping. Their meal is cooked separately.

People come from different villages or groups of villages in groups with musicians. The group is called gujung (gujūṅ). They all reach a day before the day of ceremony. The gujung of Jahlma and Yobrang come on the day of ceremony. They are considered more powerful.

Ghyat, now in the role of shirdār, by holding a drāt, long sickle, in the hand and resting it over the shoulder, receives every gujung. The goors come in spirit. One sheep is given to every gujung (called bhagat or wārnā). It is taken as a sacred distribution. The group is taken in the room and they are given meal. They are then given a place to sit in the vacant fields. They light fire and sit around it. It is called jagra (jāgrā), sitting awake. Then there arrives the next group.

People come empty handed. They don't bring anything. But the kinsmen have a bartan, have custom of exchange of presents, they bring sheep, etc.

Dhaj is raised on the day before the pungyin. At this time roti, cake, is distributed with honey, as prashad, sacred share. On the day of pungyin there is puja, prayer, in the morning. The musicians sit at the door outside. The chief chahan of the household sits there. In the room a big mashal, fire torch, is prepared. All the goors come out. The goor of the household moves first throwing fistfuls of sattu on the fire torch held in his hand. All the members of the household come in the best of their clothes and wearing ornaments and holding each other's hand. In the front go the musicians. They are followed by the goors and then the members of the household and lastly move the other people. Three kumbh, pitchers, are taken as dharni, the sacred inner holding. In it are placed 14 kinds of ratna, jewels. It is buried under the ground about four or five feet deep. One of them is buried somewhere in the marh. The second kumbh is buried at home in the ground floor where the sheep are kept. The third is buried in the field where thrashing ground is prepared every year. Here the members of the household holding hand in hand of each other take three rounds of the pud, the pole round which the cattle engaged in thrashing are tied, clockwise. They sing a song which is called Lalā. This song was known to a person from Kwang which is situated near the village of Delda. He was old in 1944 itself. After that no pungyin was held and the song is known to none.

Thereafter the murat, the carved stone slab, is established in the marh. This was kept wrapped in white cloth. The work is done by a Brahmin. After that starts the feast of the ceremony.

One lamza, a big vessel of capacity of more than 100 litres of copper or brass is kept over the fire in which butter is kept for melting. Here sits the goor of Bhagwati (Mrikula devi) of Udaipur. In this ceremony more than 100 tins (each of about 16 litres) were consumed. About 120 sheep, one khari, about four quintal, sattu and wheat flour more than this were cnsumed. The household owned four boxes of wood. A staircase was used to climb up to reach their mouth. Wheat flour was kept in them. At that time the DC (Asstt. Commissioner, Kullu) helped for bringing wheat from Amritsar. Then cakes are prepared. It is called podh (poṛh) which is thick and in size equal to about three or four roties. Every person was given seven podh, one thumbu (ladle), about 250 grams, of ghee, and a piece of meat of about the same weight.

The ceremony was attended by about five thousand persons. There come children and women. Podh is given to everybody. They can take it home. During their stay here meals are served separately. People remain here on the day of ceremony. Gujun go on the next day. Each goor is given one tin of ghee. Then they are given marchu, and clothes, and they are dropped at their home. Whenever there is any festival in the village the images are worshipped. They are smeared with tshung-mar, a pinch of ghee, and offered marpindi, a ball of sattu with ghee.

Ranah

Corresponding to the ceremony of Pungyin there is the ceremony of dGe-ba in the tradition of Buddhism which is also translated in the same way as pun-ya, virtue. This may not be as much extravagant and large in scale as pungyin. dGe-ba is also not a regular ceremony but is optional and if held it is in addition to the regular death ceremony. dGe-ba may be performed after a year or so of death of a person and may last for two-three days. It was performed by some prosperous families. The ceremony concerns only the immediately deceased and not the ancestors.

In the tradition of Buddhists the common customary funeral ceremony is named as bdun-tshig, a ceremony performed after seven weeks (knots or steps). A week may be called tshig and step wise as gchig-tshig, gnyis-tshig,.... bdun-tshig; one knot, ...seventh knot. Normally other tshigs are skipped and the funeral ceremony is performed on the seventh seventh-day, i.e. on 49th day. In some cases it may be performed at smaller scale on every seventh day and the final on a larger scale on 49th day. In certain cases the bzhi-tshig, the fourth week also may be performed at a medium scale. All sevenths including the seventh-seventh are called bdun-tshig. The last one is performed at home but some of the others may be performed in the monastery. On the last ceremony certain rites are performed by the ro-bdag, one of the persons who serves during the disposal of the corpse and attends till the last.

It appears that this tradition of bdun-tshig originated in India as a Buddhist tradition from where it was introduced in to China. One of the most ancient Tibetan books sBa-bzhed on its history (sba-bzhed: 9) records that the practice reached China on the introduction of the Doctrine there. In Tibet the practice was probably introduced in the ninth century in the period of Khri lde srong brtsan (800-815). It was brought by the Chinese princess married to the king. Before this in Tibet there was tradition that on the death of a person two meals of morning and evening were offered to the gods and the people. This was known as Tshe (life). From Tibet the custom of bdun-tshig spread to the various countries in the Indian Himalaya. In Lahul the practice came perhaps from Tibet with the Tibetan Buddhism. In the full performances memorials are raised symbolizing: sku, gsung and thugs; kāya, vāk and chitta, i.e. body, voice and the heart. The symbol for body was raised a statue of a deity like that of Avalokitesvara, Vajradhara, etc., for voice a sacred book or books were copied, like Vajrachhedika, pāpadeshnā, etc. and a chhodten was raised symbolising the heart. The kind of statue, name of book and the chaitya to be raised were suggested by a lama according to the prophecy. In a few instances such important acts were recorded at the end of the book copied at the moment with the name of the donors, other important members of the family, donor guests, and some important persons like the local ruling chief and sometimes the sovereign, and lastly it was dated. In this manner a private record acquired the status of an important historical document. This epilogue is entitled as Kar-chhag, register. Sometimes this document may be a separate sheet or even a booklet. All such instruments are named as kar-chhag.

In Pattan there is a social class named garu, formed after intermarriage between the two sections of Brahmins and Buddhists. This characteristics of fusion is also manifested in some of their important social practices. They performed a death ceremony like dge-ba but including some major features of pungyin, celebrated on a grand scale. Such performances of this class of the society was named as Raṇāh. This name was popular in Tinan also. The most difficult task in such events was documenting the event. Ranah was consecrated by the lamas. We are fortunate to discover one such document, (courtesy B.S. Rawal). It preserves complete picture of the performance. The description lists all important tasks performed, the items of expenditures, gives exact amount of expenses on different items and other kind of important information. In this case they have not constructed Marh and have not raised carvings of the Pittra. They raised statues and copied sacred books. The present document relates to village Shansha belonging to the period last quarter of nineteenth century. Below is given the translation.

Kar-chhag: The Register of Donors - Shansha

Aum Swasti! Siddhi! Pray for the welfare of all the beings! Here begins the register.

The three bodies manifest themselves: the Buddha, the teacher; the Excellent Doctrine which protect from the darkness of the two kinds of illusions; and the Arya Sangha which is adorned with three kinds of teachings. Bowing down I pay obeisance to the three Precious Ones, the place of refuge. E ma ho!

From the wheel of learning emanate thousand rays of knowledge and fall on the sphere of the disciples. I pray to Gelug, the mountain (of knowledge?). I bow at the feet of the honourable Dharamraj, Lozang Dagpa (Tsongkhapa), the lord of the world, crown of the beings, who brings benefit to the limitless beings. E ma ho!

The teacher Shakyamuni is the jewel ornament of the whole world. Padmasambhava, the mantradhara, adorns all the vidyadharas. The great tutelary deity, the most benevolent one, adorns the Himavata. This is a wonderful lineage beneficial for the complete emancipation of the sentient beings. E ma ho!

In the empire of the Jina Tsongkhapa, in the four divisions of Central Tibet, where the customs of the Doctrine are practiced in two ways, his flag flatters brilliantly. I salute at his feet bowing down hundred times. Hello!

India is land of the Doctrine which removes the darkness of ignorance of the human beings. China is the country of astrology, the store of knowledge. Tagzig (Tajik, Persia) is the country of wealth which removes the difficulties of the poor. Gesar is the country of armies which conquers the enemy forces. Himvata is the country where the Excellent Doctrine has spread. So the excellent five countries may progress and prosper! Hello!

India is an excellent country in the Jambudvipa, in the south, from where the Excellent Doctrine of Shakyamuni spread. Vajrasana (Bodhgaya) in India is the centre of Jambudvipa. Himavata (Tibet) is situated in the north of Jambudvipa. There is situated the white snowy mountain Tise (Kailash), high and pure. It is connected by an unbroken chain of mountain with Dilbu Ri here. The lady of the holy place, the self-born goddess, resides in the upper end of the valley. Vajravarahi resides at the feet, (at the lower end of the valley) at the place symbolized as thumb.

Going some distance there is situated the place of the self-born Avalokiteshvara. Mount Gandhala is very similar to Vajrasan. The auspicious Drilbu Ri is extremely wonderful. The mountain in the middle is like a lama sitting on his seat, and as if Vajradhar is surrounded by the lamas of root lineage. The mountains on the left look like the deities in wrathful manifestation sitting in frightening position, which is the sign of its being the seat of the 'Heroes of Knowledge', jnyan-shoor. Mountains on the left are like goddesses in wrathful manifestation sitting in frightful position, which is the sign of its being the seat of the 'Heroines of Knowledge'.

Moreover as prophecied in the Tantras (Phalpochhe, Avatansaka), this place, where the three mountains like Drilbu —Ri and Gandhola meet, resembles the sacred place of Tsari. It is sign of its being not different from Tsari. Joining of the two rivers here is like that of La-phyi and Chhu-bar, which is the sign of its being not different from the holy place of Chhu-bar. There are eighty great secret caves of dakinis here. There is an underground course where flows water, like the nectar of herbs. There is the river, flowing slowly (Mandakini), having eight wings. For all these reasons this valley is incomparable. Hello!

The lord, Dharamraj Dilip Singh (1870-1892, Raja of Kullu) resides at the great capital of Sultanpur. May his dominion flourish like the waxing moon. Now a days under the conditions of hardship, may the acts of the ten virtues expand and progress.

The mountains on the backside are like the assembly of the tutelary deities, the Guardians of the Doctrine. The mountains on the front look like the numerous objects of offerings (mchhodpa) arranged in rows. In the middle of the valley flows the river with green and pure water to the long distant. Chhoskhor Othang Gonpa which is adorned with the three kinds of teachings, is a wonderful place. Many scholars holding the traditions of sutra and mantra come here continuously like the garland of pearl. Lozang Nyima resides here at present. May the doctrine of the Yellow Cap expand and progress. In the prosperous village of Upper Shansha in his auspicious dominion, the laymen express happiness in the religious work and the women are faithful knowing that impermanence (of this world) is like an illusion and their family have origin from the lineage of Tho-su.

Mani the faithful landlady and her younger sister Soni, the two generally pray for the progress of the doctrine of the Buddha, progress of the kingdom, repulsing the armies of the enemies, fulfilling the wishes of the leading lamas, removing the sins of their kind parents, and for the fulfillment of the wishes of the people like Dhill-li (Dile) Ram, the husband of the two, the one who has passed away from this world for going to the other world. Rag (Raghu?) Das, father of Dile Ram, and his younger brother Kishan (uncle of Dile Ram), have survived longer than their son.

For crossing over from the ocean of the world with the force of the air and for taking the good path towards the heaven of Sukhavati, the following auspicious acts were performed.

For the advancement of the Excellent Doctrine, Vajrachhedika, the condensed collection from among the 80,000 sermons, was raised. As a receptacle of speech, Papadeshna, the dharni, was raised. As a receptacle of the body, idol of Amitabh in the form of dharamkaya and of Avalokitesvara were raised, and many tshva-tshva (icons) were raised. The good servants and the relatives lend protection from all the sides. The donation of the clothes has unlocked the knot of misery. The younger sister Soni herself mixed the nectar of the gods in the meal of the men: she prepared delicious meal. It is wonderful that the teachers and officials who are provided with intellect and are clothed with friendship were also invited. The hosts worship the god and show happiness in the good work. They show happiness towards the Doctrine like to their parents. May they have long life, have no sickness and be in pleasure. How wonderful!

For this Excellent Doctrine the list of those bringing happiness (presents) is like this.

In the beginning, Sug-gu-rama (Sukh Ram), son-in-law, from Wari brought one pitcher of chhang and one limb of meat. Zing-bhi-ga and Norbu from Go-ma offered one limb of meat and arag. Baga Nana (Bhag Nand) from Gha-da-ra gave arag. Rup Das from Lod

(Loat) gave arag and phye-mar (marpindi, dumpling of sattu, ghee and sugar). Namgyal gave arag. Norzom and Manu from Rangbey gave half a rupee. From Chhod (Tholong), Nor-jor brought arag and phye-mar. Shibu from Shang (Shansha) gave arag. Du-tsa gave two annas. Bhuddha (Buddh) Ram gave arag and phyemar. Brahamin Dhaniya gave half a rupee. Saze Ram gave a pot of chhang. Gogi gave two annas. Kho-gu gave arag. Dhaniya gave four anna. Sundra gave two anna. Dom Par, the Gur, gave arag and phyemar. Urgyan Tshering and younger sister from Gorom gave one uthi (metal pitcher) chhang and a goat. Khogu and Chhering Buthid from Ling-tog (Lindoor) gave one uthi chhang and phyemar. Chhering, Phurpa, gave one goat. Younger brother Chhering from Tshogs Zing (Tozing?) gave one rupee. Har Dhass (Das) of Yobrang gave one rupee. Tobdan from the Gonpa (monastery of Shansha) gave one uthi of chhang and phemar. Ram Sai and Dolma from Phura, the husband and wife, gave one uthi chhang and a goat. The Goor from Raaling gave four annas, arag and phyemar. Chhozom gave arag and phyemar. Paru from Wari gave one rupee.

Bhastri from Lod gave one rupee. Bhagat from Ghaling gave two annas. Chinga from Ya-nam-phel (Jahlma) gave two anna. Suku from Gorom gave four anna. Tshang Dug gave four anna. Ganga from Yobrang gave four anna. Ganga Ram from Lower Shang gave half a rupee.

The account of expenses for the consecration is like this

Fifty khal (khal = c 40 lb) of grains of Ne was spent for chhang. Thirty two khals of wheat flour was spent for khu-ra (snack). Nine khals of Ne was given to the brahmins. Twenty khals of Ne was used for sampa (sattu). Ten khals of wheat flour was used for cakes (roti). For small khu-ra one khal of wheat flour was used. Nine and half maund of oil, eight sheep and cloth (cotton cloth) costing two rupees were used.

The cost of preparation of the books of Vajrachhedika and Papdeshna was rupees three and half. Fifty two rupees were spent for the statue of Avalokitesvara. Seven rupees were offered to Suku (Sukh) Ram of Nang of Wari and to Noer dPal from Othang for the works of consecration. Su-ku Ram from Wari and Urgyan

Chhering two were Sha-pa (in charge of meat). Hasa Ram from Wari, Tsherring Buthid and younger sister three were chhang-ma (in charge of chhang). They served well as if mixing the nectar of the gods in the food for the men and brought happiness. I pray that there may come the auspicious prosperity and be the ornament of the world.

Note: This paper appears to have been written by a lama from the Othang monastery, hailing from Zanskar, and belonging to the Gelugpa sect. On the basis of the internal evidences the document may be dated c.1880 C.E.

Death ceremony in Pangi: According to Ranpatiya (1979), the ceremony after the death is called Katti (Kaṭṭī) which is done on the third, ninth or thirteenth day. On the ninth day the purohit draws picture of the deceased person on a stone slab and establishes it near the water source. It is called Dacch (Dācchh). After a month the big Katti is performed. On this day feast is given to the people. Every month the day is celebrated and after a year the final ceremony is performed called Barshi (= annuity).

As informed here by Ranpatiya dhaj are seen in Pangi but they stand isolated and are not related with any other structure. The pictures drawn by the purohit may be temporary but a legacy of a strong custom. The stone carvings on stones at the Panihar are incomparable but the custom related to it is still obscure.

Pung-yin might have been in practice in olden times besides in Lahul, as described above, in Pangi, and Kishtwar. We give below a record from Rose. Here we observe that the amount of rupees 600 during the time of Rose is enormous. He writes, "For three or five days after a death only one meal called upa:s is eaten in the house by the relatives of the deceased. On the ninth day or later a pitr is generally erected. This consists of a piece of wood or a small slab of stone on which is carved a rough effigy of the deceased. The pitr is set up near a spring or stream by a Brahman in the presence of a brother or other relatives of the deceased and a young girl. A sheep is killed in the house and some mantras are repeated at the stone and a tokri or basket containing some articles belonging to the dead person is thrown into the stream. On their return to the house clothing is given to the Brahman and the young girl. A feast is then given to the near relatives of the deceased. The pitr is sometimes placed in a small hut near a stream, or near the village and then it is called a war.

'For a year the date of the month on which the death took place is observed every month as a fast, and only one meal, also called upa:s, is eaten. At the end of a year the house is cleansed and the mourning comes to an end.

'Those who can afford it erect a dhaj in memory of a deceased relative, but this ceremony is so expensive that few can afford to perform it. A long slab of stone is brought to the village, and on an appointed day all the people of the neighbourhood assemble. A sheep is sacrificed over one end of the slab as it lies on the ground and under the direction of a Brahman it is then set up on end — one end being buried in the ground. The relatives go round the stone three times from right to left. Sometimes a rough figure of the deceased is cut on it and over this ghi is rubbed — while the Brahman repeats certain mantras. A feast is then given to all who are present, and this is the chief cause of expense. This ceremony usually takes place a year after the death. Sometimes Rs. 600 are spent," (Rose, 1883-III: 197). Existence of the custom of raising of dhaj is known from the reports. But the drawing of figure of pitrra on the wood or stone slab appears to have been a temporary phenomenon. No such remnant could be seen nor is reported.

Annexure - I

ལྷ་རྒྱུས། ༄༅།།1།།དང་པོ་ལ་བཀྲ་ཤིས།།

༄༅།། དང་པོ་ལ་བཀྲ་ཤིས་ཡོང་ཤིག། ལ་དགུང་ལ་ཕེབས་སོང་།།
ཡོང་ཤིག། ལ་ཡོང་ཤིག་དགུང་ལ།། དགུང་ལ་མ་བཀྲ་ཤིས་ཡོང་ཤིག།།
ལ་མི་དེ་ནང་དུ་ཡོང་ཤིག། ལ་ཡོང་ཤིག་མི་དེ།།
ཁྲི་རུ་དཀྱིལ་ལ་བཞུགས་ས། ཡོང་ཤིག་ལ་དགུང་སྟོད་དཀྱིལ་དུ།། ཡོང་ཤིག། ལ་ཡོང་ཤིག།།
དགུང་སྟོད་དཀྱིལ་ལ་བཞུགས་ས་ལ་ཕེབས་སོང་།། ཡོང་ཤིག། ལ་བཀྲ་ཤིས་བརྗོད།།-1

དང་པོ་ལ་བཀྲ་ཤིས་ཡོང་ཤིག། ལ་གངས་ལ་ཕེབས་སོང་།།
ཡོང་ཤིག། ལ་ཡོང་ཤིག་གངས་ལ།། གངས་ལ་མ་བཀྲ་ཤིས་ཡོང་ཤིག།།
ལ་མི་དེ་ནང་དུ། ཡོང་ཤིག།། ལ་ཡོང་ཤིག་མི་དེ། སེང་ཆེན་གྱི་ལ་བཞུགས་ས།།
ཡོང་ཤིག་ལ་གངས་སྟོད་དཀྱིལ་དུ། ཡོང་ཤིག།། ལ་ཡོང་ཤིག།།
གངས་སྟོད་དཀྱིལ་ལ་བཞུགས་ས་ལ་ཕེབས་སོང་།། ཡོང་ཤིག་་་བརྗོད།།--2

དང་པོ་ལ་བཀྲ་ཤིས་ཡོང་ཤིག།། ལ་ནགས་ལ་ཕེབས་སོང་།།
ཡོང་ཤིག། ལ་ཡོང་ཤིག་ནགས་ལ།། ནགས་ལ་མ་བཀྲ་ཤིས་ཡོང་ཤིག།།
ལ་མི་དེ་ནང་དུ་ཡོང་ཤིག། ལ་ཡོང་ཤིག་མི་དེ།། སྟག་ཆེན་གྱི་ལ་བཞུགས་ས།།
ཡོང་ཤིག་ལ་ནགས་སྟོད་དཀྱིལ་དུ།། ཡོང་ཤིག། ལ་ཡོང་ཤིག།།
ནགས་སྟོད་དཀྱིལ་ལ་བཞུགས་ས་ལ་ཕེབས་སོང་།། ཡོང་ཤིག་་་བརྗོད།།--3

དང་པོ་ལ་བཀྲ་ཤིས་ཡོང་ཤིག།། ལ་མཚོ་ལ་ཕེབས་སོང་།།

ཡོང་ཞིག། ལ་ཡོང་ཞིག་མཚོ་ལ།། མཚོ་ལ་མ་བགྲིས་ཡོང་ཞིག།།
ལ་མི་དེ་ནང་དུ་ཡོང་ཞིག། ལ་ཡོང་ཞིག་མི་དེ།། ཉ་ཆེན་གྱི་ལ་བཞུགས་ས།ཡོང་ཞིག་ལ་མཚོ་སྟོད་དཀྱིལ་དུ།།
ཡོང་ཞིག། ལ་ཡོང་ཞིག།། མཚོ་སྟོད་དཀྱིལ་ལ་བཞུགས་ས་ལ་ཕེབས་སོང་།། ཡོང་ཞིག་་་བཟོད།།--4

དང་པོ་ལ་བཀྲ་ཤིས་ཡོང་ཞིག།། ལ་མཁར་ལ་ཕེབས་སོང་།།
ཡོང་ཞིག། ལ་ཡོང་ཞིག་མཁར་།ལ། མཁར་ལ་མ་བགྲིས་ཡོང་ཞིག།།
ལ་མི་དེ་ནང་དུ་ཡོང་ཞིག། ལ་ཡོང་ཞིག་མི་དེ།། མི་ཆེན་གྱི་ལ་བཞུགས་ས།།
ཡོང་ཞིག་ལ་མཁར་སྟོད་དཀྱིལ་དུ། ཡོང་ཞིག།། ལ་ཡོང་ཞིག།།
མཁར་སྟོད་དཀྱིལ་ལ་བཞུགས་ས་ལ་ཕེབས་སོང་།། ཡོང་ཞིག་་་བཟོད།། --5

དང་པོ་ལ་བཀྲ་ཤིས་ཡོང་ཞིག།། ལ་དཔལ་ཁང་ལ་ཕེབས་སོང་།།
ཡོང་ཞིག། ལ་ཡོང་ཞིག་དཔལ་ཁང་ལ།། དཔལ་ཁང་ལ་མ་བཀྲ་ཤིས་ཡོང་ཞིག།།
ལ་མི་དེ་ནང་དུ་ཡོང་ཞིག། ལ་ཡོང་ཞིག་མི་དེ།། ཡབ་ཡུམ་གྱི་ལ་བཞུགས་ས།།
ཡོང་ཞིག་ལ་དཔལ་ཁང་སྟོད་དཀྱིལ་དུ།། ཡོང་ཞིག། ལ་ཡོང་ཞིག།།
དཔལ་ཁང་སྟོད་དཀྱིལ་ལ་བཞུགས་ས་ལ་ཕེབས་སོང་།། ཡོང་ཞིག་་་བཟོད།།--6

༄༅།།2།།གཉིས་པ་འཛོམ་གླུ།།

༄།། དགུང་སྟོད་དུ་བཞུགས་པའི། ཁྲི་གདུགས་ཉི་མ་བདེ།།
དགུང་སྨད་དུ་བཞུགས་པའི། དཀར་གསལ་ཟླ་བ་བདེ།།
དགུང་སྟོད་དཀྱིལ་དུ་འཛོམ་པའི། རྒྱུ་སྐར་འཛོམ་པོ་བདེ།།
དེ་ནས་གཅིག་དང་གཉིས་གསུམ།། འཛོམ་པའི་ཆ་གཅིག་དགོས།། ལ་ལི་བཀྲ་ཤིས་བཟོད།--1

གངས་སྟོད་དུ་བཞུགས་པའི། སེང་ཆེན་དཀར་མོ་བདེ།།
གངས་སྨད་དུ་བཞུགས་པའི། གཡུ་རལ་ལེགས་མོ་བདེ།
གངས་སྟོད་དཀྱིལ་དུ་འཛོམས་པའི། སེང་ཕྲུག་འཛོམ་པོ་བདེ།།
དེ་ནས་གཅིག་དང་གཉིས་གསུམ།། འཛོམ་པའི་ཆ་གཅིག་དགོས།།། ཏ་ལི་་་བརྗོད།--2

ནགས་སྟོད་དུ་བཞུགས་པའི། སྟག་ཆེན་ཁྲ་བོ་བདེ།
ནགས་སྨད་དུ་བཞུགས་པའི། རི་མོ་ལེགས་མོ་བདེ།།
ནགས་སྟོད་དཀྱིལ་དུ་འཛོམ་པའི། སྟག་ཕྲུག་འཛོམ་པོ་བདེ།།
དེ་ནས་གཅིག་དང་གཉིས་གསུམ།། འཛོམ་པའི་ཆ་གཅིག་དགོས།། ཏ་ལི་་་བརྗོད།--3

མཚོ་སྟོད་དུ་བཞུགས་པའི། ཉ་ཆེན་ཉུལ་མོ་བདེ།།
མཚོ་སྨད་དུ་བཞུགས་པའི། གསེར་མིག་ལེགས་མོ་བདེ།།
མཚོ་སྟོད་དཀྱིལ་དུ་འཛོམ་པའི། ཉ་ཕྲུག་འཛོམ་པོ་བདེ།།
དེ་ནས་གཅིག་དང་གཉིས་གསུམ།། འཛོམ་པའི་ཆ་གཅིག་དགོས། ཏ་ལི་་་བརྗོད།--4

མཁར་སྟོད་དུ་བཞུགས་པའི།། མི་ཆེན་གོང་མ་བདེ།།
མཁར་སྨད་དུ་བཞུགས་པའི།། རྒྱུད་རིས་མཐོན་པོ་བདེ།།
མཁར་སྟོད་དཀྱིལ་དུ་འཛོམས་པའི།། གྲོང་འཁོར་འཛོམ་པོ་བདེ།།
དེ་ནས་གཅིག་དང་གཉིས་གསུམ།། འཛོམ་པའི་ཆ་གཅིག་དགོས།། ཏ་ལི་་་བརྗོད།།--5

དཔལ་ཁང་སྟོད་དུ་བཞུགས་པའི།། ཡབ་ཡུམ་པ་མ་བདེ།།
དཔལ་ཁང་སྨད་དུ་བཞུགས་པའི།། བུ་ནོར་མོད་པོ་བདེ།།

དཔལ་ཁང་སྟོད་དཀྱིལ་དུ་འཛོམ་པའི།། གཉེན་དྲུང་འཛོམ་པོ་བདེ།།
དེ་ནས་གཅིག་དང་གཉིས་གསུམ།། འཛོམ་པའི་ཆ་གཅིག་དགོས། ཏ་ལི་་་བཟོད།།--6

༄༅།།3།། གསུམ་གུར་སྒུབ་ཅེ།།

།། དགུང་སྟོད་དཀྱིལ་དུ། གུར་ཞིག་སྒུབ་སོང་། ཅེ་དང་ཅེ་ཡི། གུར་དེ་སྒུབ་སོང་།
སེར་པོ་དར་གྱི། གུར་དེ་སྒུབ་སོང་། སུ་དང་སུ་ཡིས། ཚུགས་ཤིང་བཙུགས་སོང་།
ཁྲི་གདུགས་ཉི་མས། ཚུགས་ཤིང་བཙུགས་སོང་། སུ་དང་སུ་ཡིས། མཚམས་ཐག་སྦུལ་སོང་།
རྒྱུ་སྐར་མང་གིས། མཚམས་ཐག་སྦུལ་སོང་། མཚམས་ཐག་སྦུལ་བའི། བཀྲ་ཤིས་འདང་བཟོད།།--1

གངས་སྟོད་དཀྱིལ་དུ། གུར་ཞིག་སྒུབ་སོང་། ཅེ་དང་ཅེ་ཡི། གུར་དེ་སྒུབ་སོང་།
དཀར་པོ་དར་གྱི། གུར་དེ་སྒུབ་་་སོང་། སུ་དང་སུ་ཡིས། ཚུགས་ཤིང་བཙུགས་སོང་།
སེང་ཆེན་དཀར་མོས། ཚུགས་ཤིང་བཙུགས་སོང་། སུ་དང་སུ་ཡིས། མཚམས་ཐག་སྦུལ་སོང་།
སེང་ཕྲུག་མང་གིས། མཚམས་ཐག་སྦུལ་སོང་། མཚམས་ཐག་་་བཟོད།།--2

ནགས་སྟོད་དཀྱིལ་དུ། གུར་ཞིག་སྒུབ་སོང་། ཅེ་དང་ཅེ་ཡི། གུར་དེ་སྒུབ་སོང་།
ཁྲ་བོ་དར་གྱི། གུར་དེ་སྒུབ་སོང་། སུ་དང་སུ་ཡིས། ཚུགས་ཤིང་བཙུགས་སོང་།
སྟག་ཆེན་ཁྲ་བོས། ཚུགས་ཤིང་བཙུགས་སོང་། སུ་དང་སུ་ཡིས། མཚམས་ཐག་སྦུལ་སོང་།
སྟག་ཕྲུག་མང་གིས། མཚམས་ཐག་སྦུལ་སོང་། མཚམས་ཐག་་་བཟོད།།--3

མཚོ་སྟོད་དཀྱིལ་དུ། གུར་ཞིག་སྒུབ་སོང་། ཅེ་དང་ཅེ་ཡི། གུར་དེ་སྒུབ་སོང་།
སྔོན་པོ་དར་གྱི། གུར་དེ་སྒུབ་སོང་། སུ་དང་སུ་ཡིས། ཚུགས་ཤིང་བཙུགས་སོང་།
ཉ་ཆེན་ཉུལ་མོས། ཚུགས་ཤིང་བཙུགས་སོང་། སུ་དང་སུ་ཡིས། མཚམས་ཐག་སྦུལ་སོང་།

ཉ་སྦྲུག་མང་གྲིས། མཚམས་ཐག་སྐྱོལ་སོང་། མཚམས་ཐག་་་བཟོད།།--4

མཁར་སྟོད་དཀྱིལ་དུ། གུར་ཞིག་སྒྲུབ་སོང་། ཅི་དང་ཅི་ཡི། གུར་དེ་སྒྲུབ་སོང་།
སེ་བོ་དར་གི། གུར་དེ་སྒྲུབ་སོང་། སུ་དང་སུ་ཡིས། ཚུགས་ཤིང་བཙུགས་སོང་།
མི་ཆེན་གོང་མས། ཚུགས་ཤིང་བཙུགས་སོང་། སུ་དང་སུ་ཡིས། མཚམས་ཐག་སྐྱོལ་སོང་།
གྲོང་འཁོར་མང་གྲིས། མཚམས་ཐག་སྐྱོལ་སོང་། མཚམས་ཐག་་་བཟོད།།--5

དཔལ་ཁང་སྟོད་དཀྱིལ་དུ། གུར་ཞིག་སྒྲུབ་སོང་། ཅི་དང་ཅི་ཡི། གུར་དེ་སྒྲུབ་སོང་།
སྨུག་པོ་དར་གི། གུར་དེ་སྒྲུབ་སོང་། སུ་དང་སུ་ཡིས། ཚུགས་ཤིང་བཙུགས་སོང་།
ཡབ་ཡུམ་པ་མས། ཚུགས་ཤིང་བཙུགས་སོང་། སུ་དང་སུ་ཡིས། མཚམས་ཐག་སྐྱོལ་སོང་།
གཉེན་དྲུང་མང་གྲིས། མཚམས་ཐག་སྐྱོལ་སོང་། མཚམས་ཐག་་་བཟོད།།--6

༄༅།།4།། བཞི་པ་ཁྲི་བཞངས་ཅེ།།

སྔོན་ཆེ་བསྐལ་པ་བཟང་པོ་ལ། ཁྲི་ཞིག་བཞངས་སོང་། ཅི་དང་ཅི་ཡི། ཁྲི་དེ་བཞངས་སོང་།
སེར་པོ་གསེར་གྱི་། ཁྲི་ཞིག་བཞངས་སོང་། དེ་རུ་སུ་དང་། སུ་མི་བཞུགས་སོང་།
དེ་རུ་སྟེང་གི་། ལྷ་ཡང་བཞུགས་སོང་། དབུ་སྔོག་ཐོ་བའི་ལྷ། དེ་ལ་བཀྲ་ཤིས་འདང་བཟོད།།--1

སྔོན་ཆེ་བསྐལ་པ་བཟང་པོ་ལ། ཁྲི་ཞིག་བཞངས་སོང་། ཅི་དང་ཅི་ཡི། ཁྲི་དེ་བཞངས་སོང་།
དཀར་པོ་དངུལ་གྱི། ཁྲི་ཞིག་བཞངས་སོང་། དེ་རུ་སུ་དང་། སུ་མི་བཞུགས་སོང་།
དེ་རུ་བར་གྱི། བཙན་ཡང་བཞུགས་སོང་། གངས་རི་བཟང་པོའི་བཙན། དེ་ལ་བཀྲ་ཤིས་འདང་བཟོད།།--2

སྔོན་ཆེ་བསྐལ་པ་བཟང་པོ་ལ། ཁྲི་ཞིག་བཞངས་སོང་། ཅི་དང་ཅི་ཡི། ཁྲི་དེ་བཞངས་སོང་།
སྔོན་པོ་གཡུ་ཡི། ཁྲི་ཞིག་བཞངས་སོང་། དེ་རུ་སུ་དང་། སུ་མི་བཞུགས་སོང་།
དེ་རུ་འོག་གི་། ཀླུ་ཡང་བཞུགས་སོང་། གཡུ་མཚོ་སྔོངས་པོའི་ཀླུ་གཉན། དེ་ལ་བཀྲ་ཤིས་འང་བརྗོད།།--3

སྔོན་ཆེ་བསྐལ་པ་བཟང་པོ་ལ། ཁྲི་ཞིག་བཞངས་སོང་། ཅི་དང་ཅི་ཡི། ཁྲི་དེ་བཞངས་སོང་།
ཁྲ་བོ་ཤེལ་གྱི་ཁྲི་ཞིག་བཞངས་སོང་། དེ་རུ་སུ་དང་། སུ་མི་བཞུགས་སོང་།
དེ་རུ་མི་ཆེན་གོང་མ།བཞུགས་སོང་།། རྒྱུད་རིས་མཐོན་པོའི་མི་ཆེན། དེ་ལ་བཀྲ་ཤིས་འང་བརྗོད།།--4

སྔོན་ཆེ་བསྐལ་པ་བཟང་པོ་ལ། ཁྲི་ཞིག་བཞངས་སོང་། ཅི་དང་ཅི་ཡི། ཁྲི་དེ་བཞངས་སོང་།
སྨུག་པོ་དུང་གྱི་ཁྲི་ཞིག་བཞངས་སོང་། དེ་རུ་སུ་དང་སུ་མི་བཞུགས་སོང་།
དེ་རུ་ཡབ་ཡུམ་ཕ་མ་བཞུགས་སོང་། བུ་ནོར་འཛོམ་པོ་ཕ་མ། དེ་ལ་བཀྲ་ཤིས་འང་བརྗོད།།--5

༄༅།།5།། ལྷ་པ་ནི་ན་བཟའ་སྨྱུལ་ཅེ།།
༄། མཐོ་བ་རི་གསུམ་རྩེ་ན་བཞུགས་པ། བྲ་རྒོད་པོ་སྤུན་གསུམ་དེ་བཞུགས།
སྣམ་མེ་སྣམ་ལ་ཅི་སྣམ་། སྣམ་མེ་སྣམ་ལ་བྲ་སྤུ་སྣ་ཚོགས་སྣམ།
འདོན་ནེ་འདོན་ལ་ཅི་འདོན། འདོན་ནེ་འདོན་ལ་རྒྱ་སྐར་སྐར་ཆུང་འདོན།
སྐྱེམ་མེ་སྐྱེམ་ལ་ཅི་སྐྱེམ། སྐྱེམ་མེ་སྐྱེམ་ལ་སེ་འབྲུ་རང་ཆང་སྐྱེམ།། ལ་ཏ་ལི་བཀྲ་ཤིས་བརྗོད།། --1

ཤལ་མ་དཀར་གྱི་འདབས་སུ་བཞུགས་པའི། ཤྭ་བ་སྤུན་གསུམ་དེ།།
སྣམ་མེ་སྣམ་ལ་ཅི་སྣམ། སྣམ་མེ་སྣམ་ལ་སྤྲིན་ཙུང་ལང་ལིང་སྣམ།།

འདོན་ནི་འདོན་ལ་ཅི་འདོན། འདོན་ནི་འདོན་ལ་མེ་ཏོག་སྣ་ཚོགས་འདོན།།
སྐྱེམ་མེ་སྐྱེམ་ལ་ཅི་སྐྱེམ། སྐྱེམ་མེ་སྐྱེམ་ལ་གདངས་ཆུ་ཁྲལ་ཁྲོལ་སྐྱེམ།། ···བརྗོད།།--2

བྲག་དམར་འདབས་སུ་བཞུགས་པའི། བཙུན་པ་སྤུན་གསུམ་དེ།
སྣམ་མེ་སྣམ་ལ་ཅི་སྣམ། སྣམ་མེ་སྣམ་ལ་རས་གཟན་རྐྱང་གཅིག་སྣམ།།
འདོན་ནི་འདོན་ལ་ཅི་འདོན། འདོན་ནི་འདོན་ལ་འབྲས་དཀར་སྤོ་ལོ་འདོན།།
སྐྱེམ་མེ་སྐྱེམ་ལ་ཅི་སྐྱེམ། སྐྱེམ་མེ་སྐྱེམ་ལ་སིང་ཆང་སིང་མ་སྐྱེམ། ཏ་ལི···བརྗོད།།--3

དཔལ་ཁང་སྟོད་དུ་བཞུགས་པའི། རྒྱལ་བུ་སྤུན་གསུམ་དེ།
སྣམ་མེ་སྣམ་ལ་ཅི་སྣམ། སྣམ་མེ་སྣམ་ལ་དར་མེན་གོས་ཞེན་སྣམ།
འདོན་ནི་འདོན་ལ་ཅི་འདོན། འདོན་ནི་འདོན་ལ་ཞིམ་ཟག་མངར་བཅུད་འདོན།
སྐྱེམ་མེ་སྐྱེམ་ལ་ཅི་སྐྱེམ། སྐྱེམ་མེ་སྐྱེམ་ལ་ཨ་རག་བདུད་རྩི་སྐྱེམ།། ཏ་ལི···བརྗོད།།--4

༄༅།།6།།དྲུག་པ་དབུ་ཐོད་སྤྱུལ་ཅེ ।།

སྤོ་ལོ་གསེར་ཐོད་བསྣམས་པ་དེ། སུ་དང་སུ་ཡི་དྲིན། སྤང་མ་དམར་གྱི་དྲིན།
དེའི་དྲིན་ལན་གདངས་ཆུ་བརྗོད།། ལ་ཏ་ལི་ལ་ལང་ལ་ལ། ལ་ཏ་ལི་བཀྲ་ཤིས་བརྗོད།...1

ཉ་ལོ་དབུ་ཐོད་བསྣམས་པ་དེ། སུ་དང་སུ་ཡི་དྲིན། ཞལ་མ་དཀར་གྱི་དྲིན།
དེའི་དྲིན་ལན་ཆར་ཆུ་བརྗོད།། ཏ་ལི···བརྗོད།།--2

སླང་མ་བལ་ཐོད་བསྣམས་པ་དེ། སུ་དང་སུ་ཡི་དྲིན།
ཆུ་མིག་དངར་གྱི་དྲིན། དེའི་དྲིན་ལན་ཐང་ཆུ་བརྗོད། ཏ་ལི···བརྗོད།།--3

འོམ་བུག་དར་ཐོད་བསྣམས་པ་དེ། སུ་དང་སུ་ཡི་དྲིན།
གཙང་ཆབ་སྔོན་མོའི་དྲིན། དེའི་དྲིན་ལན་ཟླར་ཆུ་བཟོད། ཏ་ལི···བཟོད།།--4

རྒྱལ་བུ་དབུ་ཐོད་བསྣམས་པ་དེ། སུ་དང་སུ་ཡི་དྲིན།
ཡབ་དང་ཡུམ་གྱི་དྲིན། དེའི་དྲིན་ལན་དཀར་ཆུ་བཟོད། ཏ་ལི···བཟོད།།--5

༄༅།།7།། བདུན་པ་མེན་ཏོག་སྤྱུལ་ཅེ།།

རྒྱ་གར་གྱི་རྒྱལ་པོ། བདེ་འོ་སྐྱུ་ཁམས་བཟང་། རྒྱལ་མོའིས་ཚིག་ལེགས་གསུངས།
མེན་ཏོག་ཅམ་ཟམ་འབྲུངས། ཞིས་ཏ་ལོ་ཅམ་ཟམ་འབྲུངས།།
མེན་ཏོག་བརྒྱད་ཟམ་འབྲུངས། ཞིས་ཏ་ལོ་བརྒྱད་ཟམ་འབྲུངས། --1

གཅིག་ནི་ཡང་མེན་ཏོག། གཅིག་ནི་ཏ་ལོ། བདེ་བོ་སུ་ལ་སྤྱུལ། ཞིས་ཏ་ལོ་སུ་ལ་སྤྱུལ།
སྟེང་ཕྱོགས་ལྷ་ལ་སྤྱུལ། ཞིས་ལྷ་ལ་སྤྱུལ་བའི། བདེ་བོ་བཀྲ་ཞིས་བཟོད།།--2

གཉིས་ནི་ཡང་མེན་ཏོག། གཉིས་ནི་ཏ་ལོ། བདེ་བོ་སུ་ལ་སྤྱུལ། ཞིས་ཏ་ལོ་སུ་ལ་སྤྱུལ།
བར་ཕྱོགས་བཙན་ལ་སྤྱུལ། ཞིས་བཙན་ལ་སྤྱུལ་བའི། བདེ་བོ···བཟོད །།--3

གསུམ་ནི་ཡང་མེ་ཏོག། གསུམ་ནི་ཏ་ལོ། བདེ་བོ་སུ་ལ་སྤྱུལ། ཞིས་ཏ་ལོ་སུ་ལ་སྤྱུལ།
འོག་ཕྱོགས་ཀླུ་ལ་སྤྱུལ། ཞིས་ཀླུ་ལ་སྤྱུལ་བའི། བདེ་བོ···བཟོད།།--4

བཞི་ནི་ཡང་མེན་ཏོག།། བཞི་ནི་ཏ་ལོ། བདེ་བོ་སུ་ལ་སྨུལ། ཤིས་ཏ་ལོ་སུ་ལ་སྨུལ།
ཨ་བ་ཡབ་ལ་སྨུལ། ཤིས་ཡབ་ལ་སྨུལ་བའི། བདེ་བོ་་་བརྗོད།།--5

ལྔ་ནི་ཡང་མེན་ཏོག། ལྔ་ནི་ཏ་ལོ། བདེ་བོ་སུ་ལ་སྨུལ། ཤིས་ཏ་ལོ་སུ་ལ་སྨུལ།
ཨ་མ་ཡུམ་ལ་སྨུལ།། ཤིས་ཡུམ་ལ་སྨུལ་བའི། བདེ་བོ་་བརྗོད།།--6

དྲུག་ནི་ཡང་མེན་ཏོག། དྲུག་ནི་ཏ་ལོ། བདེ་བོ་སུ་ལ་སྨུལ། ཤིས་ཏ་ལོ་སུ་ལ་སྨུལ།
ཨ་ཅོ་སྤྲས་ལ་སྨུལ། ཤིས་ཨ་ཅོ་སྤྲས་ལ་སྨུལ་བའི། བདེ་བོ་་་བརྗོད།།--7

བདུན་ནི་ཡང་མེ་ཏོག་བདུན་ནི་ཏ་ལོ། བདེ་བོ་སུ་ལ་སྨུལ། ཤིས་ཏ་ལོ་སུ་ལ་སྨུལ།
ཨ་ཅེ་ལྕམ་ལ་སྨུལ། ཤིས་ཨ་ཅེ་ལྕམ་ལ་སྨུལ་བའི། བདེ་བོ་་་བརྗོད།།--8

བརྒྱད་ནི་ཡང་མེན་ཏོག། བརྒྱད་ནི་ཏ་ལོ། བདེ་བོ་སུ་ལ་སྨུལ། ཤིས་ཏ་ལོ་སུ་ལ་སྨུལ།
ཨ་བོ་རང་ལ་སྨུལ། ཤིས་ཨ་བོ་རང་ལ་སྨུལ་བའི། བདེ་བོ་་་བརྗོད།།--9

Manuscripts consulted:
1. Tashi Lhagyal, Khangsar. 2. Tashi Karingpa, Karing. 3. Amchi Gyaltshan, Tinno. 4. Old Song Lyrics in Bhoti Culture, Lahaul from Dartse. 5. sTod Ghati Kalyan Sabha, Kyelang. 7. Roerich, George De. (1934-III: 126-147). .

Annexure - II

The text of the Tho-yig – A Letter of Record, from the archives of the Thakurs of Gondhla. The document forms part of the book entitled:

འབྲོམ་སྟོན་པ་རྒྱལ་བའི་འབྱུང་གནས་ཀྱི་སྐྱེས་རབས་བཀའ་བསྡམས་བུ་ཆོས་ལེའུ་ཉི་ཤུ་པ་བཞུགས་སོ། །སྡུ་ཟི་ཤཡ་རྡོ། Some initial sentences forming prayer have been deleted.

p-1,L-4. དགྲ་བཅོམ་བཞུགས་གནས་གངས་དཀར་ཏི་སེའི་གནས། མངོས་གྲུབ་ཆབ་ཀྱི་ལ་མ་པང་གཡུ་མཚོའི་རྫབ། རི་རྒྱུད་ས་ཆད་གནས་ཆེན་དྲི་ལ་བུ་རི། རྒྱལ་བས་ལུང་བསྟན་རི་ཕྲ་རྡེ་ལ། དཔའ་བོ་དཔའ་མོའི་མདུའ་གནས་དོ་མཚར་L-4.ཆེ། ཀྱི་ལེགས། འཁོར་བྱུང་ཆེན་པོ་བརྒྱལ་ས་མཁར་སྒོ། ཆོས་བརྒྱལ་པི་ཧྲེམ་སེང་ཕྲ་དགུ་སྨོག་མཐོའ་བའི་དུས། རྒྱལ་སྲས་ཆེན་པོ་ཕྲི་ཆེན་སྐུ་མཁར་བརྩེར། སེང་གེ་གནམ་བརྒྱལ་དགུ་སྨོག་པོ་ཞིང་ཆབ་སྲིད་དར་བའི་དུས་ཡུལ་དང་གནས་ཀྱི་སྐབས་ནས་L-6.ཞལ་ཡང་མ་མཇལ་རྟུང་། ལས་དང་སྨོན་ལམ་འབྲེལ་པས། ཐོས་པའི་མཚན་ལ་རྟེན། ཉི་ཟླ་མཁའ་སྦྱོར་འདྲ་བའི་དགོངས་དབྱིངས་སུ་འཁྱིག། ཕན་ཚུན་བརྩེ་སེམས་གྲོགས་ཀྱིས་འོངས་སྐྱོད་བསྐྱིས་སུ་འཕུལ། བརྒྱ་བོད་མཆམས་ཀྱི་བྱ་ར་ལ་སེ་ལ་L-7.གློག་དམར་ཁྲུག་ཆེན་འགྲ་བའི་ཉ་ལམ་དམར་པོ་སྐྱངས། བརྒྱན་ཚིགས་སྐྱོ་མོ་འདྲ་བའི་ལུག་ལམ་དཀར་པོ་སྐྱངས། སྐྱ་དཀར་འཛོམས་པོ་འདྲ་བའི་བུ་བྲན་སྐྱིད་ལ་སྐྱིལ། དེ་འགྲའི་ཡབ་སྲས་གཉིས་ཀྱིས། ཆབ་སྲིད་དར་བའི་དུས། ཡུལ་ལ་དབུངས་ཆགས་གར་L-8.བུ་མཁའ་འགྲོའི་ལིང་། ས་ལ་འབུར་དུ་མཐོན་པའི། བསྟི་གནས་སྐུ་མཁར་ན། ལྷ་ཆེན་རིགས་བཟངས་སྐྱན་པའི་གྲགས་པ་ཅན། གདུང་རུས་རིགས་བཟངས་འོད་གསལ་ལྷ་ནས་ཆད། དཔའ་རྩལ་ཁྲལ་དང་ལྡན་པའི། ནོ་ནོ་པུ་རི། སེན་སྒོ་སྐུམ་L-9.མཛེད་གཉིས་ཀྱིས་ཀུང་། དྲིན་ཅན་ཡབ་ཀྱི་དྲིན་ལ་བསོབ་ཕྱིར་དང་། རང་རེའི་ཚེ་འདིར་འགལ་རྐྱེན་ཞི་ཕྱིར་དང་། ཕྱི་མ་དག་པའི་གོལ་འཕངས་ཐོབ་ཕྱིར་དུ། དམ་ཆོས་ཁྲུད་འཕགས་ཀ་བམ་ལགས་པོ་དང་། ཕ་ཆོས་བུ་ཆོས་ལ་སོགས་དུ་མ་བཞེངས། བསགས་པ་L-10.དོན་ཆེན་འདི་ལ་ཀུན་ཀྱིས་སྟོད། ཀྱི་ལེགས། གཞན་ཡང་བཞིན་པའི་བདག་མོ་ཨ་བྲི་ཇོ་ཇོ་ནང་ཀ་དཔལ་མོས་ཀྱང་། གསུངས་རབས་རྣམས་ལ་བཀོད་པ་མཛད་པ། ཡན་མཚན་ཆེ། ཡུམ་གྱི་མཆོག་འགྱུར་སོ་ནམ་པལ་མོ་ཀློ་གྲོ་གཉིས་ཀྱིས་ཀྱང་། མིའི་ཟས་L-11.ལ་ལྷའི་བདུད་རྩིར་སྒྱུར། དཔོན་

Bibliography

English Books

Agrawala, Vasudeva, S. (1963). *Matsya Purana - A Study*, All India Kashiraj Trust, Varanasi.

Ahluwalia, M.S. (1988). *History of Himachal Pradesh*, Intellectual Publishing House, New Delhi.

Ali, S.M. 1966. *Geography of the Puranas*, III edition, 1983. People's Publishing House, New Delhi.

Barnes, George Carnac, (1855). *Report on the Settlement of Kangra in the trans Sutluj States*, reprinted 1862, Lahore.

Beal, Samuel. (1884) *Si-yu-ki, Buddhist Records of the Western World*, translated from the Chinese of Hiuen Tsiang, reprinted 1969, Munshiram Manoharlal, Delhi.

Bruce, C.G. (1914). *Kulu and Lahoul*, Edward Arnold, London.

Chakravarty, Hemendra Nath. (1986). *Tantrasar of Abhinav Guptacharya*, Varanasi Sanskrit Sansthan, Varanasi.

Cowell, E.B. (ed.). (1895-1907). *The Jataka or Stories of the Buddha's Former Births*, Set I & II, Low Price Publications, Delhi (reprint), 1993, Jataka number 485.

Cunningham, Alexander. (1854a). *Ladak, Physical, Statistical and Historical*, reprinted, 1970, Sagar, New Delhi.

Cunningham, Alexander. (1854b). *The Bhilsa Topes*, reprinted Munshiram Manoharlal, New Delhi, 1997.

Cunningham, Alexander. (1924). *Ancient Geography of India*, reprinted 2002, Munshiram Manoharlal, New Delhi.

Drew, Frederic. (1875). *The Jammoo and Kashmir Territories, A Geographical Account*, Edward Stanford, London.

Errington, Elizabeth & Joe Cribb (Ed.). (2012). Vase with Incised scenes, The Ancient Indie & Iran Trust, *Cambridge. The Crossroads of Asia: Transformation in Image & Symbol*, pp. 163-164.

Francke, A.H. (1926). *Antiquities of Indian Tibet,* Vol. II, reprinted, Atma Ram & Sons, 1972, New Delhi.

Fraser, Baillie James. (1820). *Journal of a Tour Through part of the Snowy Range of the Himala Mountains,* Rodwell and Martin, London.

Gazetteer. (1890). *Gazetteer of Kashmir and Ladak,* The Superintendent of Government Printing, Calcutta.

Gazetteer. (1898). *Gazetteer of the Kangra District Parts II to IV, Kullu, Lahul and Spiti 1897,* reprinted Indus, 1994, New Delhi.

Gazetteer. (1910). *Chamba State Gazetteer, 1904,* Lahore.

Gazetteer. (1918). *Punjab District Gazetteer, Vol. XXX A, Kangra District, Parts II, III and IV, 1917,* Lahore.

Gazetteer. (1963). *Chamba District Gazetteer,* Himachal Pradesh.

Gazetteer. (1971). *Himachal Pradesh District Gazetteer, Kinnaur.*

Geiger, Wilhelm. (1912). *The Mahavamsa, The Great Chronicle of Ceylon,* Pali Text Society, London.

Gerard, Alexander. (1841). *Account of Koonawur in the Himalayas,* James Madden, London.

Goetz, Hermann. (1955). *The Early Wooden Temples of Chamba,* E.J. Brill, Leiden.

Grierson, G.A. (1906). *The Pisaca Languages of North-Western India,* The Royal Asiatic Society, London.

Grierson, G.A. (1919). *Linguistic Survey of India,* Vol. VIII, Part II, Indo-Aryan Family, North-Western Group, Specimens of Dard and Pisach Languages (including Kashimir) reprinted 1968. Motilal Banarsidass, Delhi.

Harcourt, A.F.P. (1871). *The Himalayan Districts of Kooloo, Lahoul & Spiti,* W.H. Allen & Co., London.

Hedin, Svin. (1909). *Trans-Himalaya, Discoveries and Adventures in Tibet,* Vol. I & II, reprinted 1968, Greenwood, New York.

Horner, I.B.(Tr.). (1963). *Milinda's Questions,* Part I, Luzac, London.

Hutchison and Vogel. (1933), *History of the Panjab Hill States,* Vol. I&II, reprinted Department of Languages and Culture, Himachal Pradesh, Shimla, 1982.

Isabella, Bird Bishop. (1894). *Among the Tibetans,* Fleming H. Revell, Newyork.

Jarrett, H.S. (Tr). (1891). *The Ain-i-Akbari by Abul Fazal Allami,* Vol.II, Asiatic Society of Bengal, Calcutta.

Joshi, Tika Ram. (1989). *A Dictionary of Pahari Dialects and a Dictionary & Grammar of Kanawari,* Himachal Academy of Arts Culture and Languages, H.P., Shimla, reprinted.

Kale, M.R. (1924). *A literal translation of Bana's Kadambari (Purvabhaga complete),* Vaman Yashwant & Co., Bombay.

Law, B.C. (1932). *Geography of Early Buddhism,* reprinted 1973, Bhartiya Publishing House, Varanasi.

Law, B.C. (1954). *Historical Geography of Ancient India,* reprinted, 1984, Munshiram Manoharlal, New Delhi.

Leitner, G.W. (1893). *Dardistan in 1866, 1886 and 1893,* reprint 1978 Manjushri, New Delhi.

Luczanits, Christian. 2004. *Buddhist Sculpture in Clay,* Serindia Publications, Chicago.

Lyall, J.B. (1874). Final Report on the Revised Settlement of Kangra District, 1865-1872, Lahore.

Madanjeet Singh. (1971). *Himalayan Art,* Macmillan, London.

Malalasekera, G.P. (1937). *Dictionary of Pali Proper Names,* Vol. I, John Murray, London.

McCrindle, J. W. (1893). *The Invasion of India by Alexander the Great,* Archibald, Westminster.

McCrindle, J. W. (1901). *Ancient India As Described in Classical Literature,* reprinted 1987, Eastern Book, Patna.

McCrindle, JW. (1926). *Ancient India as described by Megasthenes and Arrian,* reprinted 2000, Munshiram Manoharlal, New Delhi.

McCrindle, JW. (1927). *Ancient India as described by Ptolemy,* reprinted 2000, Munshiram Manoharlal, New Delhi.

Monier, Monier-Williams. (1899). *Sanskrit English Dictionary,* Reprinted,1981, Munshiram Manoharlal, New Delhi.

Moocroft, William and George Trebeck. (1841). *Travels in Hindustan,* Vol. I, reprinted, Sagar, New Delhi.

Moti Chandra. (1945). *Geographical and Economic Studies in the Mahabharata: Upayana Parva,* U.P. Historical Society, Lucknow.

Nebesky-Wojkowitz, Rene de. (1976). *Tibetan Religious Dances,* Mouton, The Hague.

Neil Howard. (2005). The Development of the Boundary between the State of Jammu and Kashmir and British India and its Representation on Maps of Lingti Plain, in *"Ladakhi Histories, Local and Regional Perspectives"*, edited by John Bray, Brill, Leiden, 217-234.

Parnavananda, Swami. (1949). *History of Kailash-Mansarovar,* S.P. League, Calcutta.

Puri, Baij Nath. (1971). *India as Described by Early Greek Writers,* Indological Book House, Varanasi.

Rose, H.A.. (1883). *A Glossary of the Tribes and Castes of the Punjab and North-West Frontier Provinces*, Government of Punjab, Lahore.

Sachau, Edward C. (1888). *Alberuni's India,* reprinted 2002, Rupa & Co., New Delhi.

Sangpo, Gelong Lodro. (2012). *Abhidharmakosa-Bhasya of Vasubandhu,* Vol.I-IV, Annotated English Translation; (Translated into French by Louis De La Vallee Pousin), Motilal Banarsidass, New Delhi.

Sherring, Charles A. (1916). *Western Tibet and the Indian Borderland,* reprinted 1974, Cosmo Publications, Delhi.

Sircar, D.C. (1973). *The Sakta Pithas,* Motilal Banarsidass, Delhi, reprinted 2004.

Snellgrove, D.L. (1957). *Buddhist Himalaya,* Philosophical Library, New York,

sTobdan, Tashi. (2005). Gyajung Nagpo, (The Centenarian Archer of sTok, pp. 181-182), in *Ladakhi Histories, Local and Regional Perspectives,* Ed. By John Bray, Brill, Leiden,

Tashi Dawa. (1994). Chandra and Bhaga, (37-38), in *Popular Antiquities, Mountains and Rivers,* ed. Gurmukh Singh Bedi, Atma Ram & Sons, Delhi.

Thomson, Thomas. (1852). *Western Himalaya and Tibet,* Reeve and Co., London.

Tobdan. (2000). *Kullu, A Study in History,* Book India, Delhi.

Tobdan. (2008). The Canda-Kinnara Jataka, and the Kinnara and the Canda Parvata, in *Expressions in Indian Art (Essays in Memory of Sh. M.C. Joshi),* II vols., 2008, Edited by B.R. Mani and Alok Tripathi, Agam Prakashan, New Delhi, (459-464).

Tobdan. (2015). *Nathapanth in Western Himalaya,* Kaveri Books, New Delhi.

Tobdan & C.Dorje. (1996). *Historical Documents from Western Trans-Himalaya,* Lahul, Zanskar and Ladakh, Book India, Delhi.

Tucci, Giuseppe. (1935). *The Temples of Western Tibet and Their Artistic Symbolism, Tsaparang,* III-2, Aditya Prakashan, New Delhi. English Translation: 1989.

Tucci, Giusseppe. (1940). *Travels of Tibetan Pilgrims in the Swat Valley,* Greater India Society, Calcutta.

Vigne, G.T. (1844). *Travels in Kashmir, Ladakh, Iskardo,* Vol. I, reprinted 2008, Gulshan Books, Srinagar.

Vogel, J.Ph. (1911). *Antiquities of Chamba State,* Part I, Archaeological Survey of India, New Delhi, reprinted 1994.

Walters, Jonathan S. (2018a). *Legends of the Buddhist Saints, - Apadanapali, Part —I, Legends of Theras,* Jonathan S. Walters and Whitman College.

Walters, Jonathan. (2018b). *Legends of the Buddhist Saints, - Apadanapali, Part II, Legends of Theris, Jonathan* S. Walters and Whitman College.

Whistler, Hugh. (1924). *In the High Himalaya,* H.F. & G. Witherby, London.

Sanskrit-Tibetan book

Vidyabhusan, Satiscandra (Ed). (1911). *Amarakosah,* - A metrical dictionary of the Sanskrit language with Tibetan version,Vol. I & II, Asiatic Society of Bengal, Calcutta.

Sanskrit-Hindi, Pali-Hindi, Sanskrit-English, Pali-English books

Abhimanyu, Shri Manna Lal. (Ed. & Tr.). (1999). *The Amar-kosha,* Chowkhamba, Varanasi.

Kashyap, J. Bhikkhu (Ed.). (1959). *The Apadana,* Part I, (Khuddaka Nikaya Vol. VI), Pali Publication Board, (Bihar Government), Motilal Banarsidass, Varanasi.

Jha, Achutyananda. (1997). *Brihatsamhita,* Chaukhamba, Varanasi.

Panda, N.C.(Ed.). (2010). *Mahavansa, Text with English Translation by Wilhelm Geiger,* Vol. I & II, Bhartiya Kala Prakashan, Delhi.

Mukund Ram, Shastri. (1918). *The Tantraloka of Abhinav Gupta,* Research Department, Jammu & Kashmir, Srinagar.

Shastri, Dwarikadas (Tr.). (1996). *Deepvansa,* Bauddh Aakar Granthmala, Varanasi.

Hindi books:

Tobdan. (2016). Chandra aur Bhaga ka Sangam aur Lahul ki sthapna, in *Shagun,* smarika, Layul Sursangam Society.

Sankrityayan, Rahul. (1948). *Tibbat me bauddh dharma,* second edition, 1979, Kitab Mahal, Illahabad.

Sankrityayan. Rahul. (1956a). *Kinner Desh* (Hindi), Kitab Mahal, Allahabad.

Sankrityayan. Rahul. (1956b). *Asia ke durgam bhookhandon me,* Navbharti, Illahabad.

Lalit CRB, Hariram Jasata, Nemchand Ajnabi and Tulsi Raman, in Tulsi Raman (ed). (2012).

Himachal ke Lok Natrya, Himachal Kala Sanskriti Bhasha Akademi, H.P., Shimla.

Sharma, Kedar (1995). Pangi Ghaati va Jukaroo Parva, (82-84) in *Kinnaur se Kilar*, ed. Sudarshan Vashishth, Shimla. in Kinnaur se Kilad.

Sharma, Banshiram, (1976). *Kinnar Lok Sahitya,* Lalit Prakashan, Bilaspur.

Sharma, Banshiram. (1986). *Himachal Lok Sanskriti ke Srot,* Arya Prakashan, Delhi.

Varma, Ramchanda. (2007). *Manak Hindi Kosh,* Vol.1I, Hindi Sahitya Sammelan, Illahabad.

Visvesvaranath, Pandita Reu. (1967). *Rigveda par ek aitihasik drishti,* Motilal Banarsidass,

Bhoti books

a-'o-rgyan gu-ru padma 'byung-gnas kyi skyes rabs rnam-par thar-pa rgyas-par bkod-pa, Dharamsala.

Gergan, Yoseb. (1976). *Ladags rgyalrabs chimed ster (History of Ladakh)*, Sterling Publishers, New Delhi.

bsTan-'dzin 'phrin-las. (1980). *'dZam-gling rgyas-par bsad-pa thag-ring gsal-bar mthong byed durba-na* (The rare 1830 redaction of the monumental Tibetan work on the geography of the world by the Fourth Btsan-po no-mon-han sprul-sku 'jam-dpal-chos-kyi bstan-'dzin 'phrin-la) published by Ngawang Sopa, New Delhi.

Dorje, Spiti. (1978). *sum-bha mkhan-pos brtsom-pa'i chos-'byung gi nang gsal stod mnga'-ris phyogs su dgon sde ji btab kyi mdsad rnam rag bsdus dngul dkar me-long*, (Extracts from the work of Sumpa Khanpo), Spiti, Himachal Pradesh.

Gondhla Kangyur — Misc. Collection, Book-5, 1/12, Shantarakshita Library, CUTS, Sarnath-Varanasi. (digitized books).

sTag-Tshang Ras-pa, (ah): *au-rgyan mkha'-'gro'i gling-gi lam-yig thar-lam bgrod-pa'i them-skas*, Hemis, Ladakh.

Godtshangpa. *rgyal-ba rgod-tshang-pa mgon-po rdo-rje'i rnam-par-thar-pa mthong-ba don-an norbu'i phreng-ba.*

Filibeck, Elena De Rossi. (1988). *Two Tibetan Guide Books to Ti-se and La-phyi*, VGH, Wisseenschaftsverlag, Bonn, contains the book in Roman transcription: bsTan 'zin chos kyi blo gros: *gangs-ri chenpo ti se dang mtsho ma dros pa bchas kyi sngon byung gi lo rgyus mdor bsdus su brzod pa'i rab byed shel dkar me long.*

sba-bzhed. btsan-po khri srong lde btsan dang. mkhan-po slob-dpon padma'i dus mdo sngags mdsad pa'i sba-bzhed zhabs btags ma, Dharamsala.

Journal: English Language

Charles Horne. (1871). Notes on an Ancient Indian Vase, with an Account of the Engravings thereupon, in *The Journal of the Royal Asiatic Society of Great Britain and Ireland*, New Series, Vol. 5, (367-375).

Cunningham, A. (1848). "Memorandum by Capt. A. Cunningham, detailing the boundary between the territories of Maharaja Gulab Singh and British India, as determined by the Commissioners P. A. Vans Agnew, Esq. and Capt. A. Cunningham, of Engineers", *Journal of the Asiatic Society of Bengal* Part 1 (January to June 1848), pp.295-297.

Das, S.K. (1954). A Note on Kinnaras, in *Man in India,* March 1954, Vol. 34, pp. 40-46.

Hutchison J. and J. Ph. Vogel. (1918). History of Nurpur State, *Journal Punjab Historical Society,* Vol. VI., pp. 101-143.,

Koels, W.N. (1932). Diary of the 1931 Expedition to Western Tibet, in *Journal of Urusvati Himalayan Research Institute of Roerich Museum,* Vol. II, Urusvati Himalayan Research Institute of Roerich Museum, 1932, (pp. 85-123).

Moorcroft, William. (1818). A Journey to Lake Manasarovara in Undes, a Province of Little Tibet, *Asiatic Researches,* volume the twelfth, London. Pp.380-53.

Pitts-Tucker, NA.(1981). Expedition to the Dharlang Valley, Pangi and Zanskar, in *Himalayan Journal,* Vol. 37 (pp.3-6).

Roerich, George De. (1934). The Tibetan Dialects of Lahul, in *Tibetica I, Journal of Urusvati Himalayan Research Institute,* Vol. III, of the Roerich Museum, Naggar and New York. (83-189).

Shuttleworth, H.Lee. (1922). Border Countries of The Punjab Himalaya, in *The Geographical Journal,* Vol. LX, No. 4, (pp. 242-264).

Shuttleworth, H.Lee. (1923). *A Wool Mart of the Indo-Tibetan Borderland,* Geographical Review, Vol. 13, No. 4, Oct. 1923, (pp. 552-558).

Strachey, Henry. (1848). Narrative of a Journey to Cho Lagan (Rakas Tal), Cho Mapan (Mansarowar), and the valley of Purang in Gnari, Hundes in Sept. and Oct. 1846, *JASB,* August-1848, pp. 327-557.

Vogel, J. Ph. 1902. Triloknath, in *Journal of the Asiatic Society of Bengal,* Vol. LXXI, Part I, Calcutta, (pp.35-40).

Widorn, Verena & Geral Kozicz. (2012). The Temple of "Triloknath — A Buddhist Nagara Temple in Lahul, in *South Asian Studies,* 28:1, 15-35.

Journals: Hindi

Tobdan. (1979). La-ra — Lahul ke devataon ki kahani, *Somsi,* July 1979, Shimla, (52-61).

Negi, Thakur Sen. (1975). Kinnauri Boliyan, in *Somsi,* October, 1975, Simla (pp. 7-16).

Ranpatiya, Amar Singh. (1994). Pangval Janjati ke Sanskar, pp. 18-22, *Somsi,* Shimla, March, 1994.

Index

D

F

G

H

I

J

K

L

M

N

P

R

S

T

V

W

Y

Z

Plate 1 : Kushan king, Triloknath

Plate 2 : Sharda inscription Triloknath, photo anonymous.

Plate 3 : Pillar base on a maane, Karing.

Plate 4 : Offering mchhodpa

Plate 5 : Khangsar Khar

Plate 6 : Khangsar Khar, Makhang.

Plate 7 : Khangsar Khar, mTshom chhedmo

Plate 8 : Lion, mchhodpa

Plate 9 : Temple of Le-be A-pa.

Plate 10 : Lha-tho and bya-tho.

Plate 11 : Lha-tho of bTsan.

Plate 12 : Mahadev, Mayling.

Plate 13 : Vasudeva Kutumbkam temple, Gushal.

Plate 14 : Gandhala monastery

Plate 15 : Bodhisattva, Chhokhor. obverse.

Plate 16 : Bodhosattva, inscription, reverse, Chhokhor.

Plate 17 : Urgyanpa, Chhukutsi.

Plate 18 : Gyamchhod, worship lamp, Zong Gonpa, Tinno.

Plate 19 : Vir, Stone carving, Srangbar, Khangsar.

Plate 20 : Baliraja, drawing on wall,

Plate 21 : Unidentified image, Margul.

Plate 22 : Unidentified image, Pangi.

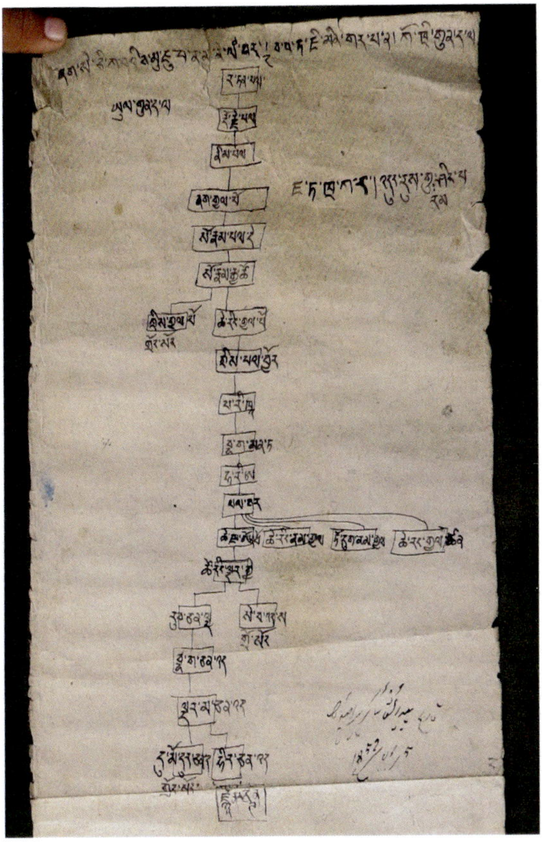

Plate 23 : Genealogical list, Tinan.

Plate 24 : A Madh, Pattan.

Plate 25 : Carvings of pitra, Pungyin, Triloknath.

Plate 26 : Sati stone carving, Triloknath.